# Bridging Troubled Waters

## Assessing the World Bank Water Resources Strategy

George Keith Pitman

2002
**THE WORLD BANK**
Washington, D.C.

http://www.worldbank.org/oed

 Printed on Recycled Paper

# Contents

## Text Tables

# Acknowledgments

This report examines the Bank's implementation experience of the 1993 Water Resources Management Policy (Operational Policy 4.07) to determine the relevance and efficacy of the Bank's overall water operations for its borrowers. It evaluates the degree to which the issues identified in the guideline document *Water Resources Management—A World Bank Policy Paper* (1993) have been internalized into Bank operations, examines the continuing relevance of the water *Strategy,* and makes recommendations for refining Bank policy and strategy in the water sectors. The report is based primarily on comparisons of events in the two six-year periods before (1988–93) and after (1994–99) the Operational Policy and covers all completed and new water and water-related economic and sector work and operations within the two periods.

The analysis also builds on earlier OED evaluations—in particular, a 1994 irrigation and drainage sector review and a 1992 evaluation of the first 23 years of Bank lending for water supply and sanitation. Conclusions were based on an evaluation of over 270 pieces of economic and sector work, 410 projects, 98 Country Assistance Strategies, and the exit performance of 306 water projects completed in the period 1988–99.

In addition to an analysis of Bank lending, the evaluation is based on an assessment of non-lending services and a review of experience in four focus countries. In-depth review and discussions between Bank staff and country/ Regional stakeholders have taken place in Brazil, Yemen, India, and the Philippines on the results of the review of activities in the four countries. A special study was undertaken with the Social Assessment Team of ESSD to examine the poverty focus and efficacy of social assessments in water projects. A questionnaire gathered feedback from the experience of over 100 Bank staff with the water *Strategy* and its implementation. Several formal and informal workshops within the Bank discussed evaluation methodology, and progress with Bank staff and other stakeholders.

The draft report was critiqued by two peer reviewers, Peter Rogers of Harvard University and David Seckler, former Director-General of the International Water Management Institute, and the final draft was circulated to Bank management for substantive review. In addition, the study report benefited considerably from the guidance of Alain Barbu, Gregory Ingram, Roger Slade, and numerous colleagues in OED. ESSD support to the Social Assessment Team and trust funds provided by the Norwegian government supported the social science and poverty evaluation.

The Task Manager for the evaluation, G.T. Keith Pitman, prepared the report. Significant written contributions were made by Hans Adler, Ayse Kudat, Bulent Ozbilgin, Eugene Stakhiv, Robert Varley, John Cunningham, Amnon Golan, Inderjeet Singh, and Mark Svendsen. Research was conducted by Kavita Mathur, Greg Browder, Saeed Rana, Monica Scatasta, Reno Dewina, and Samir Stewart. Paula Hickman, Catherine Munro, and Ted Rice provided advice and support. William Hurlbut, Bruce Ross-Larson, Caroline

McEuen, and Phillip Sawicki edited the report. Soon Wan-Pak, Marcia Bailey, Connie Frye, and Helen Philip provided administrative assistance. The paper also benefited from numerous discussions with Bank colleagues and with many individuals in development partner's countries.

This study was published in the Partnerships and Knowledge Group (OEDPK) by the Outreach and Dissemination Unit. The task team includes Elizabeth Campbell-Pagé (task team leader), Caroline McEuen (editor), and Juicy Qureishi-Huq (administrative assistant).

Director-General, Operations Evaluation: *Robert Picciotto*
Director, Operations Evaluation Department: *Gregory K. Ingram*
Manager, Sector and Thematic Evaluation: *Alain Barbu*
Task Manager: *George Keith Pitman*

## FOREWORD

**The comprehensive approach advocated in the Bank's 1993 water strategy is highly relevant to the sound and sustainable management of water resources. Implementing the strategy has advanced the Bank's corporate goals and mission, contributing to an emerging global consensus on water resource management. But implementation, although broad, has been partial and uneven, with big differences across Regions, countries, and subsectors. Work remains to adapt the strategy to diverse country contexts and to link water resource management to sustainable service delivery.**

The Bank has mainstreamed the strategy's principles in extensive economic and sector work. But Bank efforts to nurture policy reform and build domestic capacities have not matched the challenges in most countries. The water strategy has been incorporated only partially in Country Assistance Strategies (CASs). Organization for Economic Cooperation and Development countries show how difficult comprehensive water resource management is, even with sound governance, participation, institutions, and skills—all mostly missing in Bank client countries. And while some borrowers share the Bank's vision, few have implemented the comprehensive principle because of these constraints. Thus, not many Bank water projects are able to address all key elements of the strategy, such as

## PRÓLOGO

**El enfoque integral propugnado por el Banco en la estrategia sobre los recursos hídricos, de 1993, es sumamente pertinente para la ordenación racional y sostenible de dichos recursos. La aplicación de la estrategia ha promovido las metas institucionales y la misión del Banco, al contribuir a la formación de un consenso mundial sobre la ordenación de los recursos hídricos. Pero dicha aplicación, aunque amplia, ha sido parcial y desigual y se han registrado grandes diferencias entre oficinas regionales, países y subsectores. Quedan pendientes las tareas de adaptar la estrategia a diversos contextos nacionales y vincular la ordenación del agua con la prestación sostenible de servicios.**

El Banco ha incorporado los principios de la estrategia en muchos estudios económicos y sectoriales. Pero las acciones del Banco para promover reformas de políticas y fortalecer la capacidad nacional no han respondido a los retos planteados en la mayoría de los países. Esa estrategia se ha incorporado sólo parcialmente en las estrategias de asistencia a los países. Los países miembros de la Organización de Cooperación y Desarrollo Económicos muestran cuán difícil es la ordenación integral de los recursos hídricos, aun cuando exista una gestión pública eficaz, además de participación, instituciones y conocimientos, requisitos casi inexistentes en los países clientes del Banco. Si bien algunos prestatarios comparten la

## AVANT-PROPOS

**L'approche globale préconisée dans la stratégie pour l'eau élaborée par la Banque en 1993 répond tout à fait aux impératifs d'une gestion rationnelle et durable des ressources en eau. La mise en œuvre de cette stratégie a permis de faire avancer les buts institutionnels de la Banque ainsi que la mission qui lui a été assignée, et elle a contribué à dégager un début de consensus sur la gestion des ressources en eau. Mais si la stratégie a été appliquée de manière générale, sa mise en œuvre demeure néanmoins fragmentaire et inégale, avec des différences marquées entre les Régions, les pays et les sous-secteurs. Des efforts restent à faire pour l'adapter aux différents contextes nationaux et pour articuler la gestion des ressources en eau avec l'organisation de services durables.**

La Banque intègre systématiquement les principes de la stratégie aux études économiques et sectorielles de grande portée. Mais les efforts qu'elle déploie pour faire avancer les réformes et renforcer les capacités des pays ne sont pas à la mesure des problèmes auxquels sont confrontés la plupart des pays. La stratégie pour l'eau n'a été incorporée que partiellement dans les Stratégies d'assistance aux pays (SAP). Les pays de l'Organisation de coopération et de développement économiques témoignent des difficultés que présente la gestion globale des ressources en eau, même avec des atouts tels que la saine gestion des affaires publiques, la participa-

**ENGLISH**

using economic and financial instruments to efficiently allocate water and safeguard ecosystems within a national or river-basin management framework. Conversely, there has been significant progress in the adoption of the strategy's institutional, financial, and socioeconomic objectives within the water service sectors that have been the traditional vehicles for Bank assistance.

Impediments remain. Until recently, the Bank had not organized itself to treat water resources management comprehensively. Comprehensive water resources management has high transaction costs, particularly because many safeguard policies—and certainly the most controversial—apply to water-related development. Thus, country management sees many water interventions as risky ventures in a time of dwindling Bank resources.

In addition, water development transcends borders, and the international dimension is becoming increasingly important. While the main water service sectors have incorporated most of the strategy's recommendations to improve service delivery—water supply and sanitation somewhat better than irrigation and drainage—there had been no one group (until this year) charged with overseeing and developing the Bankwide institutional retooling needed to ensure a consistent approach to water resources management. Good models exist, notably in the Africa and the Middle East and North Africa Regions. And it is expected that the new Bank Water Resources Management Group cre-

**ESPAÑOL**

visión del Banco, pocos han aplicado el principio de manera integral debido a esas limitaciones. Por ende, no son muchos los proyectos del Banco en el sector del agua que pueden abordar todos los elementos fundamentales de la estrategia, como la utilización de instrumentos económicos y financieros para asignar eficientemente este recurso y salvaguardar los ecosistemas dentro de un marco de gestión a nivel nacional o de las cuencas hidrográficas. En cambio, ha habido progresos notables en la adopción de los objetivos institucionales, financieros y socioeconómicos de la estrategia dentro de los sectores de servicios de agua que han sido mecanismos tradicionales de la asistencia del Banco.

Subsisten los impedimentos. Hasta hace poco, el Banco no se había organizado para abordar integralmente la ordenación del agua, la cual tiene altos costos de transacción, debido en especial a que muchas políticas de salvaguardia —y ciertamente las más controvertidas— se aplican a proyectos relacionados con el agua. Por eso, los directivos a cargo de las operaciones del Banco en los países consideran que muchas intervenciones relativas al agua son iniciativas riesgosas en tiempos de retracción de los recursos del Banco.

Además, el aprovechamiento del agua trasciende las fronteras y es cada vez más importante el aspecto internacional. Si bien en los principales sectores de servicios de agua se ha incorporado la mayoría de las recomendaciones de la estrategia tendientes a mejorar la prestación de los servicios

**FRANÇAIS**

tion, les institutions et les compétences — qui font le plus souvent défaut aux pays clients de la Banque. Et, si certains emprunteurs partagent la vision de la Banque, rares sont ceux qui ont pu appliquer le principe de la globalité à cause de ces contraintes. C'est pourquoi, peu de projets de la Banque dans le secteur de l'eau englobent tous les éléments clés de la stratégie, tels que l'utilisation d'instruments économiques et financiers pour assurer une répartition efficace de l'eau et préserver les écosystèmes dans le cadre d'un plan national ou d'un plan de gestion d'un bassin fluvial. Des progrès notables ont toutefois été enregistrés dans l'adoption des objectifs institutionnels, financiers et socioéconomiques au niveau des services de l'eau, qui sont les instruments traditionnels par lesquels passe l'assistance de la Banque.

Des obstacles demeurent. Jusqu'à une période récente, la Banque ne s'était pas organisée pour traiter le problème de la gestion des ressources en eau dans son ensemble. La gestion globale des ressources implique des coûts de transaction élevés, en particulier parce que le développement lié aux ressources hydriques fait l'objet de nombreuses mesures de sauvegarde et notamment de la plus controversée.

C'est pourquoi les responsables-pays considèrent que les interventions dans le secteur de l'eau sont des opérations risquées à un moment où les ressources de la Banque diminuent. En outre, la mise en valeur des ressources en eau transcende les frontières, et la dimension internationale prend de

ENGLISH

ated in early 2000 within the Economic and Socially Sustainable Development Vice-Presidency will address these issues as it develops the Water Resources Sector Strategy Paper.

Perceptions of a looming global water crisis, reinforced by the Second World Water Conference at The Hague in 2000, have made policymakers aware of the need to enhance water resource management in developing countries. This is creating opportunities for the Bank to rededicate itself to implementing a comprehensive water management strategy along the lines of the following recommendations:

**Recommendation 1: *Aim country dialogue and institutional development at integrating social and environmental concerns with water resource development and project implementation.*** This requires:

- Greater attention to linking water projects with CAS and poverty strategies, to achieving better understanding of local institutions and preferences, and to monitoring and evaluating project effects on poverty
- Adopting the use of strategic environmental and social assessments, including consultations, as part of the overall water resources planning process
- More attention to be given to developing economic instruments to manage conflict in integrated water systems, including groundwater, and to balance demands at the river-basin level, and between urban and rural populations, while ensuring access of the poor to water

**ESPAÑOL**

(en el abastecimiento de agua y el saneamiento algo mejor que en el riego y el drenaje), ningún grupo (hasta este año) se ha encargado de supervisar y formular a nivel de todo el Banco la reorganización necesaria para asegurar un enfoque coherente de la ordenación del agua. Se cuenta con buenos modelos, especialmente en las regiones de África y de Oriente Medio y Norte de África; y se espera que el nuevo Grupo del Banco encargado de la gestión de los recursos hídricos, creado a principios de 2000 dentro de la Vicepresidencia de Desarrollo Social y Ecológicamente Sostenible, aborde esas cuestiones al preparar el documento de estrategia sobre recursos hídricos.

Las percepciones acerca de una inminente crisis mundial del agua, reforzadas por la Segunda Conferencia Mundial sobre el Agua celebrada en La Haya en 2000, han llevado a los encargados de formular las políticas a tomar conciencia de la necesidad de mejorar la ordenación de este recurso en los países en desarrollo. Esto está creando oportunidades para que el Banco vuelva a aplicar una estrategia de ordenación integral según las siguientes recomendaciones:

**Recomendación 1: *Procurar que en el diálogo con los países y en el desarrollo institucional se incorporen los aspectos sociales y ambientales en el aprovechamiento de los recursos hídricos y en la ejecución de los proyectos relacionados.*** Para esto es preciso:

- Prestar mayor atención a la vinculación de los proyectos

**FRANÇAIS**

plus en plus d'importance. Si les principaux services de l'eau tiennent compte de la plupart des recommandations contenues dans la stratégie pour améliorer leur organisation — de façon un peu plus rigoureuse pour ce qui est de l'alimentation en eau et de l'assainissement que pour l'irrigation et le drainage —, aucun groupe (jusqu'à cette année) n'a été chargé de procéder à la réorganisation institutionnelle de l'ensemble de la Banque qui s'impose afin de lui permettre d'adopter une approche cohérente pour la gestion des ressources en eau, et de suivre le déroulement de cette restructuration. Il existe des modèles valables, notamment dans les Régions Afrique, et Moyen-Orient et Afrique du Nord. Et le nouveau Groupe de gestion des ressources en eau créé au début de l'an 2000 au sein de la Vice-présidence Développement écologiquement et socialement durable (ESSD) s'attaquera sans aucun doute à ces questions dans le cadre de la rédaction du document de stratégie pour les ressources en eau.

La perspective d'une crise mondiale imminente de l'eau, renforcée par la deuxième Conférence mondiale sur l'eau tenue à La Haye en 2000, a sensibilisé les décideurs à la nécessité d'améliorer la gestion des ressources en eau dans les pays en développement. Cela donne à la Banque de nouvelles raisons de s'employer à mettre en œuvre une stratégie globale de la gestion de l'eau fondée sur les recommandations suivantes :

**Recommandation 1 : *Axer le dialogue avec les pays et le développement institutionnel sur la prise en compte des***

## ENGLISH

- More attention to factoring in concerns about equitable allocation of water and water rights in light of local cultural preferences and rural-urban needs
- Increased emphasis on implementation of safeguard policies during project supervision by both the Bank and the borrower.

**Recommendation 2: *Deploy Bank resources and instruments more effectively to nurture commitment to the strategy through shared objectives, realistic diagnostics, and partnerships aimed at policy reform and capacity building*.** Areas requiring particular attention include:

- Updating the Bank's water policy in the context of the forthcoming Sector Strategy Paper and supplementing it with a series of Bank procedures and good practice notes for each subsector
- Making greater use of adaptable lending instruments and developing new, cost-effective, performance-based approaches to project selection, design, procurement, and service delivery
- Strengthening economic and sector work to allow for improved diagnosis, higher-quality dialogue with stakeholders, and closer linkages with Country and Poverty Assistance Strategies
- Reorienting capacity building in the water sector toward comprehensive water management through World Bank Institute programs and global

## ESPAÑOL

del sector del agua con las estrategias de asistencia a los países y las estrategias de lucha contra la pobreza, para lograr una mejor comprensión de las instituciones y preferencias locales y observar y evaluar los efectos de los proyectos sobre la pobreza

- Realizar evaluaciones ambientales y sociales estratégicas, inclusive consultas, como parte del proceso general de planificación en el ámbito del agua
- Prestar mayor atención a la creación de instrumentos económicos para hacer frente a los conflictos en las redes de agua integradas, inclusive las aguas subterráneas, y para equilibrar la demanda a nivel de las cuencas hidrográficas y entre poblaciones urbanas y rurales, asegurando al mismo tiempo el acceso de los pobres al agua
- Prestar más atención a la incorporación de las cuestiones relacionadas con la asignación equitativa del agua y los derechos sobre el agua, teniendo en cuenta las preferencias culturales locales y las necesidades rurales y urbanas
- Hacer más hincapié en la aplicación de políticas de salvaguardia durante la supervisión de los proyectos por el Banco y el prestatario

**Recomendación 2: *Asignar los recursos y los instrumentos del Banco de manera más eficaz a fin de fomentar la adhesión a la estrategia a través de objetivos comunes, diagnósticos realistas y alianzas orientadas a la reforma***

## FRANÇAIS

*questions sociales et environnementales dans le cadre de la mise en valeur des ressources en eau et de l'exécution des projets.* Pour cela, il faut :

- veiller davantage à articuler les projets centrés sur l'eau avec les SAP et les stratégies de lutte contre la pauvreté afin d'avoir une meilleure connaissance des institutions et des préférences locales, et de pouvoir suivre et évaluer les effets de ces projets sur la pauvreté ;
- utiliser les évaluations stratégiques environnementales et sociales, et notamment les consultations, comme éléments du processus de planification des ressources en eaux ;
- veiller davantage à élaborer des instruments économiques pour gérer les conflits liés aux réseaux hydriques intégrés et notamment aux eaux souterraines, et équilibrer les ponctions sur les ressources au niveau des bassins fluviaux, et entre les populations urbaines et les populations rurales, tout en veillant à ce que les pauvres puissent avoir accès à l'eau ;
- se préoccuper davantage de l'affacturage pour les questions concernant l'allocation équitable de l'eau et les droits d'usage de l'eau en tenant compte des préférences culturelles et des besoins des zones rurales et urbaines ;
- accorder, lors de la supervision des projets, plus d'importance à l'adoption de mesures de sauvegarde, tant par la Banque que par l'emprunteur.

**Recommandation 2 : *Déployer plus efficacement les ressources***

**ENGLISH**

and regional capacity-building partnerships.

**Recommendation 3:**
*Create and sustain more comprehensive water management alliances with like-minded partners in the private sector, civil society, and the development community.* This requires:

- Sustaining involvement in global water policy networks and partnerships, with priority to cross-border, integrated, river-basin planning, driven by stakeholder demand, and to the resolution of international water disputes.
- More attention to in-country water partnerships is required to build dialogue and leverage local knowledge.
- Entering new partnerships only where the Bank has a clear comparative advantage in doing so, clearly specifying conditions for entry and exit.
- Driving the choice between private and public sector involvement by hard-nosed institutional analysis of what works and what does not in differing country contexts.

**Recommendation 4:**
*Strengthen internal management, monitoring, and evaluation of water resource management activities through a streamlined organization, more cohesive sector and country strategies, enhanced core competencies, additional operational guidance and training, and more rigorous quality assurance arrangements.* Chief among the issues to address:

**ESPAÑOL**

*de las políticas y al fortalecimiento de la capacidad.* Los siguientes temas requieren particular atención:

- Actualizar la política del Banco relativa al agua en el contexto del documento de estrategia sectorial de próxima aparición, complementándola con notas sobre procedimientos y prácticas recomendadas del Banco para cada subsector
- Aprovechar más los instrumentos de préstamo adaptables y elaborar nuevos enfoques basados en el desempeño y eficaces en función de los costos para la selección y el diseño de los proyectos, las adquisiciones y la prestación de servicios
- Mejorar los estudios económicos y sectoriales para obtener diagnósticos más precisos, diálogos de mejor calidad con las partes interesadas y vínculos más estrechos con las estrategias de asistencia a los países y de lucha contra la pobreza
- Reorientar el fortalecimiento de la capacidad en el sector de los recursos hídricos para lograr una gestión integral del agua a través de programas del Instituto del Banco Mundial y de asociaciones a nivel mundial y regional para el fortalecimiento de la capacidad.

**Recomendación 3:** *Establecer y mantener más alianzas para la ordenación integral del agua con asociados afines del sector privado, la sociedad civil y las instituciones de desarrollo.* Para esto se requiere:

- Mantener la participación en

**FRANÇAIS**

*et les instruments de la Banque afin d'encourager l'adoption de la stratégie en fondant l'action sur des objectifs partagés, des diagnostics réalistes et des partenariats axés sur les réformes et le renforcement des capacités.* Les domaines qui requièrent une attention particulière incluent :

- l'actualisation de la politique de l'eau de la Banque dans le contexte de la prochaine étude sur la stratégie sectorielle, à compléter par une série de notes sur les procédures et les bonnes pratiques de la Banque pour chaque sous-secteur ;
- le recours plus fréquent aux instruments de prêts évolutifs et la mise au point de nouvelles méthodes efficaces par rapport aux coûts et basées sur la performance pour la sélection et la conception des projets, la passation des marchés et l'organisation des services ;
- la réalisation d'études économiques et sectorielles plus approfondies afin d'affiner les diagnostics, d'engager un dialogue de meilleure qualité avec les parties prenantes et de renforcer l'articulation avec les Stratégies d'assistance aux pays et de lutte contre la pauvreté ;
- réorienter le renforcement des capacités dans le secteur de l'eau pour l'axer sur la gestion globale des ressources en eau dans le cadre des programmes de l'Institut de la Banque mondiale et des partenariats mondiaux et régionaux pour le renforcement des capacités.

**Recommandation 3 :** *Créer et maintenir des alliances plus lar-*

**ENGLISH**

- Clarifying the role of the central Water Resource Management Group and its relationship with Sector Boards and Regional staff, particularly in relation to institutional and financial aspects of the rural water portfolio, and considering the establishment of water resource management coordinating bodies in each Region.
- Providing more vigilant and independent quality assurance for safeguard policies affecting water development.
- Offering incentives and training to accelerate staff adoption of a comprehensive approach to water resources management.
- Reassessing staffing levels and skills mixes to implement the water strategy Bankwide. To ensure adequate staffing and continuity, reliance on ad hoc trust funds should be reduced and the Bank budget enhanced.

**ESPAÑOL**

las redes y asociaciones mundiales sobre políticas relacionadas con el agua, dando prioridad a la planificación transfronteriza e integrada de las cuencas hidrográficas, con el liderazgo de las partes interesadas, y a la resolución de los conflictos internacionales sobre el agua. Es preciso prestar más atención a las asociaciones dentro del país para entablar un diálogo sobre el agua y aprovechar los conocimientos locales.

- Establecer nuevas asociaciones sólo cuando el Banco tenga en ello una ventaja comparativa evidente, especificando claramente las condiciones de ingreso y salida.
- Fundamentar la elección entre la participación del sector privado y el sector público con rigurosos análisis institucionales de lo que da resultado y lo que no da resultado en el contexto de diferentes países.

**Recomendación 4:** *Fortalecer la gestión interna, el seguimiento y la evaluación de las actividades de ordenación de los recursos hídricos mediante una organización simplificada, estrategias sectoriales y nacionales más coherentes, competencias básicas mejoradas, más orientación y capacitación operacional y arreglos más rigurosos para asegurar la calidad.* Se han de abordar las siguientes cuestiones:

- Aclarar el papel del Grupo central encargado de la gestión de los recursos hídricos y su relación con las juntas sectoriales y los funcionarios de las oficinas

**FRANÇAIS**

*ges pour la gestion de l'eau avec des partenaires du secteur privé, de la société civile et de la communauté du développement qui partagent les mêmes conceptions.* Pour cela, il faut :

- maintenir la participation aux réseaux mondiaux et aux partenariats axés sur la politique de l'eau, en donnant priorité à la planification transfrontière et intégrée des basins flu-viaux fondée sur la demande des parties prenantes, et à la résolution des différends concernant les eaux internationales. Il convient d'accorder une plus grande attention aux partenariats nationaux dans le secteur de l'eau afin de renforcer le dialogue et d'approfondir la connaissance du contexte local ;
- établir de nouveaux partenariats dans les domaines où la Banque a manifestement intérêt à le faire, en spécifiant de façon explicite les conditions d'entrée et de sortie ;
- décider du choix entre la participation du secteur privé et du secteur public sur la base d'une analyse institutionnelle pratique et approfondie de ce qui marche et qui ne marche pas dans les différents contextes nationaux.

**Recommandation 4 :** *Renforcer la gestion interne, le suivi et l'évaluation des activités liées à la gestion des ressources en eau par une politique axée sur la rationalisation de l'organisation, l'amélioration de la cohérence des stratégies sectorielles et nationales, le renforcement des compétences essentielles, la*

**ESPAÑOL**

regionales, en particular en lo concerniente a los aspectos institucionales y financieros de la cartera de proyectos hidrológicos rurales, y considerar el establecimiento de órganos de coordinación de dichos recursos en cada oficina regional

- Adoptar medidas de garantía de la calidad más estrictas e independientes para las políticas de salvaguardia que afectan el desarrollo del sector del agua
- Ofrecer incentivos y capacitación para acelerar la adopción por el personal de un enfoque integral de la ordenación de los recursos hídricos
- Reevaluar la dotación de personal y la combinación de aptitudes para aplicar en todo el Banco la estrategia de ordenación de los recursos hídricos. Para asegurar que la dotación de personal y la continuidad sean adecuadas, es preciso depender en menor medida de los fondos fiduciarios especiales y mejorar el presupuesto del Banco.

**FRANÇAIS**

*fourniture de directives opérationnelles et de formations supplémentaires, et des arrangements plus rigoureux au plan de l'assurance de qualité.* Les principaux objectifs dans ce contexte sont les suivants :

- préciser le rôle du Groupe central de la gestion de l'eau ainsi que ses relations avec les commissions techniques et les Régions, en particulier pour ce qui est des aspects institutionnel et financier du portefeuille des projets centrés sur l'eau en milieu rural, et étudier la possibilité de créer dans chaque Région des organes de coordination de la gestion des ressources en eau ;
- faire preuve de plus de vigilance et d'indépendance dans le domaine de l'assurance de qualité pour les mesures de sauvegarde touchant la mise en valeur de l'eau ;
- offrir des incitations et une formation pour amener le personnel à accélérer l'adoption d'une approche globale en matière de gestion des ressources en eau ;
- réévaluer les dotations en personnel et l'éventail des qualifications disponibles pour la mise en œuvre de la stratégie de l'eau dans l'ensemble des services de la Banque. Afin de garantir une dotation suffisante en personnel et d'assurer la continuité, il conviendra de réduire les recours aux fonds fiduciaires spéciaux et d'accroître le budget de la Banque.

Robert Picciotto
Director-General, Operations Evaluation

## ENGLISH

# EXECUTIVE SUMMARY

**In 1997 more than 1.1 billion people in low- and middle-income countries lacked access to safe water supplies, and far more were without adequate sanitation. Today, 166 million people in 18 countries suffer from water scarcity, while another 270 million in 11 additional countries are considered "water stressed." By 2025 affected populations will increase to about 3 billion people, or about 40 percent of the world's population, most of them in the poorest countries. There is now a consensus that the severity of the problem requires a strategic approach that emphasizes equitable and sustainable management of water resources.**

## The Bank's Water Strategy

To inform development of the new World Bank Water Resources Sector Strategy, the Operations Evaluation Department (OED) undertook the evaluation of how effectively the Bank's current strategy has been implemented. The comprehensive approach embodied in the 1993 *Water Resources Management* (the *Strategy)* evolved in response to growing unease within the Bank that water operations were failing to deliver sustainable development—water and water-related projects were among the poorer performers in the Bank portfolio—and growing international concern about the mismanagement of global water resources and poor service levels, particularly for the poor.

The *Strategy* is highly relevant to sound and sustainable manage-

## ESPAÑOL

# RESUMEN

**En 1997, había en países de ingreso bajo y mediano más de 1.100 millones de personas que carecían de acceso al abastecimiento de agua potable y era mayor el número de personas carentes de saneamiento adecuado. Actualmente, 166 millones de personas en 18 países padecen de escasez de agua, y se considera que otros 270 millones, en otros 11 países, están en situación de "estrés" por carencia de agua. Hacia 2025, las poblaciones afectadas aumentarán a unos 3.000 millones de personas, o un 40% de la población mundial, la mayoría de ellas en los países más pobres. Hoy día hay un consenso acerca de que la gravedad del problema requiere un enfoque estratégico que haga hincapié en la ordenación equitativa y sostenible de los recursos hídricos.**

## La estrategia del Banco sobre ordenación de los recursos hídricos

Para fundamentar la formulación de la nueva estrategia para el sector del agua del Banco Mundial, el Departamento de Evaluación de Operaciones (DEO) realizó una evaluación de la eficacia en la aplicación de la actual estrategia del Banco. El enfoque integral consagrado en el documento titulado *La ordenación de los recursos hídricos* (la *Estrategia)* de 1993 se elaboró en respuesta a la creciente preocupación suscitada en el Banco en el sentido de que las operaciones relativas al agua no eran conducentes a un desarrollo sostenible —los proyectos sobre recursos

## FRANÇAIS

# RÉSUMÉ ANALYTIQUE

**En 1997, plus de 1,1 milliard d'habitants des pays à faible revenu et à revenu intermédiaire ne pouvaient avoir accès à une source d'eau salubre et un nombre bien plus important encore ne disposait pas d'équipements d'assainissement adéquats. Aujourd'hui, 166 millions d'individus vivant dans 18 pays souffrent d'une pénurie de l'eau, et 270 millions d'individus dans 11 autres pays sont considérés comme souffrant d'un « stress hydrique ». D'ici à 2025, les populations touchées passeront à quelque 3 milliards de personnes, soit à peu près 40 % de la population mondiale, la plupart vivant dans les pays les plus démunis. On s'accorde maintenant à reconnaître que la gravité du problème exige une approche stratégique mettant l'accent sur une gestion équitable et durable des ressources en eau.**

## La stratégie de la Banque pour l'eau

Dans le cadre de la mise au point de la nouvelle Stratégie sectorielle pour les ressources en eau de la Banque mondiale, le Département de l'évaluation des opérations (OED) a entrepris d'examiner l'efficacité avec laquelle la stratégie actuelle de la Banque avait été appliquée. La philosophie de l'approche globale dont s'inspirait la *Gestion des ressources en eau* (la *Stratégie)* de 1993 a pris corps lorsque la Banque a constaté avec une inquiétude grandissante que les opérations concernant le secteur de l'eau ne permettaient pas de promouvoir un développe-

## ENGLISH

ment of water resources. It recognizes that improving performance in meeting water needs requires borrowing countries to reform their water management institutions, policies, and planning systems. It also acknowledges that this would mean changes in the Bank's internal processes, training, skill mix, and the resources assigned to water and water-related operations.

The comprehensive analytical frameworks advocated in the *Strategy* paper are designed to help guide decisions about water. There are two major thrusts: to produce an overarching water resources management framework that integrates the needs of the water service subsectors, and to present a reform agenda and innovations to improve the relevance, effectiveness, and sustainability of the main water service subsectors.

### Implementation Is Broad— but Partial and Uneven

Implementing the 1993 *Strategy* has advanced the Bank's corporate goals and mission, contributing to an emerging global consensus on water resource management. But implementation, while broad, has been partial and uneven, with big differences across Regions, countries, and subsectors. Work remains to adapt the *Strategy* to diverse country contexts and to link water resource management to sustainable service delivery.

### Reform is Difficult

While many *Strategy* principles have been mainstreamed in economic and sector work, and have

## ESPAÑOL

hídricos y los proyectos relacionados con este sector figuraban entre los de menor rendimiento de la cartera del Banco— y a la creciente inquietud internacional acerca de la ordenación deficiente de los recursos hídricos mundiales y los insuficientes niveles de servicios, particularmente para los pobres.

La *Estrategia* es sumamente pertinente a la ordenación racional y sostenible de los recursos hídricos. En ella se reconoce que para mejorar el desempeño en la satisfacción de las necesidades de agua es preciso que los países prestatarios reformen sus instituciones, políticas y sistemas de planificación relativos a la ordenación de este recurso. También se reconoce que esto entrañará cambios en los procedimientos internos del Banco, la capacitación, la combinación de aptitudes y los recursos asignados a operaciones sobre los recursos hídricos y relacionadas con este sector.

Los marcos analíticos integrales propugnados en el documento de la *Estrategia* se han diseñado para ayudar a orientar las decisiones relativas al agua. Hay dos aspectos principales: producir un marco global de ordenación de los recursos hídricos que integre las necesidades de los subsectores de servicios de agua, y presentar un programa de reforma e innovaciones a fin de mejorar la pertinencia, la eficacia y la sostenibilidad de los principales subsectores de dichos servicios.

### La aplicación es amplia, pero parcial y desigual

Al aplicar la *Estrategia* de 1993 se han impulsado los objetivos insti-

## FRANÇAIS

ment durable — dans le portefeuille de Banque, les projets centrés sur l'eau ou liés à l'eau étaient ceux dont les résultats étaient les plus décevants — et que la mauvaise gestion des ressources mondiales en eau et la mauvaise qualité des services, en particulier pour les pauvres, ont suscité des préoccupations croissantes au sein de la communauté internationale.

La *Stratégie* répond tout à fait aux impératifs d'une gestion rationnelle et durable des ressources en eau. Elle tient dûment compte du fait que les pays emprunteurs doivent réformer leurs institutions, leurs politiques et leurs systèmes de planification dans le domaine de la gestion de l'eau s'ils veulent pourvoir de meilleure façon aux besoins en eau de leurs populations. Elle reconnaît aussi que cela implique de la part de la Banque qu'elle modifie ses processus internes, les formations dispensées, la répartition des qualifications et les ressources consacrées aux opérations centrées sur l'eau ou liées à l'eau.

Les cadres d'analyse d'ensemble que préconise le document de *Stratégie* sont conçus pour guider les décisions concernant l'eau. Ils reposent sur deux grandes lignes de force : mettre au point un système global de gestion des ressources en eau, qui intègre les besoins des sous-secteurs des services d'eau, et présenter un programme de réformes et des innovations afin d'améliorer la pertinence, l'efficacité et la viabilité des principaux sous-secteurs des services d'eau.

**ENGLISH**

guided Bank involvement in an increasing number of international water partnerships, awareness of water development issues at the level of Country Assistance Strategies remains elusive.

Bank actions are a modest driving force behind water management reforms, except in small countries. Even then, reform requires aligning Bank interventions with country conditions and the activities of other international actors. Other development institutions, including multilateral and bilateral development agencies, nongovernmental organizations (NGOs), and the private sector can, and do, influence the pace and direction of reform. Promoting collaboration with these participants is an important element of the *Strategy*.

The Bank has not widely adopted the comprehensive principles at the heart of the *Strategy*. This is less a failure, however, than an indication of the complexity of water sector reform. Even with sound governance, participation, institutions and skills—all largely missing in Bank client countries—such reform takes 10–20 years.

Reform also takes time. All too often the Bank has expected reform to quickly follow investment. But in water supply and sanitation, making investment conditional on reform frequently leads to more successful outcomes.

### Leadership and Ownership

Where there are champions for reform, the results can be remarkable. In Brazil the Bank's water programs are successful in the state of Ceara because of the per-

**ESPAÑOL**

tucionales y la misión del Banco y se ha contribuido a un consenso mundial incipiente sobre la ordenación de los recursos hídricos. Pero la aplicación, aunque amplia, ha sido parcial y desigual, con grandes diferencias entre las oficinas regionales, países y subsectores. Quedan pendientes tareas para adaptar la *Estrategia* a diversos ámbitos nacionales y vincular la ordenación de los recursos hídricos con la prestación de servicios sostenibles.

### La reforma es difícil

Si bien muchos principios de la *Estrategia* han sido incorporados en los estudios económicos y sectoriales y han orientado la participación del Banco en una creciente cantidad de asociaciones internacionales relativas al agua, aún no se ha creado suficiente conciencia sobre las cuestiones relativas al aprovechamiento de los recursos hídricos a nivel de las estrategias de asistencia a los países. Las intervenciones del Banco son una pequeña fuerza impulsora de las reformas en la ordenación del agua, salvo en países pequeños; aun en ellos, la reforma requiere que las intervenciones del Banco se armonicen con las condiciones reinantes en el país y las actividades de otros participantes internacionales. Otras instituciones de desarrollo, entre ellas organismos multilaterales y bilaterales de desarrollo, organizaciones no gubernamentales (ONG) y entidades del sector privado, pueden influir sobre el ritmo y la orientación de la reforma, y así lo hacen. Promover la colaboración con esos partici-

**FRANÇAIS**

## La stratégie est appliquée de manière générale — mais sa mise en œuvre est fragmentaire et inégale

La mise en œuvre de la *Stratégie* de 1993 a permis de faire avancer les buts institutionnels de la Banque ainsi que la mission qui lui a été assignée, et elle a contribué à dégager un début de consensus sur la gestion des ressources en eau. Mais si la stratégie est appliquée de manière générale, sa mise en œuvre demeure néanmoins fragmentaire et inégale, avec des différences marquées entre les Régions, les pays et les sous-secteurs. Des efforts restent à faire pour adapter la *Stratégie* aux différents contextes nationaux et pour articuler la gestion des ressources en eau avec l'organisation de services viables.

### Les réformes sont difficiles

Un grand nombre des principes qui sous-tendent la *Stratégie* sont systématiquement inclus dans les études économiques et sectorielles, ce qui a conduit la Banque à participer à un nombre croissant de partenariats internationaux pour l'eau, mais la sensibilisation aux problèmes de la mise en valeur de l'eau dans le cadre des Stratégies d'assistance aux pays demeure un vœu pieux. Les interventions de la Banque ont peu d'influence sur les réformes concernant la gestion des ressources en eau, sauf dans les petits pays. Et si c'est le cas, encore faut-il adapter les interventions de la Banque à la situation des pays et aux activités des autres acteurs internationaux. D'autres institutions de développement, et notamment les organismes multilatéraux

**ENGLISH**

sonal interest of the governor and grassroots operations and management. In India the chief minister of Andhra Pradesh pushed through an extensive reform program of the irrigation sector.

### Cross-Sectoral Operations, Subsectoral Differences

The number of cross-sectoral water resources management operations is increasing, but slowly. Most Bank operations remain project-focused because that is seen as the most effective way of building capacity, introducing reforms, and enabling economic and sector work in a time of declining budgets. Indeed, tailoring project design to the *Strategy*'s service-delivery—rather than comprehensive—initiatives appears to result in fewer problem projects and catalyzes reform. In consequence, Bank efforts to nurture policy reform and build domestic capacities have not matched the challenge in most countries.

A major problem is that the main water subsectors (water supply, irrigation and drainage, hydropower, flood control, and environment) function independently, with little cross-sectoral planning and cooperation, and there has been only modest progress toward integrating water resources management activities within river basins. Greater attention is being devoted to making existing infrastructure and institutions work more effectively, but there is a long way to go.

There are also marked subsectoral differences—reform in public sector irrigation and drainage

**ESPAÑOL**

pantes es un importante elemento de la *Estrategia*.

El Banco no ha adoptado en forma generalizada los principios integrales básicos de la *Estrategia*. Sin embargo, esto no es tanto una falla, sino más bien un indicio de la complejidad de la reforma del sector de recursos hídricos. Aun cuando se cuente con una adecuada gestión de gobierno, participación, instituciones y conocimientos —todo lo cual suele faltar en gran medida en los países clientes del Banco—, las reformas suelen llevar de 10 a 20 años.

Con frecuencia, el Banco ha esperado que la reforma ocurra rápidamente después de las inversiones. Pero en materia de abastecimiento de agua y saneamiento, supeditar las inversiones a la reforma suele redundar en resultados más satisfactorios.

### Liderazgo e identificación con los proyectos

Cuando hay paladines de la reforma, los resultados pueden ser notables. En el estado de Ceará (Brasil), los programas del Banco sobre el agua son eficaces debido al interés personal del Gobernador y a las operaciones y gestión por las comunidades de base. En la India, el primer ministro de Andhra Pradesh impulsó un amplio programa de reforma del sector de riego.

### Operaciones intersectoriales, diferencias subsectoriales

Está aumentando, aunque lentamente, el número de operaciones intersectoriales para la ordenación de los recursos hídricos. La mayoría de las operaciones del Banco

**FRANÇAIS**

et bilatéraux de développement, les organisations non gouvernementales (ONG) et le secteur privé, peuvent influer sur le rythme et le cours des réformes, et c'est ce qu'elles font. La promotion de la collaboration avec ces participants est un élément important de la *Stratégie*.

Les principes généraux qui sont au cœur de la *Stratégie* n'ont pas été largement adoptés par les services de la Banque. C'est moins là le signe d'un échec qu'une indication de la complexité de la réforme du secteur de l'eau. Même avec les atouts que représentent une saine gestion des affaires publiques, la participation, les institutions et les compétences — atouts qui font le plus souvent défaut aux pays clients de la Banque —, il faut de 10 à 20 ans pour mener ces réformes à leur terme.

Les réformes demandent également du temps. Trop souvent, la Banque a pensé que les investissements seraient rapidement suivis de réformes. Mais, dans le secteur de l'alimentation en eau et de l'assainissement, on obtient souvent de meilleurs résultats lorsque l'investissement est subordonné à la mise en œuvre de réformes.

### De l'importance du leadership et de la prise en charge des opérations par les acteurs concernés

Dans les pays où la cause des réformes est entendue, les résultats peuvent être remarquables. Au Brésil, le bilan des programmes de la Banque dans le secteur de l'eau est très satisfaisant dans l'État du Ceara parce que le Gouverneur s'y intéresse personnellement et que ce sont les pop-

**ENGLISH**

is now significantly behind that in water supply and sanitation, which is increasingly accepting commercialization and privatization. Other important elements of the *Strategy*— legal and policy aspects, institutional development, participation of stakeholders in decisionmaking and decentralization, a focus on the most needy— remain partially implemented. While there was increased attention to cost recovery, water quality concerns, and the environment, the broader issues of the economic value of water, water and property rights, and mechanisms to equitably allocate an increasingly scarce resource have been neglected, even when Bank attention to the management of trans-boundary and international waters increased.

## Managing Complexity

Determining the right level of complexity and phasing is one of the unresolved dilemmas of a more comprehensive and integrated approach. Not everything can be done at once. The Turkey Izmir Water Supply and Sewerage Project demonstrates the inadvisability of committing funds for large-scale expansion of facilities before addressing critical institutional issues. The Lesotho Highland Water Project, in contrast, largely complied with the *Strategy*, but its sheer size and complexity created an influential national implementation agency that government will have trouble controlling, and dam building crowded-out attention to water supply and sanitation. While it is essential to plan comprehensively,

**ESPAÑOL**

siguen centradas en los proyectos porque se considera que ésta es la manera más eficaz de fortalecer la capacidad, introducir reformas y realizar estudios económicos y sectoriales en tiempos de retracción presupuestaria. En efecto, al adaptar el diseño de los proyectos a iniciativas de prestación de servicios conforme a la *Estrategia* —y no a iniciativas integrales— se obtienen, al parecer, en menos proyectos problemáticos y se favorece la reforma. En consecuencia, las actividades del Banco para promover la reforma de políticas y fortalecer la capacidad nacional no han estado a la altura de los retos que enfrenta la mayoría de los países.

Un problema importante es que los principales subsectores del agua (abastecimiento de agua, riego y drenaje, energía hidroeléctrica, defensa contra las inundaciones y medio ambiente) funcionan independientemente, con escasa planificación y cooperación intersectoriales, y sólo se ha logrado un progreso relativo hacia la integración de la ordenación de los recursos hídricos en el ámbito de las cuencas hidrográficas. Se está prestando mayor atención a que la infraestructura y las instituciones existentes funcionen más eficazmente, pero es muy largo el camino que queda por recorrer.

También hay marcadas diferencias subsectoriales: la reforma en cuestiones de riego y drenaje en el sector público va ahora muy a la zaga de la reforma en abastecimiento de agua y saneamiento, donde hay una aceptación cada vez mayor de la comercialización

**FRANÇAIS**

ulations locales qui ont pris en charge les opérations et la gestion des programmes. En Inde, le ministre en Chef de l'Andhra Pradesh a pu mener à bien un programme de réformes de vaste portée dans le secteur de l'irrigation.

## Opérations intersectorielles, différences sous-sectorielles

Le nombre des opérations intersectorielles de gestion des ressources en eau augmente, mais lentement. La plupart des opérations de la Banque restent centrées sur les projets parce qu'elle considère que c'est la façon la plus efficace de renforcer les capacités, d'introduire des réformes et d'effectuer des études économiques et sectorielles à un moment où les budgets diminuent. De fait, il apparaît que, lorsque les projets sont centrés sur l'organisation des services, comme le requiert la *Stratégie* — plutôt que sur un programme d'action global —, il y ait moins de projets à problèmes et que la dynamique des réformes y gagne. C'est la raison pour laquelle les efforts déployés par la Banque pour faire avancer les réformes, et renforcer les capacités ne sont pas à la mesure des gageures auxquelles sont confrontés la plupart des pays.

L'une des difficultés majeures tient au fait que le fonctionnement des principaux sous-secteurs de l'eau (alimentation en eau, irrigation et drainage, hydroélectricité, maîtrise des crues et environnement) est compartimenté et qu'il y a peu de planification et de coopération intersectorielles. En outre, peu de progrès ont été réalisés pour intégrer les activités de

## ENGLISH

greater success could be achieved through discrete, manageable, and sequenced development.

### Impediments Remain

There is tension between the demands of the Bank's water strategy, country priorities for water development, and what the Bank can deliver within the constraints imposed by internal organization, budgets, and staffing and incentive structures. In water supply and sanitation, and more recently in environment, the Bank has exercised its strategic advantage. But in other areas, particularly irrigation, the Bank needs internal reform to become more effective.

Links across the Bank—particularly in sharpening the development focus on poverty alleviation and institution building—need to be strengthened and mainstreamed. Comprehensive treatment of water resource management has high transaction costs, particularly because many safeguard policies apply to water-related development. Country management thus sees many water interventions as risky ventures in a time of dwindling Bank resources. In addition, water development often transcends borders, and the international dimension adds to the complexity.

Until 2000, no one group had been charged with overseeing and developing the Bankwide institutional retooling needed to ensure a consistent approach to water resource management. But there are some good models, notably in the Africa and the Middle East and North Africa Regions. And it is expected that the new

## ESPAÑOL

y la privatización. Otros elementos importantes de la *Estrategia* —aspectos jurídicos y de políticas, desarrollo institucional, participación de los interesados en la adopción de decisiones y descentralización, y atención a los más necesitados— aún se aplican parcialmente. Si bien se prestó mayor atención a la recuperación de los costos y las cuestiones de calidad del agua y medio ambiente, se han descuidado las cuestiones más amplias del valor económico del agua, los derechos al agua y a la propiedad y los mecanismos para asignar equitativamente un recurso cada vez más escaso, aun cuando el Banco prestó mayor atención a la ordenación de aguas transfronterizas e internacionales.

### Gestión de la complejidad

Uno de los dilemas aún no resueltos de un enfoque más completo e integrado es la determinación del nivel correcto de complejidad y de las etapas. No es posible hacer todo al mismo tiempo. El proyecto de abastecimiento de agua y alcantarillado en Izmir (Turquía) demuestra que no es conveniente comprometer fondos para una expansión en gran escala de las instalaciones si no se han abordado antes las cuestiones institucionales de importancia crítica. En cambio, el proyecto de recursos hídricos en las regiones montañosas de Lesotho se adhirió en gran medida a la *Estrategia*, pero debido a su gran tamaño y complejidad se creó un influyente organismo nacional de ejecución que el gobierno tendrá dificultad en controlar, y se prestó excesiva

## FRANÇAIS

gestion des ressources en eau au niveau des bassins fluviaux. Des efforts sont faits pour améliorer l'efficacité des infrastructures et des institutions existantes, mais il reste encore beaucoup à faire.

Il y a aussi des différences notables entre les secteurs : dans les secteurs publics de l'irrigation et du drainage, les réformes accusent maintenant un sérieux retard par rapport au secteur de l'alimentation en eau et de l'assainissement, où les principes de l'exploitation commerciale et la privatisation gagnent de plus en plus de terrain. Les autres éléments importants de la *Stratégie* — aspects juridiques et aspects relevant de l'action gouvernementale, développement institutionnel, participation des parties prenantes aux prises de décision et décentralisation, priorité accordée aux plus pauvres — ne sont encore appliqués que de façon fragmentaire. Si les problèmes de recouvrement des coûts, de qualité de l'eau et de la protection de l'environnement sont davantage pris en ligne de compte, les questions plus générales que sont la valeur économique de l'eau, les droits d'usage de l'eau et les droits de propriété, les mécanismes permettant de répartir équitablement des ressources de plus en plus rares ont été négligées, même lorsque la Banque a entrepris de s'intéresser davantage à la gestion des eaux transfrontières et internationales.

### Gérer la complexité

Déterminer le bon degré de complexité et d'échelonnement des opérations est l'un des dilemmes non résolus de l'approche globale

## ENGLISH

Bank Water Resources Management Group created in early 2000 within the Environmentally and Socially Sustainable Development Vice-Presidency (ESSD) will address these issues in the Water Resources Sector Strategy Paper.

### Better Guidelines Are Needed

OED's staff survey found that overall satisfaction with the *Strategy* document is high: about 75 percent considered it thorough, consistent with Bank objectives, and relevant to current Bank work and borrower needs. But among informed staff, almost 60 percent thought that the recommendations are difficult to monitor and somewhat platitudinous. Many comments described the *Strategy* as "another unfunded mandate." Independent reviews commissioned by OED also found that the Operations Policy is difficult to use as a guidance document: "It is too brief and abstract for most practitioners and Bank staff," noted one respondent. Compounding this, the reviews found that the *Strategy* needs to be revised, based on lessons and international best practices. In this, the Bank needs to develop sensitive, flexible guidelines that permit staff to set assistance priorities and to determine acceptable tradeoffs in cases where the water *Strategy* imposes competing demands or where elements of the *Strategy* are not likely to be successful.

### A Truly Comprehensive Strategy

The prediction of a global water crisis makes it important for the

## ESPAÑOL

atención a la construcción de presas, en desmedro del abastecimiento de agua y el saneamiento. Si bien es imprescindible que la planificación sea integral, podrían lograrse mejores resultados mediante intervenciones de desarrollo discretas, manejables y realizadas en secuencia.

### Subsisten los impedimentos

Hay tensión entre las exigencias de la estrategia del Banco sobre recursos hídricos, las prioridades de los países para el aprovechamiento del agua y los servicios que el Banco puede prestar dentro de las limitaciones impuestas por la organización interna, los presupuestos, la dotación de personal y las estructuras de incentivos. En materia de abastecimiento de agua y saneamiento, y más recientemente, de medio ambiente, el Banco ha aprovechado su ventaja estratégica; pero en otras esferas, particularmente la del riego, el Banco necesita una reforma interna para aumentar su eficacia.

Es preciso fortalecer los vínculos internos en el Banco e incorporarlos en las actividades de desarrollo, en particular en cuanto a centrar el enfoque del desarrollo en la mitigación de la pobreza y el fortalecimiento institucional. Para un tratamiento integral al tema de la ordenación de los recursos hídricos entraña altos costos de transacción, sobre todo debido a que muchas políticas de salvaguardia se aplican al desarrollo relacionado con el agua. Por eso, los directivos a cargo de las operaciones en los países consideran que muchas intervenciones relati-

## FRANÇAIS

et intégrée. On ne peut tout faire à la fois. Le Projet d'alimentation en eau et d'assainissement d'Izmir (Turquie) montre qu'il n'est pas souhaitable d'engager des fonds pour de vastes travaux d'expansion des équipements sans avoir au préalable réglé les problèmes institutionnels fondamentaux. Par contre, le Projet eau dans les zones montagneuses du Lesotho s'appuyait dans une large mesure sur les principes de la *Stratégie*, mais la taille et la complexité mêmes de l'opération a conduit à mettre en place un organisme d'exécution national influent que le gouvernement aura du mal à contrôler, et la construction du barrage a éclipsé les problèmes d'alimentation en eau et d'assainissement. Une planification d'ensemble est certes essentielle, mais on peut obtenir de meilleurs résultats avec des opérations de développement spécifiques, d'une envergure raisonnable et échelonnées dans le temps.

### Des obstacles demeurent

Il est difficile de concilier à la fois les impératifs de la stratégie de l'eau de la Banque, les priorités des pays en matière de mise en valeur de l'eau et ce que la Banque peut accomplir compte tenu des contraintes qu'imposent l'organisation interne, les budgets, la composition du personnel et les structures d'incitation. Dans les domaines de l'alimentation en eau et de l'assainissement, et plus récemment dans celui de l'environnement, la Banque a exploité son avantage stratégique. Mais dans d'autres domaines et particulièrement dans celui de l'irriga-

## ENGLISH

Bank to reposition itself to meet the challenge. This is creating opportunities for the Bank to implement a comprehensive water management strategy along the following lines:

- Aim country dialogue and institutional development at making water development more responsive to social and environmental concerns and give more attention to allocation issues.
- Nurture commitment to the strategy through shared objectives, realistic diagnostics, and partnerships aimed at policy reform and capacity building.
- Create and sustain comprehensive water management alliances with like-minded partners in the private sector, civil society, and the development community.
- Strengthen internal Bank management and monitoring and evaluation of water resources management activities through a more streamlined organization. Foster more cohesive country and water sector strategies, enhanced core competencies, additional operational guidance and training, and more rigorous quality assurance arrangements.

## ESPAÑOL

vas al agua son iniciativas riesgosas en momentos en que disminuyen los recursos del Banco. Además, el aprovechamiento de los recursos hídricos suele trascender las fronteras y la dimensión internacional aumenta la complejidad.

Hasta 2000, no se había encomendado a ningún grupo la supervisión y formulación a nivel de todo el Banco de la reorganización institucional necesaria para asegurar un enfoque coherente de la ordenación de los recursos hídricos. Existen buenos modelos, especialmente en las regiones de África y de Oriente Medio y Norte de África; se espera que el nuevo Grupo del Banco encargado de la gestión de los recursos hídricos, creado a principios de 2000 dentro de la Vicepresidencia de Desarrollo Social y Ecológicamente Sostenible, encarará esas cuestiones en el documento de estrategia sobre recursos hídricos.

### Es preciso contar con mejores directrices

En la encuesta del personal realizada por el DEO se comprobó que en general, hay gran satisfacción con el documento de la *Estrategia*: un 75% de los encuestados opinaron que era completo, que guardaba coherencia con los objetivos del Banco y que era pertinente a la labor actual del Banco y las necesidades de los prestatarios. Pero de los funcionarios competentes, casi 60% opinaron que las recomendaciones son difíciles de supervisar y algo triviales. Muchas observaciones aludieron a la *Estrategia* como "otro mandato sin financiamiento". En exámenes independientes enco-

## FRANÇAIS

tion, clle doit engager des réformes internes pour devenir plus efficace.

Il faut renforcer et systématiser les liens entre les services de la Banque — en particulier pour mieux centrer les actions de développement sur la lutte contre la pauvreté et le renforcement des institutions. Le traitement global de la gestion des ressources en eau implique des coûts de transaction élevés, en particulier parce que beaucoup de mesures de sauvegarde s'appliquent au développement lié aux ressources hydriques. C'est pourquoi les responsables-pays considèrent que les interventions dans le secteur de l'eau sont des opérations risquées à un moment où les ressources de la Banque diminuent. En outre, la mise en valeur de l'eau transcende souvent les frontières, et la dimension internationale ajoute à complexité des opérations.

Jusqu'en 2000, aucun groupe n'a été chargé de procéder à la réorganisation institutionnelle de l'ensemble de la Banque qui s'impose afin de lui permettre d'adopter une approche cohérente pour la gestion des ressources en eau, et de suivre le déroulement de cette restructuration. Mais il existe des modèles valables, notamment dans les Régions Afrique, et Moyen-Orient et Afrique du Nord. Et le nouveau Groupe de gestion des ressources en eau créé au début de l'an 2000 au sein de la Vice-présidence Développement écologiquement et socialement durable (ESSD) s'attaquera sans aucun doute à ces questions dans le document de Stratégie sectorielle pour les ressources en eau.

**ESPAÑOL**

mendados por el DEO también se comprobó que la política operacional es difícil de utilizar como documento de orientación: "Es demasiado breve y abstracta para la mayoría de los profesionales y de los funcionarios del Banco", dijo un encuestado. En los exámenes también se comprobó que es preciso modificar la *Estrategia* sobre la base de las enseñanzas recogidas y las prácticas óptimas internacionales. Al respecto, es preciso que el Banco elabore directrices perceptivas y flexibles que permitan al personal establecer prioridades de asistencia y determinar soluciones de compromiso aceptables cuando la *Estrategia* sobre recursos hídricos imponga exigencias en pugna o cuando sea improbable que algunos de sus elementos surtan efecto.

## Una estrategia realmente integral

Habida cuenta del pronóstico de una crisis mundial del agua, es importante que el Banco se reposicione para responder ante ese reto. Esto crea oportunidades para que el Banco aplique una estrategia integral de ordenación de los recursos hídricos acorde con los siguientes lineamientos:

- Procurar que en el diálogo con los países y en el desarrollo institucional el aprovechamiento de los recursos hídricos responda mejor a cuestiones sociales y ambientales y preste más atención a los problemas de asignación de recursos.
- Fomentar la adhesión a la estrategia a través de objetivos comunes, diagnósticos realistas y alianzas orientadas a la

**FRANÇAIS**

## Il faut améliorer les directives

L'enquête menée par l'OED auprès des services de la Banque montre que le taux de satisfaction concernant la *Stratégie* est élevé : environ 75 % des agents considèrent que ce document présente une analyse fouillée, cohérente avec les objectifs de l'institution et qui correspond bien aux activités actuelles de la Banque et aux besoins des emprunteurs. Mais près de 60 % des agents informés ont estimé que les recommandations sont difficiles à contrôler et qu'elles sont assez banales. Beaucoup décrivent la *Stratégie* comme « un autre mandat qui ne fait pas l'objet d'un financement ». Des enquêtes indépendantes demandées par l'OED montrent aussi que la politique opérationnelle est difficile à utiliser comme document de référence : « C'est trop succinct et trop abstrait pour la plupart des hommes de terrain et des agents de la Banque » a noté une personne interrogée. Plus grave encore, les enquêtes montrent qu'il faut réviser la *Stratégie* sur la base des enseignements tirés et des pratiques optimales internationales. À cet égard, il faut que la Banque élabore des directives rationnelles et souples qui permettent aux agents d'établir les priorités d'intervention et d'opérer les arbitrages nécessaires lorsque la *Stratégie* impose des exigences antinomiques ou lorsque certains de ses éléments risquent de se solder par un échec.

## Une stratégie véritablement globale

Avec la crise mondiale de l'eau qui se profile à l'horizon, il est important que la Banque se repo-

**ESPAÑOL**

reforma de las políticas
y al fortalecimiento de
la capacidad.
- Establecer y mantener
más alianzas para la
ordenación integral del
agua con asociados afines del sector privado,
la sociedad civil y los círculos
de desarrollo.
- Fortalecer la gestión interna, el
seguimiento y la evaluación del
Banco de las actividades de
ordenación de los recursos
hídricos, mediante una organización simplificada, estrategias
sectoriales y nacionales más
coherentes, competencias básicas mejoradas, más orientación
y capacitación operacional y
arreglos más rigurosos para
asegurar la calidad.

**FRANÇAIS**

sitionne pour être en
mesure de relever cette
gageure, ce qui lui offrira
l'occasion de mettre en
œuvre une stratégie globale de l'eau fondée sur les
principes suivants :
- axer le dialogue avec les
pays et le développement institutionnel sur la prise en
compte des questions sociales
et environnementales dans le
cadre de la mise en valeur de
l'eau et se préoccuper davantage du problème de répartition des ressources en eau ;
- encourager l'adoption de la
stratégie en fondant l'action sur
des objectifs partagés, des
diagnostics réalistes et des
partenariats axés sur les
réformes et le renforcement
des capacités ;
- créer et maintenir des alliances
larges pour la gestion de l'eau
avec des partenaires du secteur
privé, de la société civile et de
la communauté du développement qui partagent les mêmes
conceptions ;
- renforcer la gestion interne de
la Banque ainsi que le suivi et
l'évaluation des activités de
gestion des ressources en eau
par des mesures tendant à
rationaliser l'organisation de
l'institution. Encourager l'adoption de stratégies plus
cohérentes pour les pays et le
secteur de l'eau, renforcer les
compétences essentielles,
fournir des directives opérationnelles supplémentaires,
élargir l'éventail des formations
et prendre des dispositions
plus rigoureuses en matière
d'assurance de la qualité.

# ABBREVIATIONS AND ACRONYMS

| | |
|---|---|
| ADB | Asian Development Bank |
| AFR | Africa Region |
| APL | Adaptable Program Loan |
| BP | Bank Procedure |
| CAS | Country Assistance Strategy |
| CDD | Country-driven Development |
| CDF | Comprehensive Development Framework |
| CODE | Committee on Development Effectiveness |
| DFID | Department for International Development, U.K. |
| EAP | East Asia and Pacific Region |
| EC | European Commission |
| ECA | Europe and Central Asia Region |
| ESSD | Environmentally and Socially Sustainable Development Network |
| ESW | Economic and sector work |
| EU | European Union |
| FAO | Food and Agriculture Organization |
| GEF | Global Environment Facility |
| GP | Good practice |
| I&D | Irrigation & drainage |
| ICR | Implementation Completion Report |
| IDA | International Development Association |
| IFC | International Finance Corporation |
| IUCN | International Union for the Conservation of Nature |
| LAC (LCR) | Latin America and Caribbean Region |
| LIL | Learning and Innovation Loan |
| M&E | Monitoring and evaluation |
| MNA | Middle East and North Africa Region |
| NGO | Nongovernmental organization |
| O&M | Operation and maintenance |
| OECD | Organization for Economic Cooperation and Development |
| OED | Operations Evaluation Department |
| OP | Operational Policy |
| PIP | Project Improvement Plan |
| PROSANEAR | Water and Sanitation Program for Low-Income Urban Population, Brazil |
| PSI | Private Sector Infrastructure Board |
| PSP | Private sector participation |
| QAG | Quality Assurance Group |
| RDV | Rural Development Board |
| RWSS | Rural Water Supply and Sanitation |
| SA (SAR) | South Asia Region |
| SAL | Structural Adjustment Loan |
| SEA | Sectoral Environmental Assessments |
| UNDP | United Nations Development Program |
| UWSS | Urban Water Supply and Sanitation |
| WATSAL | Water Sector Adjustment Loan, Indonesia |
| WBI | World Bank Institute |

| WRM | Water Resources Management |
| WSS | Water Supply and Sanitation |
| WUA | Water User Association |
| WWV | World Water Vision |

# The 1993 *Strategy*— Still Relevant Today

T he *Strategy* embodied in the 1993 *Water Resources Management: A World Bank Policy Paper* is the benchmark for this evaluation.[1] It evolved in response to growing unease within the Bank that water operations were failing to deliver sustainable development and growing international concern about the mismanagement of global water resources and poor service levels, particularly for the poor.

## A Strategy Was Overdue

When the Bank's water *Strategy* was issued, water-related projects were among the poorer performers in the Bank's portfolio. This was emphasized by the influential Wapenhans Report of 1993, which was highly critical of the quality of the Bank's water lending as shown in the findings of OED sector reviews of water supply and sanitation and of irrigation and drainage, and trends in OED outcome ratings.[2]

These sectors had neither comprehensive water development policy nor guidelines. Almost half the water supply and sanitation projects were begun without an established policy for the sector—and without studies in the sector context. Most failed to tap the synergy available from complementary investments in sanitation and environmental protection. Poverty considerations were mostly bypassed as the Bank responded to the pressure from influential segments of the population for better water and sanitation services. There was a general failure to promote compliance with cost-recovery provisions and the implementation of water tariffs and charges that reconciled economic efficiency, social equity, financial criteria, and autonomous and independent regulatory systems.[3] Thus, to improve water supply and sanitation in borrowing countries, OED recommended that the Bank should embark on medium-term programs focused on sectoral adjustment and technical assistance—followed by investment lending only when minimum and monitorable conditions for healthy expansion were met.

Minimal policy and institutional content were also the hallmarks of the irrigation and drainage portfolio—despite a marked shift in the late 1980s toward sector loans and a definite trend away from new construction, toward rehabilitation. An increasing aversion to projects involving safeguard policies prevailed, particularly involuntary resettlement and land acquisition. Insufficient integration of engineering and social science jeopardized better irrigation service to people, lower unit costs, and water conservation. Financial sustainability was elusive because incentive structures that enabled stakeholders to work together to improve performance were ignored. While effective in reaching the rural poor, the perceived success of irrigation projects was strongly affected by macroeconomic conditions, emphasizing the need for comprehensive appraisal. Clearly, there was a need for better policies and a strategic approach to guide the Bank's water investment and non-lending work.

### The Bank *Strategy*

The 1993 Bank *Strategy* described water policies needed to guide internationally sponsored water development. And today, most of the major multilateral development agencies and several bilateral agencies have adopted, or are formulating, water policies. With few exceptions, these policies derive from the Dublin principles (box 1.1) and are consistent with the Bank's *Strategy*.

The relevance of the key principles underlying the Bank's *Strategy* was reaffirmed by the 1997 United Nations General Assembly Special Session, which called for urgent action to address a looming freshwater crisis—and respond to increasing Organization for Economic Cooperation and Development (OECD) concern about persistent water quality problems, the need for heavy investment in water delivery and treatment infrastructure, and growing competition for finite supplies (OECD 1998). Indeed, a consensus

endures that the severity of the world's water problems requires a strategic approach that emphasizes the equitable and sustainable management of water resources.

### Strategic Approach to Equitable and Sustainable Water Management

The *Strategy* paper was the outcome of a hot debate. It fell hostage to another debate over public access to information—a debate not resolved until 1993—making it doubly contentious. Following protest letters from nongovernmental organizations (NGOs) representing 24 borrowing and 8 other countries, the Bank convened a consultative workshop in Washington, D.C., in May 1992. The lessons from this workshop made a substantial difference to the eventual content of the *Strategy* paper—but not without extensive lobbying pressures. The penultimate draft reflected divisions within the Bank between those who would rely on privatization and market forces to solve the problems of the water sector and those who preferred a more comprehensive and participatory approach. The final paper accommodated both perspectives.

The Dublin and Rio Conferences, as well as contemporary Bank work, influenced the *Strategy*. These ideas and principles were driven by the concerns of global NGOs in the late 1980s and earlier Bank statements, operational directives, and notes—the most important of which emerged in 1989–92.[4] They were largely developed by a coalition of water professionals from developing and developed countries. An overriding concern of all involved was that dwindling water resources had to be distributed more widely (figure 1.1) and protected from degradation (Shiklimanov 2000a).

The *Strategy* paper recognized that improving performance in meeting water needs requires borrowing countries to reform their water management institutions, policies, and planning systems. It also acknowledged that this would require changes to the Bank's internal processes, training, skills mix, and resources assigned to water and water-related operations. The main recommendation was that a new approach—recognizing that water is a scarce natural resource, subject to many interdependencies in con-

---

**Box 1.1** — **The Dublin Guiding Principles on Water**

- Fresh water is a finite and valuable resource, essential to sustain life, development, and the environment.
- Water development and management should be based on a participatory approach, involving users, planners, and policymakers at all levels.
- Women play a central part in the provision, management, and safeguarding of water.
- Water has an economic value in all its competing uses and should be recognized as an economic good.

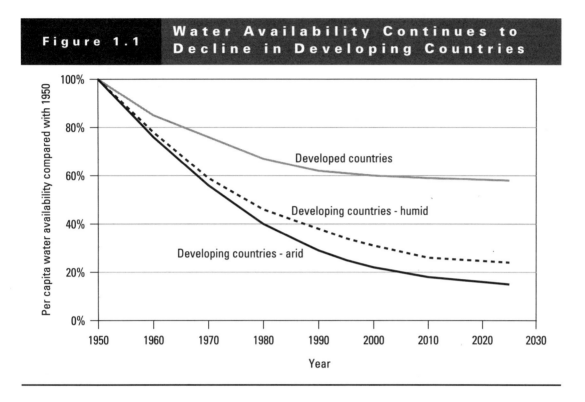

**Figure 1.1** Water Availability Continues to Decline in Developing Countries

veyance and use—should be adopted by the Bank and its member countries.

The twin requirements of comprehensiveness and country-specificity are the centerpiece. Together, they challenge the Bank to avoid cookie-cutter blueprints for institutional reform and water-sector management—and challenge borrowers to look beyond the short-term gains from discrete projects. The aim is to:

- Maximize the contribution of water to countries' economic, social, and environmental development while ensuring that resource and water services are managed sustainably.
- Encourage and help countries establish comprehensive analytical frameworks to foster informed and transparent decisionmaking, with an emphasis on demand management.
- Promote decentralized implementation processes and market forces to guide the appropriate mix of public and private sector provision of water services.

The comprehensive analytical frameworks advocated in the *Strategy* paper are to help guide decisions about water resources and "enable coherent, consistent policies and reg-

ulations to be adopted across sectors . . . in countries where significant problems exist, or are emerging, concerning the scarcity of water, the efficiency of service, the allocation of water, or environmental damage" (World Bank 1994d, pp. 10–11, 13). There thus are two major thrusts: to produce an overarching water resources management framework that integrates the needs of the water service subsectors and a reform agenda and innovations to improve the relevance, effectiveness, and sustainability of the main water services subsectors (figure 1.2). Traditionally, the majority of the Bank's operations dealt with subsector development.

Country situations and constraints provide the pattern to tailor the comprehensive frameworks. Recognizing that many borrowers would need help in designing a suitable analytical framework and implementing the corresponding reform effort, the *Strategy* committed the Bank to assist governments in institutional reforms and in establishing a strong *legal and regulatory framework* for dealing with pricing, monopoly organizations, environmental protection, and other aspects of

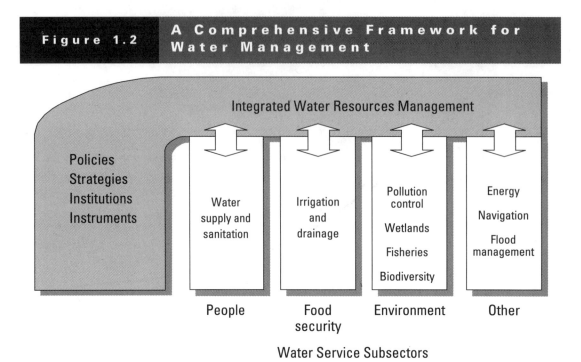

**Figure 1.2    A Comprehensive Framework for Water Management**

Integrated Water Resources Management

Policies
Strategies
Institutions
Instruments

| Water supply and sanitation | Irrigation and drainage | Pollution control<br>Wetlands<br>Fisheries<br>Biodiversity | Energy<br>Navigation<br>Flood management |

People          Food security          Environment          Other

**Water Service Subsectors**

*Source:* After Global Water Partnership (2000).

water management (World Bank 1994d). The main areas of emphasis in the 1993 *Strategy* are to:

- Build institutional and regulatory capacity in borrower countries sufficient to enable borrowers to implement and sustain the comprehensive approach to water-sector planning and management.
- Support international cooperation on management and use of international waterways and bodies, recognizing that a truly comprehensive approach to water-resource management extends beyond the borders of individual borrowers and beyond the timeframe of individual projects.
- Draw on the comparative advantages of organizations outside the Bank and involve stakeholders in decisions that affect them. Decentralization, participation, and partnerships are key instruments to increase stakeholder ownership and accountability, build capacity, and ultimately lower the cost and improve the effectiveness of operations, maintenance, safeguards, and monitoring and evaluation.

- Adopt water rights, pricing, and incentives (including adoption of new technologies and managerial approaches) to encourage rational and efficient allocation of water among competing uses, discourage waste, and ensure adequate water services.
- Ensure that water operations enhance human and natural environments, with special attention to safeguards, social impacts (particularly on women), and meeting the needs of the poor.

## New Approaches and Initiatives Are Even More Critical Today

Apart from the attention needed to reform old institutions and organizations and build new ones to deal with the strategic issues in water development, the most daunting challenge is to mobilize funds. World Water Vision (WWV) 2000 estimates that the annual investment to meet all water supply and sanitation, irrigation, industrial, and environmental management needs by 2025 will be $180 billion—today it is $70–80 billion (table 1.1). The WWV team postulated that investment for agriculture (mainly irrigation and

| Table 1.1 | Annual Investment for Water Must Increase | | |
|---|---|---|---|
| | **Investment ($ billion)** | | **Increase** |
| **Water use** | **1995** | **2025** | **1995–2025 (%)** |
| Agriculture | 30–35 | 30 | -8 |
| Environment and industry | 10–15 | 75 | 500 |
| Water supply and sanitation | 30 | 75 | 150 |
| Total | 70–80 | 180 | 140 |

*Source:* WWC 2000.

| Table 1.2 | A Much Greater Role for the Private Sector | | |
|---|---|---|---|
| | **Investment ($ billion)** | | **Increase** |
| **Source** | **1995** | **2025** | **1995–2025 (%)** |
| National | | | |
| Public sector | 45–50 | 30[a] | -37 |
| Private firms | 12–15[b] | 90[c] | 620 |
| International | | | |
| Donors | 9 | 12 | 33 |
| Private investors | 4[b] | 48 | 1,100 |
| Total | 70–80 | 180 | 140 |

a. Assumes direct government subsidy of $20 billion to the poor.

b. Does not include investment by industry.

c. Includes investment by industry, excluding hydropower.

*Source:* WWC 2000.

drainage) declined because the era of costly, large-scale public capital investment in new irrigation is almost at an end—and that more efficient user-managed rehabilitation, operation, and maintenance are likely.[5] The public sector provides most of the investment (table 1.2), but private investments (including contributions by industry) of $138 billion a year, or almost 70 percent of the total, will be essential.

Even international donors are expected to increase their contribution by a third—to $12 billion. This massive increased investment—which would be even greater if irrigation and drainage investment were to increase—can be achieved only if developing countries are able to create an investment climate conducive to the private sector and able to absorb these investments. This requires political stability and attention to governance and institutions—particularly property rights, rule of law, transparency, and participation.

The Commission Report of the Second World Water Forum (March 2000) stated that:

To ensure that environmental quality is improved and people's needs are met, there must be a redoubled effort at technological, financial, and institutional innovation. With regard to technological innovation this means mobilizing the knowledge and investment capacity of the private sector and supplementing it with strategic investments. With regard to institutional innovation, the core challenges are stimulating new forms of involvement of citizens in managing water and providing incentives for private sector involvement. The Commission emphasizes that unless full-cost pricing for water services becomes accepted practice, none of these will succeed. With commitment, however, the problems can be overcome. A secure world is possible, but we must change the ways we manage water.

This statement supports the assertion that the Bank's 1993 *Strategy* is highly relevant to current global priorities. Fine-tuning will enable the Bank to make adjustments in response to lessons from positive and negative changes in the operating environment. That will involve updating the *Strategy* to ensure congruence with over-arching Bank priorities (poverty reduction, governance, sound economic and fiscal management) and the greater focus on achieving results consistent with the Comprehensive Development Framework (CDF).

# The Bank's Water Assistance and Portfolio

T he Bank has substantially realigned the composition of water operations and non-lending work to incorporate crosscutting water *Strategy* issues in a diverse set of countries.

## Different Countries Present Different Challenges

Bank actions are generally only a modest driving force behind water management reforms, except in small countries. Even then, reform requires aligning Bank interventions with country conditions and other international actors. Other development institutions, including multilateral and bilateral development agencies and nongovernmental organizations and the private sector, can and do influence the pace and direction of reform. Promoting collaboration with these international actors is an important element of the water *Strategy*, particularly in large countries—China, India, Mexico, and Brazil—where it is essential to improve selectivity by leveraging the relatively small external assistance. For example, India is the second-biggest Bank borrower for water, yet the Bank's credits have provided only about 10 percent of national water investment and less than half of all external assistance for water development (Pitman 2001).

The design of relevant reforms and the time frame for their implementation crucially depend on the internal dynamics and water situation of the country:

- Water-short Mexico and Yemen are striving to sustainably manage groundwater in the face of competing urban and agricultural water demand.
- The rapidly urbanizing populations of Brazil, China, and India face the key challenges of providing water and sanitation while controlling pollution that reduces the resource base.
- In the central Asian republics, triage to determine appropriate maintenance and rehabilitation of failing irrigation systems is among the major development issues.
- In Honduras and St. Lucia, land use policies and regulation are key to sustainable watershed management.
- While Pakistan is focused on solving its massive drainage problems and resultant salinization, flood control has traditionally dominated the agenda in Bangladesh.

The challenge of comprehensive water resource management continues to be addressing these critical development issues, and coping with such natural disasters as drought and the results of El Niño—all without neglecting environmental management, institutional development, and financial, economic, and social sustainability. While the impact, scale, and timing of global warming on water resources and sea levels are contentious, the likely effects need to be included in the discussion of long-term regional and global water strategies.

## The Mix of Instruments Has Changed

The Bank's work has remained primarily at the country level, complemented by selected global programs. The custom package of assistance depends on a country's needs. Over time, the mix and nature of Bank products and services has changed and the Bank has increasingly leveraged its other assets—cross-country experience, and relationships and capacity to connect clients with additional sources of finance, technical expertise, and partnerships.

### Lending

The range of instruments has changed in the last decade. Traditional specific investment lending dominates (80 percent), followed by specific investment and maintenance loans (10 percent). But within this category, loans have financed a wide range of activities, from single small-scale projects to complex programmatic sectoral operations. Poor experience with technical assistance loans caused them to be reduced by a third, and only six were made post-*Strategy*. Adaptable Program and Learning and Innovation Loans, introduced Bankwide in 1997, accounted for only 7 of the 201 operations since 1993. Sectoral Adjustment Loans (SALs) have been used sparingly, most notably to leverage reform in Jordan, and an ambitious SAL for water is currently being completed for Indonesia.

Since 1989, the Bank has successfully facilitated the privatization process to leverage large private investment. Private sector participation (PSP) in water supply and sanitation has grown remarkably, and took off in 1992 in response to global liberalization and the easing of fiscal restraints. To date, more than $21.8 billion has been invested for 86 water supply utilities, most of it in the well-governed middle- to higher-income developing countries. The Bank, with the International Finance Corporation (IFC) and the Global Environmental Facility (GEF), has been involved in 17 PSP operations. Bank Group investments in PSP, which exceed $680 million, cover 12 countries, of which a third are in the low-income category eligible for IDA funding.

### Economic and Sector Work

Economic and sector work (ESW) for water has more than doubled since 1991. In 1992–98 the number of ESW reports rose from 25 a year to about 30, falling back slightly during the Bank reorganization of 1997. Unlike much of the earlier work, which dwelt on traditional technical issues, ESW after 1992 fully embraced the themes, policy instruments, and objectives of the new *Strategy*, moving away from traditional water management toward roles for the private sector, participation, and comprehensive water management (figure 2.1). ESW on the private sector, pricing, and markets has seen the biggest increase in attention, but most of this work concerned water supply rather than either sanitation or irrigation and drainage. Social assessments have been notably absent. Partnerships to promote global public water and capacity building are the most notable innovation post-*Strategy*.

### Partnerships

*Building global and regional public policy.* The Bank has been instrumental in forming and supporting a growing number of international partnerships. Notable are the Global Water Partnership and the World Water Council in 1996. The two bodies have similar and overlapping objectives, but they differ in the way they contribute to sustainable water resources management. The World Water Council is more a forum than a network, views itself as the world's water policy think tank, and is publishing a new journal, *Water Policy*, which focuses on policy aspects of water resources. Conversely, the Global Water Partnership, initially chaired by a Bank Vice President, attempts to translate recommendations for action on water management into specific services for developing countries and to catalyze funding mechanisms for service implementation. Through a consultative process, the partnership developed the Framework for Action, establishing a shared view of appropri-

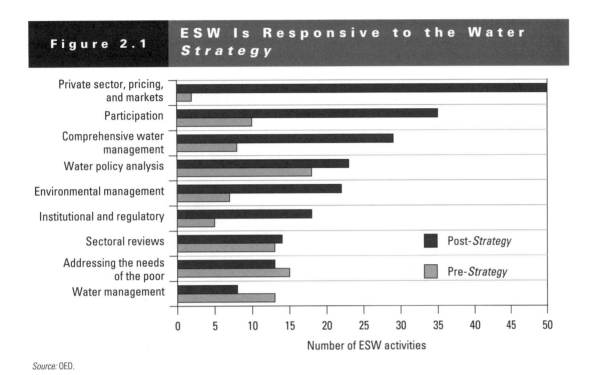

**Figure 2.1   ESW Is Responsive to the Water Strategy**

Private sector, pricing, and markets
Participation
Comprehensive water management
Water policy analysis
Environmental management
Institutional and regulatory
Sectoral reviews
Addressing the needs of the poor
Water management

■ Post-*Strategy*
■ Pre-*Strategy*

Number of ESW activities

*Source:* OED.

ate strategies, mechanisms for implementation, and priorities for immediate action and investment to obtain a World Water Vision. The framework was presented at the Second World Water Conference organized by the World Water Commission at The Hague in 2000. The UNDP-World Bank Partnership on International Waters was established in 1998.

Not all global policy partnerships are long-term or formal. The World Commission on Dams received substantial buy-in across the globe, but was dissolved after issuing its final report in November, 2000.[1] An informal partnership between the Bank and Germany has sponsored four international roundtables on transboundary water policy and management to support the Global Water Partnership's Integrated Water Resources Management Window. In addition, the Business Partners for Development partnership has a three-year water and sanitation component sponsored by the Bank, the U.K. Department for International Development (DFID), and private water companies. It is studying public-private partnerships in eight countries to see what determines success.

The Africa and Middle East and North Africa (MNA) Regions of the Bank are facilitating re-gional dialogue on water policy, development, and management. The 1997 MNA Regional Water Policy Initiative is a partnership with the European Union (EU) and the European Investment Bank. The Africa Region hosted the Africa Water Resources Management Policy Conference in Nairobi (May, 1999), leading stakeholders to establish an African Water Resources Forum to exchange knowledge among African professionals and practitioners. The Council of Ministers of Water Affairs of the Nile Basin has asked the World Bank and its partners to organize and host a consultative group—the International Consortium for Cooperation on the Nile—that will seek coordinated and transparent support for cooperative projects in the Nile Basin. The Consortium will emphasize sharing the benefits of development rather than focusing on allocation alone.

*Capacity-building Partnerships.* The oldest global water partnership—the 1977 UNDP-World Bank Water and Sanitation Program—has been a model of governance for subsequent partnerships. Supported by 11 bilaterals, it seeks to "influence without taking over" in 30 countries. Aiming to meet the needs of the poor, it thus developed self-standing demonstration programs outside the scope of the Bank's lending program. Managed by the Bank, it leverages bilateral experience into larger-scale investments by the Bank and others—and builds capacity to strengthen national policy reforms for community-based approaches.

The World Bank Institute's (WBI) Water Policy Capacity Building Program meets the demand for knowledge and learning dissemination supported by formal training. Supported by four UN agencies and five bilateral partners since 1994, borrowers qualify if they show commitment to water reform and if Bank staff judge the sustainability of program impact to be likely. Rated as successful by clients, the program has reached 9,000 participants in 90 countries. Almost half of participants surveyed said that WBI-sponsored activities initiated country reforms of water management policy.

The Bank has also been successful in enabling local initiatives to grow into international partnerships to build capacity and country ownership for sectoral reform. A 1995 WBI workshop in Mexico gave rise to the International Participatory Irrigation Network, which now has members in over 44 countries and national chapters in the 10 biggest borrowers for irrigation. The Network supplements the former Bank-sponsored International Program for Research in Irrigation and Drainage that moved to the Food and Agriculture Organization (FAO) in 2000.

Since 1996, the Bank has supported the African Water Utilities Partnership for Capacity Building, which organizes management assistance from more experienced partners to utilities serving rapidly growing urban populations. A similar partnership is being developed for South Asia. In 2000, a new Bank-Netherlands Water Partnership emanating from the Second World Water Forum began mobilizing significant Dutch funding to apply practical experience, lessons, and innovation to Bank-supported operations.

## A Larger Portfolio Whose Quality Has Improved, Albeit Unevenly

The Bank is the only lending institution with a global mandate to improve water management, and its most visible assistance has been investment lending. Each year, developing countries

invest $70–80 billion in water development. Of this, multilateral and bilateral agencies supply about $9 billion, of which the World Bank provides from $2 to $3 billion, or about 3 percent of the global funding for water.

Between 1988 and 1999, the Bank approved $28.8 billion (1996 dollars) for water projects, including 319 country-based investment operations and one regional program (the Aral Sea), rising from 56 countries before 1993 to 70 after.[2] In addition, the Bank lent about $6.2 billion for water-focused investments in 91 other projects that included significant water development components.[3] Comparing lending for water before and after the *Strategy* shows an increase of 21 percent, from $14.5 to $17.5 billion, while overall Bank lending increased by 9.4 percent. As a result, the Bank's portfolio of water projects rose steadily from 10 percent of total projects in 1988 to 14 percent today, even though the share of lending for water has declined since 1997 (figure 2.2).

Of the lending for water, a third went to East Asia and the Pacific (EAP), a fifth each to South Asia (SA), and to Latin America and the Caribbean (LAC), with the balance divided among Africa (AFR), Europe and Central Asia (ECA), and the Middle East and North Africa (MNA). This distribution is similar to that of overall Bank lending. The volume of lending for water remained heavily concentrated before and after the *Strategy*, with more than half going to only five countries: Brazil, China, India, Indonesia, and Mexico (figure 2.3). The share going to China and India increased from 25 percent before 1993 to almost 40 percent after. Indeed, the overall portfolio became more concentrated: 85 percent of lending covered 48 countries before the *Strategy*, but only 24 countries after.

Because the Bank's water activities are fragmented across many sectors, Bank involvement in water development is considerably greater than suggested by Bank statistics for the traditional water sectors. The composition of the Bank's water portfolio has been realigned significantly since 1993, mainly because of an increased focus on the environment and on multisectoral projects, watershed development in agriculture projects, and social sector, transport, and urban investments (figure 2.4).[4]

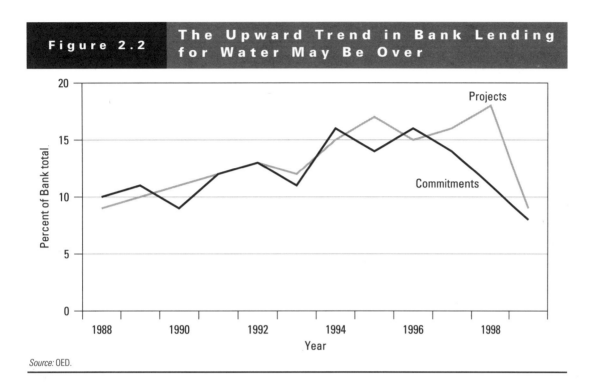

**Figure 2.2** The Upward Trend in Bank Lending for Water May Be Over

*Source:* OED.

Bank commitments to the "other sectors" category grew eightfold after 1993 to reach $6.2 billion. And most of this was for water development embedded within more general agricultural development projects and social sector projects (table 2.1). As a result, the amount lent (but not **the number of** projects) to the traditional water subsectors (water supply and san-

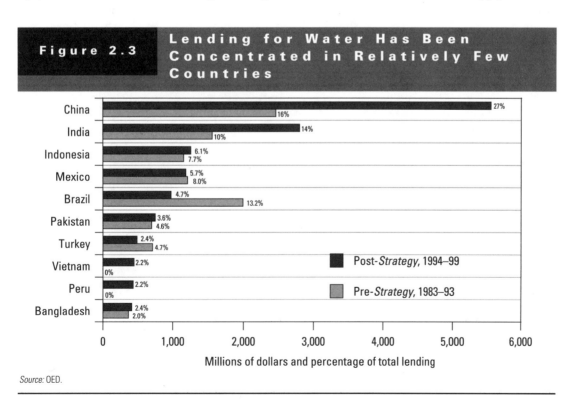

**Figure 2.3** Lending for Water Has Been Concentrated in Relatively Few Countries

*Source:* OED.

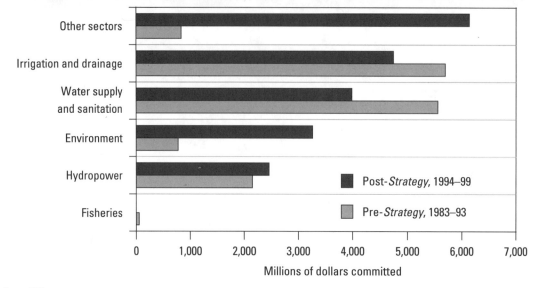

Figure 2.4 — Lending to the Traditional Water Sectors Has Declined Since the 1993 *Strategy*

Post-*Strategy*, 1994–99
Pre-*Strategy*, 1983–93

Millions of dollars committed

*Source:* OED.

itation, irrigation, and drainage) declined. Given that most "other sector" water projects are embedded in operations managed by nonwater staff or are not managed at all in demand-led social funds, there is growing concern that water policy oversight and coherence is being diluted. That makes it more difficult to apply the principles of the *Strategy*.

## The Poverty Focus of Water Operations Is Getting Better

The *Strategy* gives priority to the provision of adequate water and sanitation services to the poor. OED's analysis of Bank Quality Assurance Group (QAG) data found that water projects were not as good as other sector projects in complying with the Country Assistance Strategy (CAS) poverty strategy.[5] Despite this, more water investment goes to poorer countries than Bank investment as a whole, primarily because irrigation and drainage investments have become more sharply focused on the poorest countries. Indeed, the poverty focus of irrigation and drainage projects rose by 23 percent after the *Strategy*. Conversely, formal water supply and sanitation operations declined by 13 percent—primarily because of the increased focus on lending to financially viable urban utilities that outweighs the new generation of pro-poor rural Water Supply and Sanitation (WSS) projects. Indirect lending

| Table 2.1 | Water Supply and Sanitation Investments in Nontraditional Sectors Are Increasing | | | | |
|---|---|---|---|---|---|
| Investment ($millions)[a] | 1988–93 | 1994–99 | Projects (number) | 1988–93 | 1994–99 |
| Official WSS | 5,556 | 3,984 | Official WSS | 64 | 67 |
| Other sectors | 56 | 1,181 | Other sectors | 8 | 53 |
| Total | 5,612 | 5,165 | Total | 72 | 120 |

a. Constant 1996 US $.

*Source:* OED data.

for WSS implemented through community-driven social funds is strongly pro-poor.

Compelling evidence exists that social concerns are being increasingly addressed in water operations (figure 2.5), but it is too soon to judge outcomes.[6] Increasing poverty analysis and establishing institutional mechanisms to target the poor and monitor impacts of Bank investments on poverty enhanced the focus on poverty alleviation through water operations. But substantial room remains for targeting the poor and vulnerable populations within water sector operations. Of most concern across the Bank is the scant attention given to the direct impact of these operations on the poor.

## Overall Project Design Has Been Improving

The quality of water operations at approval is generally better than the quality of all other Bank investments, according to QAG data, but with some deficiencies. While water operations address social and stakeholder analysis better than other Bank subsectors, they are notably deficient in forming appropriate partnerships with other development partners, in pushing for ap-

propriate and realistic reform measures, or in tailoring project design to meet the needs of target populations.

## But There Are Subsectoral Differences

Water projects as a whole ranked behind Bankwide projects in conducting adequate analysis of the institutional framework—and were less realistic in financial appraisal. This was primarily because of the rural sector's weakness in designing financial management systems and poor assessment of project risks in irrigation and drainage. In their approaches to social development concerns in project design, irrigation and drainage projects fare significantly better than water supply and sanitation. They are more participatory, incorporate the views and wishes of various stakeholders better in the project design, and do a much better job of putting in place social impact and poverty monitoring mechanisms. Water supply and sanitation projects, by contrast, articulate their development objectives more clearly—and they are 25 percent better than the irrigation and drainage portfolio on satisfactory analysis and treatment of insti-

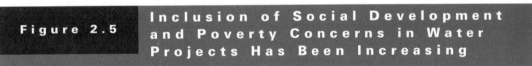

**Figure 2.5** Inclusion of Social Development and Poverty Concerns in Water Projects Has Been Increasing

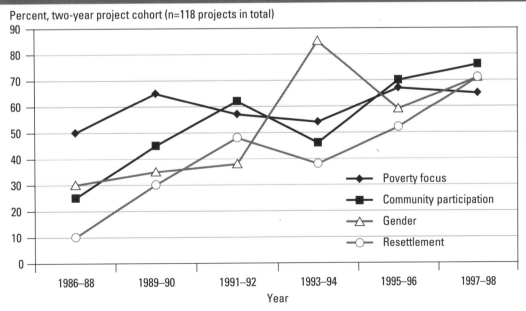

tutional issues, and on the quality and coherence of economic justification.

The weakness of rural sector water operations also increases the risk of implementation problems. Factors contributing to the risk are country conditions threatening achievement of development objectives—economic management and past portfolio performance—and the vigilance of sector management. In "realism," which flags chronic overoptimism and a failure to recognize implementation problems early on, natural resources management and water supply and sanitation were near the Bank average (74 percent), while irrigation and drainage were much less realistic. Sector management was also less proactive in addressing lingering problems in irrigation and drainage than in water supply

and sanitation. But it was not as bad as natural resources management, which was way below the Bank average.

The irony here is that more "realism" will lead to a more problematic portfolio. In the MNA Region the high-risk water supply and sanitation portfolio appears to reflect the Bank's tough and principled stand on urban water reform in a difficult Region, rather than flawed project design and supervision.[7] Of the 16 Bankwide water supply and sanitation problem projects, 3 had risk factors that were political; 3, institutional; and the remaining 10, financial and managerial. None of the Bank's irrigation operations highlighted financial or utility management risks because there were few benchmarks against which to judge them.

# The Water *Strategy* Has Been Only Partially Implemented

T he Bank has not widely adopted the comprehensive principles at the heart of the *Strategy*. This is less a failure, however, than it is an indication of the complexity of water sector reform, which even in OECD countries takes 10–20 years.

Only two of the six Bank Regions (AFR and MNA) have produced regional water strategies in line with the Bank *Strategy,* and only one (MNA) has developed country and sector strategies driven by a regional sequencing of priorities for action. By contrast, some Regions (LAC) are bundling subsector strategies to determine national and regional strategies. Few borrowers take a long-term holistic view that water is a vital resource that needs careful stewardship to ensure sustainability, equitable access, and use.

The number of cross-sectoral water resources management operations is increasing only slowly. Most Bank operations remain project-focused because that is seen as the most effective way of building capacity, introducing reforms, and enabling economic and sector work in a time of declining budgets. Indeed, tailoring project design to the *Strategy's* service-delivery initiatives appears to result in fewer problem projects and catalyzes reform.

## Treatment of Water Issues in CASs Has Been Weak

The *Strategy* emphasizes the critical importance of embedding projects in country water strate-

gies within the CAS framework, a benchmark of successful *Strategy* implementation. But this requires significant cross-sectoral coordination, a duty for which Bank staff have few incentives and inadequate resources. If water is mentioned in a CAS, it is more likely to be water supply and sanitation, not irrigation or comprehensive water resources management.[1] Water supply and sanitation, raised as an issue in 57 countries, is promoted as a way of improving health and labor productivity and, hence, reducing poverty. Irrigation is mentioned in only 34 percent of CASs, and such issues as water user groups, participatory management, and water rights occur in less than a tenth. Of most concern is the near absence of water supply and sanitation issues for Africa CASs—a Region that is not only poor but is also experiencing rapid urbanization.

Only one CAS, for water-short Yemen, explicitly promotes sustainable water resource use and a need to focus on water. For the other 97 countries covered by CASs, 64 have no reference to a comprehensive framework, a core requirement of the *Strategy*. A comprehensive approach was found in the CASs for seven of eight mainly arid MNA countries (with significant water issues), but only Ethiopia and Senegal in AFR. Thailand, Vietnam, and the Philippines in EAP raise all three comprehensive management issues: water policy, water management, and a national framework plan. In ECA, the management of international waters and the control of water pollution have been a major theme in CASs.

The mention of water strategy issues in a CAS is not enough to bring attention to needed reforms and not a very good measure of the efficacy of the water strategy and of ESW.[2] Negligible comment in the CAS could mean there are no problem issues—or that they are addressed either satisfactorily through Bank operations or outside the framework of Bank country assistance. In Ghana, active reform efforts have strong domestic ownership and multidonor involvement. Tunisia is recognized as the most advanced country in water management in MNA, while South Africa has an exemplary water law and process for implementing reform. But even where water issues are important, there may be no mention in the CAS because the Bank's country macroeconomists have other perspectives and concerns.

These interpretation difficulties could be overcome if the CAS included a table showing the country's status in all sectors and the reasons for the Bank's level of involvement in each sector or subsector. This would also have the advantage of making the selectivity criteria for Bank involvement more transparent, probably enhancing synergistic partnerships with other assistance agencies.

## Projects Have Become More Responsive to the *Strategy*

The new generation of economic and sector work has changed the design of Bank water projects. Evaluation of the design of 177 water projects against the key principles of the *Strategy* shows that they are increasingly responsive, with the average trend upward since 1993 (figure 3.1).[3] Each project was evaluated only against relevant *Strategy* principles. For example, a rural water supply project is not a relevant instrument for reforming regional or river basin water resources management, just as a dam safety or flood prevention project is not a relevant instrument for reform of water tariffs and subsidies. So it is

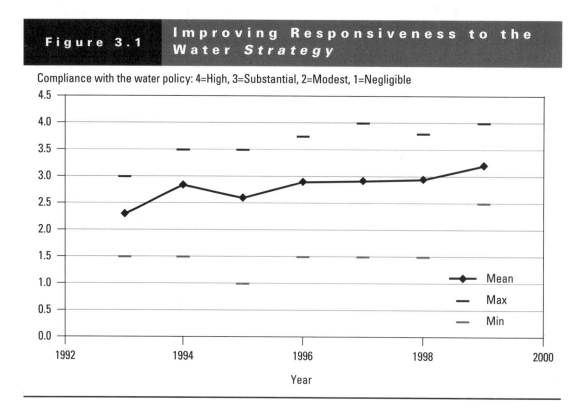

**Figure 3.1**    Improving Responsiveness to the Water *Strategy*

Compliance with the water policy: 4=High, 3=Substantial, 2=Modest, 1=Negligible neither practical nor appropriate for any one project to fully respond to all the recommended components of the water *Strategy*. Indeed, OED's analysis found that highly rated projects were those that focused on four or fewer elements of the *Strategy* in project design.

Water projects fell into two classes—the minority (20 percent) considered comprehensive water resources management at the river basin and national scales, and the majority (80 percent) focused only on the project, with negligible larger-scale linkages. Because very few projects took the comprehensive view before 1993, this is a notable achievement. Despite the lack of large-scale linkages, project-focused operations scored highly on the comprehensiveness rating if they included other *Strategy* elements in design. In many cases, while projects delivering water service infrastructure were not appropriate vehicles for reforming basin-wide or national water management, they did tackle systemic institutional reform issues. And many projects appeared to avoid issues involving high transaction costs, long gestation periods, and high perceived risk.

Other important elements of the *Strategy*—legal and policy aspects, institutional development,

and a focus on the most needy—remain partially implemented (figure 3.2). The inadequate attention to the legal and policy aspects of institutional development is cause for concern. These issues, critical to ensuring the sustainability of water reform initiatives, embrace appropriate mechanisms for cross-sectoral coordination, participation of stakeholders in decisionmaking and decentralization, sufficient powers to enable policy institutions to operate effectively, and the quality of the regulatory environment.

## Regions Have Pursued Different Approaches to Comprehensive Water Management

There are substantial differences in the way regional lending operations address comprehensive water resources development.[4] Adherence by Region to the comprehensive principle is varied (figure 3.3). Some of this is due to differences in hydrologic endowment, level of economic development, willingness to reform, or pre-*Strategy* starting point. MNA scored low on its national and basin-level approach because many of its large countries do not have large perennial river basins. The exceptions are

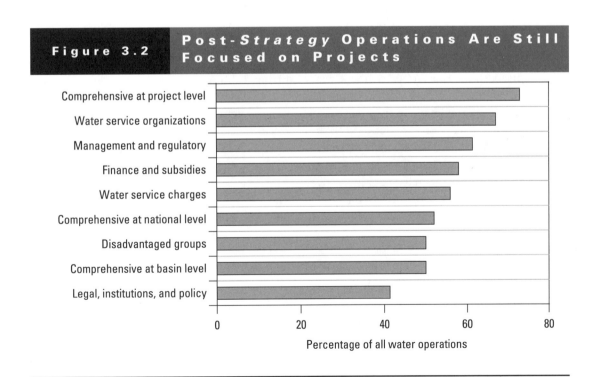

**Figure 3.2** Post-*Strategy* Operations Are Still Focused on Projects

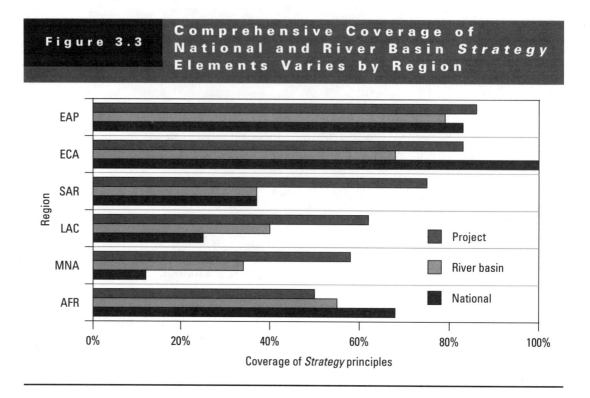

**Figure 3.3** Comprehensive Coverage of National and River Basin *Strategy* Elements Varies by Region

Morocco, where the Water Resources Management project is piloting a River Basin Agency, and Jordan, where the Jordan River Valley Authority is central to Bank assistance for reform.

The real cause for concern is the scant progress made at the national and basin level in South Asia and in Latin America and the Caribbean, although there are exceptions in Brazil, Nepal, and Bangladesh. In Latin America, Bank water operations are most active in water supply and sanitation and are not linked to river basin management. Three exceptions are flood protection assistance in Argentina, water quality management in Brazil's Guarapiranga project, and integrated water resources management in the river basins of Brazil's Ceara state. Most of the Bank's water-related efforts in Latin America are strongly linked to commercialization or to ensure environmental and social sustainability.

The Bank scores highly on its responsiveness to the *Strategy* at the basin level in the ECA and EAP regions, frequently because water projects dovetail neatly into existing regional sea or river basin management organizations. Even so, the Bank has been very effective in improving operation and longer-term planning—and, particu-

larly in China, in augmenting measures to improve financial and environmental sustainability.

The improvement in strategy responsiveness of regional water portfolios since 1993 is a measure of the Regions' effectiveness in promoting the water *Strategy* (figure 3.4). While MNA and AFR started at the bottom, they show the most improvement over the past six years. Starting higher, Latin America and the Caribbean shows the smallest improvement. In all cases, the level of improvement is strongly related to the regional organization for water resources management, as discussed in Chapter 5.

## As Have Subsectors

The various water subsectors also differ in the extent to which they have followed the *Strategy*. Subsectors vary substantially in integrating projects into policy, institutional, development, and planning frameworks (figure 3.5). Except for the water resource management and sector projects, all other subsectors give the greatest attention to project design issues that attempt to internalize local externalities. Irrigation—the traditional home of water resources planning and management in most client countries—is below

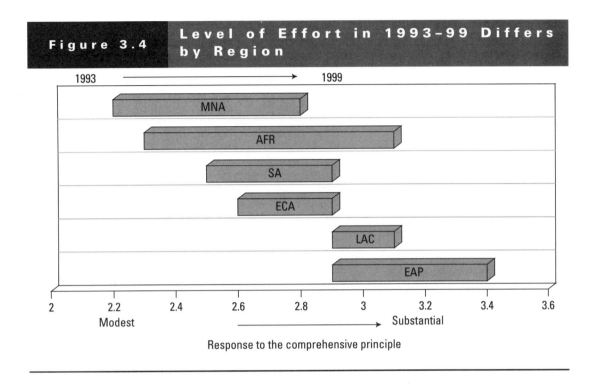

**Figure 3.4** — Level of Effort in 1993–99 Differs by Region

Response to the comprehensive principle

the water supply and sanitation projects in incorporating *Strategy* issues.

One reason is that irrigation organizations generally have substantial power and vested interests that resist reforms that would lessen their power base and influence, particularly in South Asia and in East Asia and the Pacific, where most irrigation projects are located. In many irrigation projects, policies and investments to ensure service delivery take priority over more global

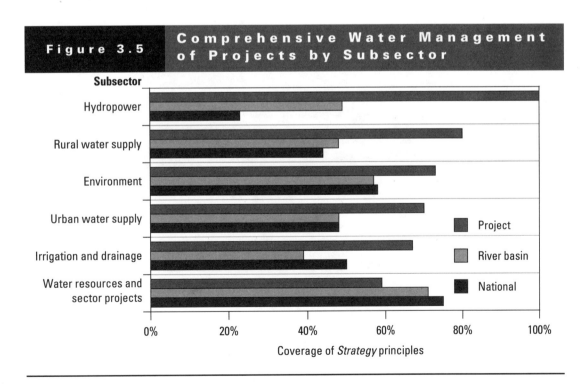

**Figure 3.5** — Comprehensive Water Management of Projects by Subsector

Coverage of *Strategy* principles

concerns. Hydropower projects meet the highest standards at the project level, but they score badly at the national level—that is surprising, because their relatively large scale should argue for a more integrated approach.

Appropriately, environmental and water resource management projects are better at dealing with the bigger picture of water resource management than with the four subsectors dealing with service delivery, which are only modestly involved in comprehensive water management at the river basin and national levels. This is a problem for both the Bank and its clients. Water reform is inherently political, and the Bank can only facilitate change, not enforce it. Profound organizational problems plague most countries, where water jurisdiction and management are fragmented across many agencies and split among states and provinces. Compounding this in some Regions is a dearth of technical skills—and different foci. Water supply utilities have to deal only with securing supplies and delivering them—effectively a closed system. Irrigation, by contrast, is only one input in a complex agricultural crop production system that is vital to rural development and a national econ-

omy. Emerging requirements for addressing the broad environmental aspects of water resources management and maintenance of the ecological functions of freshwater systems present new challenges in water resources management.

Each subsector addresses the *Strategy's* recommendations on water and pricing policy, management, the regulatory environment, and institutional reforms in different ways (figure 3.6). Water resource management and water sector projects are superior on all criteria, followed by water supply and sanitation projects on six. Irrigation and drainage projects are the worst for five of the eight criteria. Attention to the needs of disadvantaged groups (poverty, resettlement) and water policy is inadequate.

Attention to water service management and regulation received the greatest attention, except in irrigation and drainage. Water service organizations considered decentralization of the organization, its regulatory framework for pricing and service quality, operational and financial autonomy, and customer participation in management decisions. Again, irrigation and drainage gave the least attention to finance and subsidies and to water service charges. Because irrigation

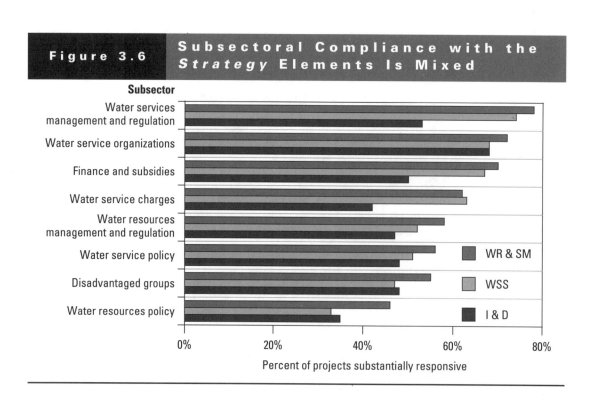

**Figure 3.6  Subsectoral Compliance with the Strategy Elements Is Mixed**

uses more than three-quarters of the developing world's water resources, this is a cause for concern. In most respects these findings show that there are fundamental philosophical differences in the way the sectors are treated. Irrigation and drainage are still very much in the public goods domain, dominated by conservative public sector agencies. Water supply and sanitation have moved toward commercialization and, in some cases, privatization.

## Water Projects Tackle Environmental Issues from Different Fronts

Water development has profound impacts on the environment and its management. The Bank has addressed these concerns directly through environmentally focused water projects—and indirectly with safeguard policies to evaluate alternatives and provide plans that minimize or mitigate harmful effects. AFR, ECA, and MNA have initiated a series of major initiatives with GEF to support integrated management of the basins of regional seas and major rivers. A new initiative for cooperative management of the Mekong River basin has been undertaken by EAP. In LAC, a new GEF-supported regional groundwater management program has been initiated. Environmental projects in the water sector represent a major growth area in the work of the Bank and are a source of innovation in approaches to their identification, preparation, and implementation.

Environmental projects are now the third largest category of water-related institutional support and investment in the Bank's portfolio. This category increased from 11 projects pre-*Strategy* to 48 projects post-*Strategy*, and $3.3 billion has been committed since 1993. Many national programs deal with environmental management through legislation and regulation that includes water and institution-building. Under the Baltic Sea, Danube Basin, and Black Sea environmental programs, the Bank is supporting new initiatives to address the impacts of non-point pollution from agriculture and rural settlements on surface and ground water resources. Specific projects are concerned with pollution control, drainage, watershed management, and erosion prevention. Groundwater management,

neglected for so long, is beginning to receive the attention it deserves.

### Groundwater Has Been Mismanaged

Groundwater mismanagement has profound social and environmental impacts. Most of the world's poor rely on groundwater for drinking, and as much as half the irrigation that sustains the green revolution has come from groundwater. But the lack of regulation and effective water pricing have led to the salinization of aquifers on which people rely for water supplies and agricultural employment. Notable examples of such contamination include the coastal aquifers of Gaza, Gujarat, west Java, and Mexico.

The Bank, having nearly ceased to finance public sector groundwater development, is starting to focus on managerial and remedial measures, an effort it needs to expand rapidly. Mexico has a new water management regime based on transferable property rights, management by users, and the elimination of distorting subsidies, and results are encouraging. In India, rural power subsidies promote overpumping of groundwater. These distortions are at last being recognized and addressed through Bank-supported state fiscal reform programs.

### Investment Can Improve Drainage, but Sustainability Is Key

Poor drainage spoils as much land as new irrigation creates. Bank projects have been particularly effective in addressing this issue through investment, as in Pakistan, but sustainability remains a problem. In Egypt and Turkey, investment in drainage projects enabled irrigated crop yields to double in many areas, but weak links between irrigation and drainage agencies and the emerging water user associations threaten operation and maintenance. Community involvement underlies the success of soil reclamation through better groundwater management and drainage in Uttar Pradesh.

### Successful Watershed Management Requires Participation and a Long-term Perspective

Although almost $1 billion has been invested in watershed management, only a few projects are free-standing, with three-quarters of the 42 watershed operations embedded in more general development projects cutting across 11 subsectors.[5] The primary focus of the majority of watershed projects is on improving soil and water conservation, not on managing watersheds as a whole. A quarter of the projects deal with reducing siltation, fewer than 10 percent with pollution reduction, and less than 5 percent with integrated water management. Projects in Europe and Central Asia and in East Asia and the Pacific are concerned more with the effects of pollution and siltation, those in LAC with agricultural management, and those in Africa with community resource management.

The most successful projects have high government and community ownership, mainly because they have sharply focused objectives. Poorly performing projects tended to focus on short-term goals supported by project subsidies that could not be sustained in the long term, were not supported by an enabling environment, and depended too much on ineffective government agencies unable to coordinate effectively at the local level or scale up the few successes.

Compare them with the successful Madagascar Second Environment Program prepared entirely by Malagasy agencies that took a long view—15 years—with the strategy of mainstreaming environmental concerns into macroeconomic management and sector programs. Under the program, Malagasy agencies, assisted by 10 donors and four international NGOs, worked in teams to formulate the institutional and investment program. With this broad consensus on strategy and coordination, implementation of water-related components is proceeding well.[6] Another notable success, China's Loess Plateau Watershed Rehabilitation Project, has substantially reduced local soil erosion by 20–30 million tons annually (and the total sediment load of the Yellow River by about 1 percent). It has also brought substantial socioeconomic benefits to marginal farmers on the plateau.

## Compliance with Safeguards Is Demanding

Since the water *Strategy* was issued, almost three-quarters of all water projects have been classified as environmentally sensitive—a marked increase. Seven safeguard policies particularly apply to water operations (box 3.1). Those classified as likely to have potentially adverse environmental impacts that are sensitive, diverse, or unprecedented (category A) have tripled in number and doubled their share in the total portfolio. There is now greater willingness to acknowledge site-specific impacts (category B) that can be mitigated or reversed. Presumably a result of more careful project design and/or selection, the proportion of water projects forcing involuntary resettlement has fallen by a tenth—to 37 percent of all Bank projects. Dam safety requirements are routinely applied to any project involving the impoundment of water. The India and Indonesia dam safety projects have been the first Bank operations addressing dam safety per se.[7] Based on the lessons from these projects is a second generation of dam safety projects and components under the Aral Sea Basin Program and in Albania, Armenia, the Kyrgyz Republic, Peru, and Sri Lanka.

The compliance at entry of water projects with safeguards is higher than that of other Bank projects. But this assessment comes largely from a desk review that dealt with only two environ-

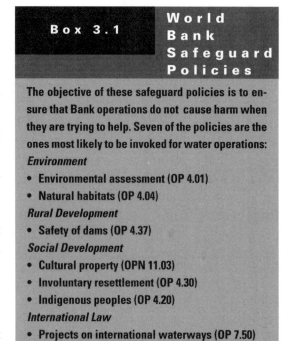

**Box 3.1** **World Bank Safeguard Policies**

The objective of these safeguard policies is to ensure that Bank operations do not cause harm when they are trying to help. Seven of the policies are the ones most likely to be invoked for water operations:

*Environment*
- Environmental assessment (OP 4.01)
- Natural habitats (OP 4.04)

*Rural Development*
- Safety of dams (OP 4.37)

*Social Development*
- Cultural property (OPN 11.03)
- Involuntary resettlement (OP 4.30)
- Indigenous peoples (OP 4.20)

*International Law*
- Projects on international waterways (OP 7.50)

mental questions—Was the environmental analysis adequate? Did it cover analysis of alternatives and economic evaluation?—and three stakeholder and social analysis questions. The quality of safeguards at supervision, however, was worse.[8] Recently QAG, with the support of the Bank's new Quality Assurance and Compliance Unit, has expanded the review of projects for quality at entry and quality of supervision to include review of all ten safeguard policies.

Of projects in the A environmental category, 82 percent were satisfactorily supervised; for category B, this dropped to 55 percent. Why the discrepancy? Policy guidance of category A projects is well defined; the projects are highly visible to Bank management and relatively well resourced. But policy guidance and compliance standards for category B projects are poorly defined, allowing considerable discretion for task managers. Much depends on the borrower, who frequently feels that safeguards are an expensive Bank imposition (as in the Nicaragua Social Fund) and who does not have the institutional, technical, and organizational skills to meet Bank requirements. Within the Bank, incentives to implement safeguard policies are weak. Recent decentralization of responsibility and budgets to the Regions and country units eroded the capacity of the Environment Department to monitor implementation of policies, and competition for resources reduced the environment to a low-priority sector. Task managers often viewed environmental inputs as an added cost and chose to do without specialist help unless absolutely necessary. These changes diminished the Bank's capacity to mainstream the environment into country programs and to implement its safeguard policies effectively (Liebenthal 2002).

Some countries have found the Bank's safeguard policies too demanding and too costly, and have sought alternative funding with fewer conditions. In Morocco, a large dam component (a key element of its water resources management project) was dropped after completion of essential preparation work by the Bank. There are still echoes from the Narmarda controversy. While safeguard policies have proven to be successful in integrating environmental and social issues into the design of projects, greater efforts are needed to more effectively implement national environmental and social legislation, develop country ownership of the safeguard concept, and foster mainstreaming by borrowers. This reveals the dilemma of the safeguard policies. Unless mainstreamed by borrowers, they primarily protect the Bank from risk and criticism. After intense opposition by environmentalists, Nepal's Arun III project was dropped by the Bank—yet Nepal is now embarking on a dam twice the size on the same site, using private sector financing.

## Addressing Institutional Concerns by Involving Stakeholders and the Private Sector

The water strategy insists that policies affecting water rights be carefully evaluated to ensure that they do not harm the poor, who often need water rights to earn income. There are well-documented instances of such harm. Dams reduce the downstream flow of water. Irrigation wells dry up traditional springs and shallow indigenous wells. Agricultural drainage pollutes downstream water sources. But this evaluation was unable to find any Bank projects that systematically reviewed pre-project water uses to determine the effects of the project on water access and use by different socioeconomic groups.

The current emphasis on water rights comes from experience in Chile, which has been trading water rights and increasing economic efficiency since 1981. While Chile's short rivers and small drainage basins make it a special case, water trading has been particularly effective in adjusting the allocation of water between urban and agriculture uses. Several preconditions—including a strong link between water and land rights, a prior history of informal water trading, a sound legal system, a system for registering water rights, and good governance—make water trading work. An independent regulatory system to allocate water rights and safeguard essential users is crucial, as are a good hydrological information base and titling system.

A major impediment to awarding water rights is the resistance of borrowers to relinquishing control. Many borrowers fear that private rights will lead to private monopolies. Many of these fears are unfounded. Research shows that informal water trading of de facto rights takes place even when expressly forbidden by law, as in Fordwah-Sadiqia in Pakistan and Gujarat in India. The issue for the Bank is how to leverage these examples into public policy discussions with borrowers. Major efforts are under way on water rights and pricing in Brazil and Mexico, but substantial resources and time are required to identify users and register water rights.

## Decentralization and Participation Have Been Key to Success

Decentralization involves users in planning and managing water projects, and encourages stakeholders to contribute to policy formulation. Traditionally considered in a government context, decentralization also applies to such large projects as irrigation, with operation and management devolved to farmers. The Bank recognizes that a variety of organizations—private firms, financially autonomous entities, and community organizations—contribute to decentralizing water delivery. That is why it supports projects that introduce different forms of decentralized management and that focus on division of responsibilities between public and private entities. About 70 percent of the Bank's projects address decentralization of water resource management.

Including beneficiaries has been central to better management, and water projects, particularly irrigation and rural water supply, have done much better than other Bank projects in this regard. Beneficiary involvement has facilitated better system operation and management. Despite this, women all too frequently are overlooked as important stakeholders in land and water management. Irrigation performance in Albania, India (Andra Pradesh), Mexico, Niger, and Turkey improved when the Bank moved away from mandating cost-recovery goals through covenants to persuading governments that empowering stakeholders was more effective. The lesson: operation and maintenance improve when water user groups have financial autonomy and arrange operation and maintenance themselves.

Second-generation problems are now emerging from evaluation of participatory irrigation management (Svendsen and others 2000). Most

notably, this has to be correctly sequenced with upstream reform of irrigation agencies. In Nepal's Sunsari Morang Irrigation project, the initial delegation of operation and maintenance to water users' groups took place before the reliability of water supplies was assured and the groups lost their raison d'etre. Investment in group formation activities was premature and had to be repeated. In the Philippines, several groups found the operation and maintenance task too technical—or too onerous, given their limited access to heavy equipment—and reverted to state management. Conversely, a Bank credit enabled water user associations in Turkey to import their own heavy maintenance equipment.

## Community-driven Development Works— But Is It Sustainable?

Projects that focus on community-driven development have much more social policy content and poverty focus than other water projects. They use a bottom-up approach in which community organizations, as both stakeholders and beneficiaries, have authority over decisions, including direct responsibility to manage internal and external resources. These characteristics should mean more ownership and sustainability, because they are sensitive to social development concerns and include the poor.

Community-driven development water projects are often funded through social funds. Most of the water investment components under social funds—between 2 percent and 44 percent of a fund—tend to be for water supply, drainage works, and small irrigation schemes. In Laos, under the Luang Namtha Provincial Development project, social funds provide local water schemes and enable technical assistance for training to develop, supervise, and operate water and sanitation systems. In Angola the Social Action project focuses on rehabilitation and expansion of water supply using appropriate and cost-effective technologies (hand-dug wells) and improves the capacity of NGOs and communities to plan, manage, and maintain investment. This is occurring even in more developed economies—in the Russian Federation, the Community Social Infrastructure project rehabilitates and upgrades existing water and wastewater infrastructure.

Evidence shows that water projects managed by social funds do not pay enough attention to developing organizations and institutions that ensure long-term sustainability. The Honduras social fund evaluation found that 83 percent of the systems assisted by the project had too little revenue to cover operational costs, and half had no technical assistance from either the government or NGOs.

A concern that cuts across all social fund lending is that while the investments are community- and demand-led, there are weak linkages to the sectoral apex agencies and almost no linkage with national or Bank sectoral strategy. While responsive to the Bank's water *Strategy*, which encourages subsidiarity and demand-led approaches, the laissez-faire approach may not necessarily focus on the areas of greatest need. It is difficult to judge whether the poor are given priority in these projects because the funds are dispersed on a first-come, first-served basis, and the poor are not normally in a position to take advantage of such opportunities unless special efforts are made.

### Private Provision Is Cost-Effective—But Has It Helped the Poor?

The Bank facilitated the commercialization of public water utilities and regulatory frameworks to leverage substantial private investment. Privatization of municipal water supplies in Africa and in Latin America and the Caribbean has achieved greater area coverage at no public cost. But getting the private sector to focus on the alleviation of poverty and to design tariffs in a way that does not discriminate against the poor has proved hard to achieve in practice. Even so, typical full-cost tariffs charged by private sector utilities range from $0.20 to $0.90 per cubic meter, much cheaper than water vendor or trucked supplies, which can be more than 10 times more expensive.[9]

To date, only a few private sector participation management ventures have failed, and these mainly because of poor governance. In The Gambia, instability following a 1995 military coup undermined lease and management contracts for operation and maintenance. The 1995 Aguas del Aconquija concession in Argentina is subject to bitter legal disputes, which the Bank has tried to mediate, and the losses to the concessionaire may exceed $16 million.

There is concern among NGOs that the new focus on private sector participation will have adverse consequences for the water and sanitation needs of the poor. Non-urban areas lack the economies of scale so attractive to private investment. And peri-urban areas pose the biggest service challenge to public and private sectors alike, particularly as they tend to house migrants escaping from rural poverty. Where the private sector cannot deliver or sees the risks as too high, there may be a case for the Bank to intervene to improve capacity and policy to upgrade public sector utilities.

### Pricing Promotes Efficiency and Conservation, but There Are Few Successful Examples

Water pricing is key to the Bank's water strategy and water allocation (Rogers 1992). In theory, underpriced resources are frequently misallocated, mismanaged, and wasted. In practice, however, water resources have only a nominal price set by a small license fee because of the economic and cultural difficulties of putting a value on a natural resource. Consequently, allocation is almost always made by prior appropriation or administrative fiat.

Within the water services sectors, efficient water pricing combined with appropriate fee collection and good management ensures water service delivery by enabling system operation and maintenance—and thus meets the Bank's poverty alleviation objectives. The corollary of pricing—attention to cost minimization—focuses managerial attention on staffing overheads, system efficiency, water loss reduction, and efficient billing systems. This has positive environmental impacts, since more efficient water use and attention to production costs (particularly for agriculture) generally reduce water pollution and increase conservation. And when water is seen as a commodity, more attention is paid to its allocation in the market environment.

The Middle East and North Africa was the best-performing Region, thoroughly covering pricing and financial issues in the design of projects.

East Asia and the Pacific, boosted by China's extremely well-developed financing regulations, performed almost as well. The best-performing sector was water supply and sanitation, in which two-thirds of all projects covered these issues substantially. Irrigation, heavily influenced by India's low ratings, was the poorest-performing sector.

Were there specific cost-recovery targets? How did these relate to the financial health of the agency? Were efficiency and equity taken into account? And did the revenues collected go back into service provision? Globally, most Bank projects pay lip-service to cost recovery, but only two-thirds of Bank projects have addressed it substantially. Of the sector loans, those for water supply sector adjustment were the best-performing. Conversely, those for the environment seldom addressed cost-recovery issues.

The Bank has been trying to widen the knowledge base for water supply benchmarks through a Web site for participating utilities. The international benchmarks, such as those disseminated by the Asian Development Bank, provide only "order of magnitude" comparisons of efficiency. For the irrigation sector there are virtually no benchmarks because the technical, social, and institutional features of irrigation service arrangements are complex and geographically diverse. Many Bank capacity-building efforts in water supply and sanitation utilities are directed at developing cost accounting and financial management frameworks as the basis for a pricing policy. This is lacking for irrigation, which relies mainly on financing from budget transfers.

The battle to mainstream the economic and financial aspects of pricing policy in both sectors has largely been won inside the Bank but not in client countries or the international arena.

A large external constituency of stakeholders still wants to maintain social water pricing, which is difficult to manage with formulaic guidelines. For policies to be effective, countries need an apparatus for setting prices and the capacity to administer them. Most client countries have neither and are hindered by loading the pricing mechanism with multiple objectives.

The Bank's ability to give practical advice on pricing is diminished because few staff or consultants have experience in setting tariffs or managing the finances of utilities and irrigation authorities. This shortcoming is being addressed by the Bank's Water and Sanitation Sector Board. Only a few Bank operations contain irrigation service–fee components within a work program for a functioning and financially autonomous irrigation service provider. Given the political sensitivity of pricing, it is essential to be realistic in setting performance targets and linking them with institutional reform.

## The Bank's Effectiveness on Key *Strategy* Elements Varies Widely

The results of the qualitative and quantitative evaluation described above were classified in terms of how effectively the Bank has implemented the *Strategy* and are summarized for cross-sectoral comparison in figure 3.7. Clearly, much remains to be done, particularly on better alignment with the Bank's overarching goal to alleviate poverty, on ensuring that a comprehensive planning framework is adopted, and that more attention is given to allocation and pricing, water rights, gender, and addressing systemic institutional problems that have slowed the path to reform. But, as the next chapter shows, getting results will remain a major challenge.

**Figure 3.7 — The Bank's Effectiveness in Implementing the *Strategy* Varies Considerably by Sector**

| Very effective | Moderately effective | Ineffective |
|---|---|---|
| **Comprehensive water resources management** | | |
| ❏ Working in partnership with other international development agencies to build consensus on management of international waters | ❏ Raising awareness of comprehensive water resources management at country level | ❏ Alignment with the Bank's poverty strategy |
| | ❏ Environmental management and pollution control | ❏ Getting borrowers to adopt comprehensive water resources management |
| | | ❏ Introducing the river basin as a unit of account |
| | | ❏ Improving the management and conservation of groundwater |
| | | ❏ Improving coordination among all water users |
| | | ❏ Allocation issues and opportunity cost of water |
| **Water supply & sanitation** | | |
| ❏ Setting standards and regulatory environment for utilities | ❏ Decentralization | ❏ Increasing access to sanitation |
| ❏ Enabling commercialization and/or privatization of urban water supplies | ❏ Cross-subsidies | ❏ Gender concerns |
| ❏ Cost-recovery and tariffs | ❏ Expanding access and participation in rural and deprived areas | ❏ Addressing concerns about affordability |
| | ❏ Ensuring institutional and organizational standards for other sector WSS | |
| | ❏ Sector poverty strategy | |
| **Irrigation & drainage** | | |
| ❏ Participatory management and water user associations | ❏ Improving system operation and maintenance | ❏ Water rights |
| ❏ Poverty impact | ❏ System redesign for more efficient operation | ❏ Decentralization |
| | ❏ Water quality and drainage | ❏ Gender issues |
| | ❏ Increasing user charges | ❏ Transparency and full cost accounting of water delivery service |
| | ❏ Organizational reform and unbundling activities | ❏ Reforming the legal and regulatory framework |
| | | ❏ Conjunctive use of surface and groundwater |
| | | ❏ Addressing subsidies that discourage water conservation—e.g. rural electricity tariffs |
| **Hydropower** | | |
| ❏ Regulatory environment and dam safety safety | ❏ Environmental concerns and involuntary resettlement | ❏ Multipurpose development |
| | ❏ Integrated water sector strategy | |
| **Environmental management** | | |
| ❏ Watershed management and conservation | ❏ Decentralized management | ❏ Strategies to address underlying institutional constraints |
| | ❏ Institutional and regulatory environment | ❏ Gender issues |
| | ❏ Participation and Social Concerns | |

# Why It's Difficult to Get Good Results

T he core business of water resources management is to establish incentives for water users to protect and conserve the resource, allocate it to higher-value uses, and reallocate as demand changes. This needs to be done in a holistic way at the river basin level because externalities and opportunities for reallocation do not occur just within sectors. Each use has an impact on the resource that affects its value and the perceived risks to other users.[1] In the Philippines, for example, private sector investors ranked the lack of watershed protection against polluters as the second most critical risk for urban water supply investment, the first being the risk of nonpayment for bulk water supplied to public sector distributors.

## Comprehensive Water Management Is Inherently Difficult

Integrated water resource management by river basin organizations is difficult to set up. To be effective, it requires sophisticated institutions and good governance—things lacking among most of the Bank's borrowers. A review of global experience suggests that a more hybrid approach to integrated water resource management (the *Strategy* aims to create a perfect super-institution) would focus on enhanced cooperation among existing institutions (table 4.1) (Millington 2000).[2] The Bank's approach to *Strategy* implementation has matured along this path since 1993.

The hybrid approach recognizes that while water resources management needs to focus on

defining and enforcing water rights through administrative and economic instruments,[3] this is viable only when it is supported by specialist knowledge that varies by subsector. More important, these subsectors perform better when they have autonomy and clearly defined governance and accountability. Each subsector's specific policy and financing challenges differ from those of the other subsectors and from those of overall water resource management.

A recent global review of holistic approaches to planning (OED 2000b) found that it is best to avoid delegating responsibility for integrated planning to separate "super-institutions" created specifically for the task. Experience suggests that these are either ineffectual in the short term or unproductive or unsustainable in the long term.

| Table 4.1 | Mature Water Resource Management Organizations Do Not Run Water Businesses | | |
|---|---|---|---|
| **River basin organization function** | **Status of river basin organization** | | |
| | **New** | **Developing** | **Mature** |
| **Planning.** Water and natural resource data collection and processing, systems modeling, water and natural resource planning | • | • | • |
| **Project management.** Feasibility, design, implementation, operation and management, raising financing | • | • | |
| **Allocation.** Allocating water shares (quality and quantity), cost sharing principles, and user/license to support RBO activities | | • | • |
| **Policy and strategy development.** For economic, financing, and environmental issues, community awareness and participation | | | • |
| **Monitoring and evaluation.** Water use and shares, pollution and environmental conditions, oversight and review of projects promoted by subsector partners | | | • |

*Source:* Modified after Millington (2000).

The biggest problem for river basin organizations is that they tend to take the form of regional structures that attempt to claim (but often merely duplicate) the responsibilities of existing regional departments of national ministries.

A pervasive problem facing these new organizations is securing adequate funds for water resources management activities. To mitigate this problem, new bodies should be given responsibility for coordinating the relevant elements of existing organizations and ensuring the participation of stakeholders, including NGOs, civil society, and the private sector: the goal should be integrated planning, but not integrated implementation. Decentralized governance—subsidiarity—is a key component of this approach. In practice, however, lack of local capacity and basic data are frequently critical constraints in Bank client countries. Another difficulty is that river basins frequently transcend national borders, and this adds another dimension.

## International Water Cooperation Is Essential but Controversial

International waters are always a potential source of conflict, even more so when they are shared by water-short countries. The Bank's primary interest in these situations is to foster economic cooperation for natural resource management. But it also has a strong interest in reducing the economic and human costs of water conflicts that lead to suboptimal development and sometimes wasteful investment.

The Bank, with its ability to mobilize funding, its knowledge, and its convening power, has the capacity to lead on the issues associated with international waters. The Bank's first foray into this area, the Indus Water Treaty in the 1960s, clearly demonstrated this. It also showed that solutions take a long time and require a high level of commitment. The Indus problem was solved only because the Bank worked at it for 10 years and had the personal commitment of Bank President Eugene Black. It is notable as being the only case where the Bank helped establish formal procedures for allocating water between countries. Over the last decade a series of regional programs focused on basin-level environmental management of freshwater, coastal, and marine resources have been undertaken in ECA, MNA, and AFR. The key lessons learned are that success is based on a shared vision, sustained commitment, and broad-based partnerships.

The lesson from the Bank's current portfolio is that each international and intrastate water problem has a unique blend of political, environmental, and socioeconomic factors. As the

Aral Sea program illustrates, there are no easy solutions. Before significant funds can be committed, much needs to be done to facilitate partnerships, agree on approaches, and formulate policies for each situation. For Bank staff and managers there are few institutional incentives for undertaking such risky cross-regional endeavors in times of declining budgets, despite the requirements of the Bank's water *Strategy*. Consequently, corporate culture will need to change significantly before the Bank can assume its appropriate leadership role in international waters. And because these usually are high-risk situations, often taking years to establish and ensure stakeholder ownership, the Bank should have a clear exit strategy.

## Water Is Not Seen as an Important Economic Resource

Reforming water management requires concerted action to elevate social and environmental concerns, set development priorities, correct poor governance and ineffective public-sector institutions, and redress large knowledge and skill gaps. Most important, unless the enabling conditions are in place—a conducive political economy and strong local leadership—a water reform agenda is unlikely to be viable. The agenda is extremely ambitious, and agreeing on the sequence and scope of activities in a country setting is difficult, time-consuming, and risky.

One major difficulty is in linking water development to the CAS agenda. Water sector interventions in CASs are generally subsumed under broader development goals, such as securing macroeconomic stability, alleviating poverty, improving natural resource use and the environment, or removing infrastructure bottlenecks.

The explicit valuation of water as an input to public health, food production, and environmental maintenance is fraught with difficulty, leaving it undervalued until there are problems. Indeed, water issues tend to attract political attention mainly for extreme events—Bangladesh's Flood Action Plan, El Nino Emergency Loans for Peru and Bolivia, or the Sudan and Zimbabwe Drought Recovery Credits—or when things go wrong—arsenic in Bangladesh's groundwater and India's Narmarda controversy.

## Transforming *Strategy* into Action Is Difficult

The Bank's water reform agenda has been unclear to most stakeholders and insufficiently linked to national economic issues.[4] This shows the value of developing and disseminating short country water strategies closely linked to CASs. All stakeholders complained about lack of knowledge and the asymmetry of available knowledge, which skewed decisionmaking. They argued that the Bank needs to be more inclusive, moving beyond the usual government department clients to involve politicians and the public in discussing water strategy and development priorities.

OED's Rural Vision to Action study of five countries found significant differences between Bank staff and local stakeholders on what was important.[5] Almost two-thirds of country stakeholders believed that the central government should directly allocate their country's water resources among competing users; only a quarter of Bank staff did. Similarly, Bank staff were three times more likely than country stakeholders to believe that small rural communities could plan and manage water supply systems.

A recent review by the Bank's Quality Assurance Group (QAG) of five water-related pieces of ESW concludes that the relevance of water policy reform needs to be improved, primarily through greater management of and attention to major pieces of ESW.[6] Management is criticized for providing support systems for ESW that are "largely unclear and inadequate." This lack of clear priorities is especially true of ESW to support water reform. QAG noted that with staff typically over-programmed, ESW tends to get lower priority, and quality can suffer because of this.

QAG criticizes traditional ESW for failing to strike a balance between short, quick-response, informal tasks and longer gestation, more costly formal tasks.[7] In commenting on the India water management review, QAG suggests that these old-style ESW products "may not be the appropriate vehicle for effecting policy change. Crisp, timely, analytical pieces, based on well-conceived and broadly representative workshops in the country, can much better serve as instruments for Bank dialogue and engagement in the sector."

Major recommendations are that stakeholders should be more closely involved in preparing and reviewing ESW task teams for major sector reports and should include adequate representation of macro and sector economists to avoid the dialogue being restricted to technicians of the Bank and client. In reviewing a sewerage project in Indonesia, for example, QAG commented that the limited results and impact of the study could have probably been achieved quicker, and at a much lower cost, by organizing a workshop in Indonesia at which each of the seven cities surveyed by the study could have provided a description of issues they face as they try to expand service. In contrast, the review of the Water Sector Adjustment Loan environmental assessment is given high marks for an outstanding effort to address this issue in a participatory fashion, while raising doubts as to whether this kind of approach was either replicable or affordable for the Bank.

Country stakeholders (in Brazil and India) observed that there seems to be an unwillingness by the Bank to continually learn from evolving implementation lessons—process seemed more important than substance once a project was approved. The staff focus was on meeting disbursement targets and responding to directives and mandates from headquarters that the stakeholders saw as having little relevance to local issues or concerns. Lack of continuity of Bank staff was also seen as a problem (Chapter 5). There was frustration that Bank staff, because of these pressures, could not take more time for non-lending work and for facilitating public policy debate on water issues.

## Detailed Guidelines Have Been Lacking

Even though *Water Resources Policy Review and Strategy Formulation* (FAO 1995) guidelines were jointly prepared by the UNDP, FAO, and the World Bank at the request of the Subcommittee on Water Resources of the UN Administrative Committee for Coordination, these were only modestly effective. There was no follow-through in the Bank (or elsewhere) to make the guidelines fully operational, based on the lessons. Nor was there a realistic assessment of the resources required to implement them through lending and nonlending operations.

## Selectivity and Good Management Are Important

The theoretical underpinnings of comprehensive water management are sound, but such a large task cannot be accomplished everywhere at once—or quickly. Selectivity is therefore important, as is recognition that the Bank's project horizon of five to seven years is simply too short to carry out the reforms needed to establish comprehensive management. The usual solution—a series of projects—can work, but only if properly sequenced within the comprehensive framework. China's Tarim Basin II, the Brazil Second Water Modernization, and the Morocco Water Resource Management projects demonstrate good practices in this area. They need to be adapted and adopted in other water-related sectors. It is also important to focus on doing a few things right to demonstrate new approaches that work. While it is necessary to be comprehensive, it is not necessary to be complex.

## Seven Ways to Improve Results

The Bank has many options for improving performance in the water sector:

- Establish ownership and leadership.
- Find win-win solutions and opportunities.
- Judge results, not plans.
- Step up the country and sector dialogue.
- Manage complexity and accept tradeoffs.
- Use partnerships to build capacity.
- Be patient—reform takes time.

### Establish Ownership and Leadership

Much of the success of institutional reform is owed to an independent agency outside the concerned ministries and agencies. In Mali and Albania, the government ensured the agency's independence and freedom to reform. In Brazil, the Bank's water programs are highly successful in the state of Ceara because of the personal interest of the governor and grassroots operations and management. In India, the chief minister of Andhra Pradesh pushed through an extensive reform program of the irrigation sector. But in other states and countries there are few champions, and water sector reform is mired in political indifference and bureaucratic malaise.

## Find Win-Win Opportunities and Solutions

The Bank is in a unique position of being able to see the macroeconomic and political conditions that provide opportunities for comprehensive reform. In all cases, the precursors to water reform were outside the water sector—and reform of water is typically second or third generation, following in many cases reform of the power sector. Macroeconomic crises of the late 1980s were the motivating force for irrigation reform in Mexico and for debates on water sector reform in Australia, Chile, and India. In South Africa, water sector reform has been part of reconstruction of the economy in the post-apartheid era. A major change in Poland's environmental and water management, supported by the Bank and other donors, was accelerated by the ongoing EU accession process. Financial crisis drove water sector reform in Brazil, France, Mali, Niger, Senegal, Turkey, and the United Kingdom, and more recently in the Philippines Metro-Manila water concession. In many of these cases, water reform also benefited from the synergy of political and economic liberalization. All too frequently, however, Bank water staff promote reform when the enabling conditions are absent.

## Judge by Results, Not Plans

Water development requires multisectoral cooperation and safeguards that can be costly to clients. In the Yemen Taiz Water Supply project, water supply staff pursued their quest for water by administrative reallocation from rural to urban use—neglectful of insufficient groundwater—while agriculture and social sector staff, cognizant of the importance of water in the rural economy and local needs and customs, argued that a more socially inclusive approach was required. The compromise, a project with many social safeguard components, is proving too complex to implement effectively. Consequently, there is a standoff between the local landowner and the Taiz water supply agency. The key resource issue of how to address the groundwater mining on which all livelihoods depend is still unresolved. Similar problems occurred in the Trinidad and Tobago Water Sector Institutional Strengthening project. Bank staff in different subsectors worked independently with limited interaction, sending mixed signals to the client. Frequent changes of task manager due to Bank reorganization caused significant problems for the government after Bank delays led to the eventual cancellation of a $100 million complementary investment.

While the water strategy stresses the importance of sound environmental and social assessment and compliance with the Bank's safeguard policies (box 3.1), the borrower's costs of compliance may be significant. Involuntary resettlement is generally among the important social safeguard issues in water projects. In a Bankwide review of projects that involved resettlement, the average number of affected people per project had declined from 30,500 to 11,600 post-*Strategy* (Annex F). While a vast majority of these are only affected by acquisition of land, a much smaller number need to be physically relocated. Resettlement action plans are agreed with the borrower prior to project approval for regular investment projects, though 16 percent are finalized during implementation, due to the programmatic nature of projects.[8] Given the need to construct dams to conserve as much water as possible for future demand and the current lack of capacity to implement safeguard policies in some borrower countries, the Bank faces significant technical and public relations challenges in water sector development.

The main lesson OED drew from its 1998 resettlement review was that results rather than plans should be the touchstone of quality management.[9] The main lesson for water operations is that there needs to be a clear shift from resettlement policy and planning to procedures and practice. There is an urgent need for the Bank to review quality control procedures, including the adverse effects of water management, to ensure that reviews are transparent and independent. More emphasis needs to be given to sectoral environmental assessment and moving upstream to help borrowers solve root safeguard problems—institutions, governance, and knowledge gaps—before they get in the way of development. There also is rising demand for taking more explicit account of borrowing countries' policy and regulatory regimes and for making determined efforts to seek harmonization be-tween domestic legislation and Bank policies prior to project processing.

## Step Up the Country and Sector Dialogue

Understanding the country and sector context is vital for developing a comprehensive develop-ment strategy. Morocco's strong government ownership, sound sector administrative capacity, and an organization allied with decentralized water distribution utilities (Régies) enabled a successful outcome. In Metro-Manila, knowl-edge transfer and dedication over a number of years translated into success. The various water sectors naturally differ in their readiness for re-form. In Chile the successful Environmental In-stitutions Development project established an effective national environmental management agency, yet regulation of water pollution by min-ing failed because of vested interests. Where political and administrative transaction costs are high, reform may be cosmetic—passing a water law, for example—with no attempt to enforce it.

Low client commitment and institutional ca-pability allied with ambitious project objectives account for much of the poor performance of four of the six water supply and sanitation adjustment loans. In Colombia and Honduras, the loans achieved their objective of providing increased access to water by the poor. But they failed in their institutional objectives, mainly because the project scope exceeded the capacity of sector in-stitutions that suffered from frequent managerial changes and political interference. In Algeria and Ghana, similar problems and ill-defined per-formance objectives, poor governance, and cor-ruption prohibited financial sustainability.

Insufficient country and sector dialogue dooms projects to failure, sometimes blinding the Bank to changed circumstances. The ambitious Brazil NE Irrigation Engineering project ignored the macroeconomic situation and wavering po-litical commitment to continued investment in public sector irrigation. The result? The project delivered products no one wanted. Subsectoral reviews can ensure that investment priorities are clearly linked to a development strategy led by borrowers. In India and Pakistan, public tubewell development projects underestimated

the scale of farmers' private sector initiatives, making the projects irrelevant because of in-sufficient beneficiary involvement in project de-sign and unreliable power supplies.[10]

Failure to heed the findings of the Argentine public sector investment review led to pro-longed and expensive involvement in the Yacyreta Dam project long after it was shown to be subeconomic. Changed project manage-ment compounded the Bank's failure to appre-ciate government sovereignty over procurement regulations and led to withdrawal from Turkey's Berke Hydroelectric project in 1995, two years after approval of the loan. Similar problems had also affected the national drainage project, but were resolved. A major difficulty is the Bank's continued optimism about the public sector's in-tent to reform, in spite of substantial evidence to the contrary.

When there is deep country dialogue the re-sults can be outstanding, as Mali's Office du Niger Consolidation Irrigation project demon-strates. The Office was restructured, its financial health restored, government monopolies were unbundled, and agricultural production bur-geoned—helped by improved land tenure and market liberalization. This success led other donors to invest more, leveraging the Bank's in-vestment by 250 percent. In the Baltic Sea En-vironment Program and the Nile Basin Initiative, the strong and sustained commitment of the cooperating governments has been critical for their success to date.

## Manage Complexity and Accept Tradeoffs

Determining the appropriate level of complex-ity and phasing is one of the unresolved dilem-mas of a more comprehensive and integrated approach. Not everything can be done at once. Turkey's Izmir Water Supply and Sewerage proj-ect, completed in 1996, demonstrates the inad-visability of committing funds for large-scale expansion of facilities before addressing critical institutional issues. A gradual program aimed first at building management capacity and encour-aging efficient use of existing facilities would have been a better approach.

At the other end of the scale, the Lesotho Highland Water Project is one of the few that largely complied with the Bank's water *Strategy*. A complex project facilitating interregional and interbasin water transfer, its ambitious engineering objectives are nearing full achievement. Its sheer size has created an influential national implementation agency that government will have difficulty in controlling. The environmental and social aspects remain only partially implemented, and are now being given increased attention—as is Lesotho's water supply and sanitation subsector after a decade of benign neglect.[11] All these examples indicate that while it is essential to plan comprehensively, greater success can be achieved through discrete, manageable, and sequenced development.

Indeed, unbalanced growth approaches to institutional development are seen as superior to centralized planning approaches (Ellerman 2000; Hirschman 1994). Successful "unbalanced" interventions set up tensions and highlight unforeseen problems that catalyze additional and sequential reform efforts. Thus the Bank's experience suggests developing country water strategies as a means to highlight where and when to selectively intervene—and then ensure that the targeted interventions are realistically scheduled and funded.

A comprehensive attack on all the problems faced by an institution cannot hope to achieve final results in a specified time.[12] Instead, a few aspects can be identified on which progress is feasible given the general operational level of the institution, and the program can concentrate on those aspects for a reasonable period—say, three years. After that, the progress made will have ripple effects on other parts of the institution. At that point, a new program can be designed that takes account of the new situation—including changes in personnel—but that focuses on another limited number of objectives. In sum, institutional development efforts should abandon comprehensiveness of scope and schedule, pursuing instead a partial, cumulative, and highly focused approach (Israel 1987). Good examples of interventions that create ripple effects are governance and institution building efforts that make service providers accountable to customers (water user associations), and full cost accounting that frequently reveals both administrative and technical inefficiencies—not least, volumetric measurement of water supply and consumption.

## Use Partnerships to Build Capacity

Creating a shared vision among the Bank, borrowers, and other development partners is the key to successful implementation of the Bank's water *Strategy*, and the Bank has made some major accomplishments on the international stage (Chapter 2). The biggest challenge is converting donor-led partnerships into country-led partnerships. In most countries, the finance ministry does not share the Bank's vision about the importance of water in their economies. The Bank needs to ensure that the highest levels of the government and the Bank understand how critical water development and management are to the future of the countries. But one can hardly fault ministers of finance when the bulk of the Bank's country assistance strategy ignores the importance of water.

A major concern, however, is that inability to meet the costs of proliferating partnerships may have reputational risks when the Bank fails to deliver. For example, the Bank allocated far less than anticipated for the WBI water program, leaving a greater burden for its partners. Indeed, budget cuts have recently skewed the WBI water program toward the area of strongest demand—water and sanitation reform. That deemphasizes sectors that need reform the most—national water management, and irrigation and drainage. Such induced selectivity may prove short-sighted. Another area of risk is that performance standards to judge the efficacy and relevance of partnerships and arrangements for monitoring and evaluation are still nascent.

## Be Patient—Reform Takes Time

All too often, the Bank has expected reform to quickly follow investment. But in water supply and sanitation, making investment conditional on reform frequently leads to more successful outcomes. The Indonesia and Jordan water SALs are good examples of the challenges and achievements, while Mexico's Second Water Modernization shows the advantage of the long-term programmatic approach. The success of a sequenced and incremental approach that balances learning with doing and building stakeholder ownership is illustrated by the first phase of the Uttar Pradesh Sodic Soils Reclamation project. It increased agricultural productivity and had a marked impact on poverty. OED's recent evaluation of the rural water supply sector emphasized that building stakeholder ownership takes time (OED 2000c).

# 5

# Improving Bank Management and Internal Incentives

Long before the Bank's 1993 water *Strategy* and policy were published, many staff believed that the lending and nonlending initiatives
of the water sector should focus primarily on policies to improve water
service delivery operations.[1] Task managers knew that adding a multisectoral water resources management dimension to a lending operation would
greatly complicate it, especially when resources allocated to delivery
operations were already too low and decreasing. The consensus of staff was
that water-scarce countries needed special attention—otherwise, resource
management should be evaluated (perhaps through a nonlending program)
when the viability of water investment was at risk.

The challenge was to design a Bank implementation strategy based on processes and procedures that were cost- and resource-effective.
Resolving this challenge became important because policy and strategy formulation had included widespread participation, coordination,
and dialogue with other donors and NGOs. One
group of leading NGOs, supportive of the Bank's
water *Strategy*, was concerned that the Bank
would not be able to deliver on its promises of
action.[2]

Thus alerted, management agreed that the
Bank's capacities and abilities to implement the
*Strategy* would have to be reviewed and substantially increased if the policy objectives were
to be effectively addressed. But three issues
clouded management's perception of the prob-

lem. First, the demand-led approach made it difficult to define resource requirements. Second,
the Bank was then expanding its environment
and social sector staff. And third, the Bank was
aggressively trying to cut overhead costs.

While some uncoordinated action was taken
to assess the resources required, the implementation plan agreed to when the *Strategy*
was presented to the Board was never prepared
in detail, and thus never institutionalized. So,
adoption has been voluntary, depending on
whether operational units have the interest—or
more important, the resources—to give attention
to water resource management.

Advisory staff in the Bank did translate the conceptual framework into practical implementation guidelines for client countries. But the joint

UNDP-World Bank technical paper—*A Guide to the Formulation of Water Resources Strategy* (FAO 1995)—was seen as an end in itself. As with the *Strategy*'s implementation plan, there was no follow-through in the Bank to make the guidelines fully operational or to assess the internal resources required to implement the guidelines through lending or nonlending interventions.

## The Bank Is Poorly Organized to Implement the Water *Strategy*

In 1995 the operational Regions reverted to a two-tier system with country management units directly supported by sector management units. The sector units functioned like the old technical departments, providing specialist staff to respond to a country director's needs—despite the fact that water knows no borders. Most sector units are large (70 to 120 staff) and structured such that water resources management cannot be treated in a holistic manner. Urban water supply is separated from rural development (and thus irrigation and drainage), and in some Regions from environment and social development. In addition, demand for sector support is unpredictable because it is controlled by budgetary provisions from the country units, and the continuity of staff involvement cannot be guaranteed. Until 1999 the Africa and MNA Regions were the only ones with a functioning water resources management unit capable of delivering a regional approach. Since then, all Regions have begun to set up regional water teams, and all have lead water specialists/advisors.

Strategic leadership for water resources management remains fragmented within the Bank. Rural development (including irrigation and rural water supply) and the environment are under the vice-president for *Environmentally and Socially Sustainable Development Network* (ESSD). Urban water and sanitation (WSS) is under the vice-president for *Private Sector and Infrastructure Network (PSI),* primarily to reflect the Bank's strategy of encouraging privatization of public sector activities, such as water supply and sanitation. The division of water-related development into two separate organizational units may promote other Bank policy strategies (privatization), but specific Bank pol-

icy objectives that require a holistic approach—such as implementation of its water *Strategy*—get lost by subdivision.

Councils and Sector Boards within ESSD and PSI differ in their effectiveness on water issues. Both sector boards have produced a series of performance improvement plans focused on the efficiency of their operations. The Urban Water Supply and Sanitation Board has been developing a coherent plan to improve the efficiency of its operations and water service delivery function. But the same is not true of the Rural Sector Board. Under this board, water-related operations—even though they account for half its lending—are only part of a mandate that spans a complex of 16 rural development activities. As a result, managerial guidance and oversight on water development get lost in bigger rural development issues. It was only in the spring of 2000 that a new *Water Resources Management Group* was formed under ESSD to address this. It is too early, however, to judge the effectiveness of this new set-up and the way that energy, environment, infrastructure, rural development, and WBI training will be coordinated.

One possible solution for better water service delivery in the rural sector is to focus exclusively on the efficiency and sustainability of water delivery in the same way that urban water supply concerns itself only up to the household tap. The delivery systems for urban water and for irrigation and drainage are both capital-intensive, with similar economies of scale, organization, subsidies, and financial viability issues. In irrigation, this would require full attention only up to the bulk delivery and sales point—where farmers' water user groups would then take responsibility for further management and allocation. Indeed, there may be a case for greater involvement of PSI staff in Bank efforts to reform public sector irrigation agencies to capitalize on their expertise in unbundling complex public sector utilities. That would focus attention on getting water delivery right and make utilities financially viable. It could also focus the attention of irrigation staff on improving the management of water below the utilities' delivery point and strengthening the linkages between irrigated agriculture and rural development.

Bankwide thematic groups that focus on the water service sectors have been successful at knowledge management, particularly in water supply and sanitation. There is some cross-coordination among the various thematic groups on subsectoral issues, and Bankwide discussion to advocate the case for holistic water resources management is just beginning, aided by the Bank-Netherlands Water Partnership. But the knowledge function is now seriously eroded by recent budget cuts in the Bank.

## But Successful Institutional Approaches Are Evolving

Despite the fragmented approach in the Bank, there have been successful examples where water resource issues were treated in a holistic manner, with the encouragement and active support of the regional management. None, however, has been institutionalized. And they depend heavily on unpredictable non-Bank budgetary support and the use of consultants.

The African Water Resources Management Initiative unit, set up in 1995, is the only self-contained unit in the Bank that has performed as anticipated in the recommendations for implementation of the *Strategy*. It is a "bottom-up" initiative led by staff with the ability to organize and attract non-Bank staffing and funding resources. Not dependent on budgetary support from Bank country lending programs, the initiative has considerable flexibility in choosing priorities. This obviously works, since it is gaining strength from partnerships with stakeholders to meet borrowers' demand for assistance in formulating their water strategies across sectoral boundaries.

The comprehensive approach has also made it possible for the Bank to influence almost all the key national and international water resources challenges in the Region, including river basin management. It is still too early to evaluate the full impact of the initiative, but substantial increases in Bank budgetary support by the Africa Region clearly indicate management's recognition of its positive role.

In MNA, a sector manager attracted enough staff to one of the sector units to maintain a regional initiative on comprehensive water policy reform. But as in the Africa Region, the water service sectors remain split under separate sector units, and MNA staffing and funding arrangements make it difficult to respond to regional water challenges in a timely and comprehensive manner.

## Staff Resources Are Stretched Too Thinly

Since 1993, there has been a substantial increase of specialist staff in natural resources and environment, a modest increase in water supply and sanitation, but a substantial decrease in irrigation and hydropower. There has also been a substantial decrease in senior technical staff, primarily due to retirement.

The results of an OED survey (Annex G) show that Bank staff clearly believe they lack the funds and personnel to carry out the *Strategy* (figure 5.1). Few internal incentives favor the long-term, comprehensive, cross-sectoral view required for water resource management. Strongly favored is the project-oriented enclave approach that focuses on service delivery. Staffing needs and recruitment are contentious issues, with most staff believing that the Bank had made little effort to quantify staffing at the regional and sectoral levels or in the networks. Inadequate recruitment of new staff is a significant concern, as is the loss of skills to implement the *Strategy*—a view not shared by less-experienced staff.

## External Stakeholders Also See Problems

NGO interviews also raise some serious questions about the perceived barriers to successful *Strategy* implementation: "The high degree of internal disagreement over fundamental aspects of the policy, such as whether to adopt a comprehensive planning approach, coupled with a low level of interest in the policy shown by water project task managers, indicates that without concerted efforts by concerned governments and NGOs, the policy and its new approaches are fragile and may never be fully implemented." From this and other evidence, the NGOs expressed concern that "the pressure to lend . . . has not been removed and continues to work against aspects of the water policy that recommend greater

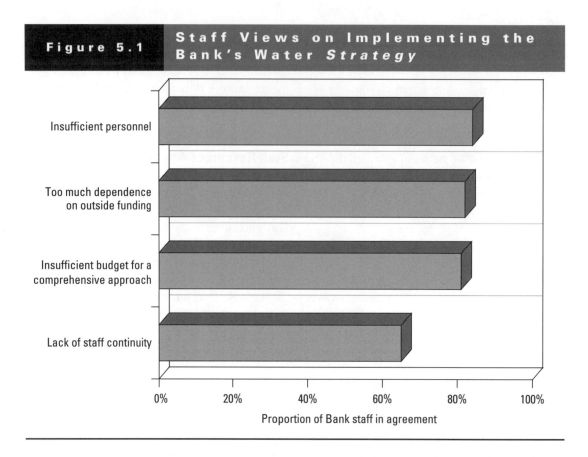

**Figure 5.1** Staff Views on Implementing the Bank's Water *Strategy*

Insufficient personnel

Too much dependence on outside funding

Insufficient budget for a comprehensive approach

Lack of staff continuity

0%   20%   40%   60%   80%   100%

Proportion of Bank staff in agreement

attention to smaller and cheaper alternatives." And they believe that "there is no clear constituency—either inside or outside the Bank—strong enough to ensure that the water policy will be implemented and enforced."

Local stakeholders are confused by the lack of coordination between the Bank's water subsectors, and the mixed messages this sends. Country stakeholders say that the Bank appears to be internally divided on one of the basic principles agreed at Dublin (to deal with water holistically)—and that the internal division limits Bank effectiveness, and thus the pressure it can put on governments to develop a comprehensive regulatory and institutional environment. Even within the various subsectors, the Bank does not practice what it preaches about integrating the approaches to water development and incorporating environmental concerns. Stakeholders in Brazil thought that the Bank's urban water group seemed fixated on privatization and water tariffs, driven more by Washington's agenda than by local concerns.

## Better Guidelines Are Needed

The water sector needs better guidelines. OED's staff survey found that overall satisfaction with the *Strategy* document is high: about 75 percent considered it thorough, consistent with Bank objectives, and relevant to current Bank work and borrowers' needs.[3] But among informed staff, almost 60 percent thought that the recommendations are difficult to monitor and somewhat platitudinous. Many written comments described the *Strategy* as "another unfunded mandate."

Independent reviews commissioned by OED also found that the operations policy statement (OP 4.07; see Annex A) is difficult to use as a guidance document: it is too brief and abstract for most practitioners and Bank staff. Compounding this, they found that the *Strategy* needs to be revised, based on lessons learned and international best practices. In this, the Bank needs to develop sensitive, flexible guidelines that permit staff to set assistance priorities and to determine acceptable tradeoffs in cases where the water *Strategy* imposes competing demands or where elements of the *Strategy* are unlikely to be successful.

# Recommendations

**R**ecommendation 1: Aim country dialogue and institutional development at integrating social and environmental concerns with water resource development and project implementation.

This requires:

- Greater attention to linking water projects with CAS and poverty strategies, to achieving better understanding of local institutions and preferences, and to monitoring and evaluating project effects on poverty.
- Adopting the use of strategic environmental and social assessments, including consultations, as part of the overall water resources planning process.
- More attention to be given to developing economic instruments to manage conflict in integrated water systems, including groundwater, and to balance demands at the river basin level, and between urban and rural populations, while ensuring access of the poor to water.
- More attention to factoring in concerns about equitable allocation of water and water rights, in light of local cultural preferences and rural-urban needs.
- Increased emphasis on implementation of safeguard policies during project supervision by the Bank and borrower.

**Recommendation 2:** Deploy Bank resources and instruments more effectively to nurture com-

mitment to the *Strategy* through shared objectives, realistic diagnostics, and partnerships aimed at policy reform and capacity building. Areas requiring particular attention include:

- Updating the Bank's water policy in the context of the forthcoming Sector Strategy Paper and supplementing it with a series of Bank procedures and good practice notes for each subsector.
- Making greater use of adaptable lending instruments and developing new, cost-effective, performance-based approaches to project selection, design, procurement, and service delivery.
- Strengthening ESW to allow for improved diagnosis, higher-quality dialogue with stakeholders, and closer linkages with Country and Poverty Assistance Strategies.
- Reorienting capacity-building in the water sector toward comprehensive water management through WBI programs and global and regional capacity-building partnerships.

**Recommendation 3:** Create and sustain more comprehensive water management alliances with like-minded partners in the private sector, civil society, and the development community. This requires:

- Sustaining involvement in global water policy networks and partnerships, with priority to cross-border integrated river-basin planning, driven by stakeholder demand, and to the resolution of international water disputes. More attention to in-country water partnerships is required to build dialogue and leverage local knowledge.

- Entering new partnerships only where the Bank has a clear comparative advantage in doing so, clearly specifying conditions for entry and exit.

- Driving the choice between private and public sector involvement by hard-nosed institutional analysis of what works and what does not in differing country contexts.

**Recommendation 4:** Strengthen internal management, monitoring, and evaluation of water resource management activities through a streamlined organization, more cohesive sector and country strategies, enhanced core competencies, additional operational guidance and training, and more rigorous quality assurance arrangements. Chief among the issues to address:

- Clarifying the role of the central Water Resource Management Group and its relationship with Sector Boards and Regional staff, particularly in relation to institutional and financial aspects of the rural water portfolio, and considering the establishment of water resource management coordinating bodies in each Region.

- Providing more vigilant and independent quality assurance for safeguard policies affecting water development.

- Offering incentives and training to accelerate staff adoption of a comprehensive approach to water resources management.

- Reassessing staffing levels and skills mixes to implement the water strategy Bankwide. To ensure adequate staffing and continuity, reliance on ad hoc trust funds should be reduced and the Bank budget enhanced.

# ANNEXES

## ANNEX A:  WORLD BANK OPERATIONAL POLICY 4.07, WATER RESOURCES MANAGEMENT

1. Bank[1] involvement in water resources management entails support for providing potable water, sanitation facilities, flood control, and water for productive activities in a manner that is economically viable, environmentally sustainable, and socially equitable.
2. The Bank assists borrowers in the following priority areas:
   (a) Developing a comprehensive framework for designing water resource investments, policies, and institutions. Within this framework, when the borrower develops and allocates water resources, it considers cross-sectoral impacts in a regional setting (e.g., a river basin).
   (b) Adopting pricing and incentive policies that achieve cost recovery, water conservation, and better allocation of water resources.
   (c) Decentralizing water service delivery, involving users in planning and managing water projects, and encouraging stakeholders to contribute to policy formulation. The Bank recognizes that a variety of organizations—private firms, financially autonomous entities, and community organizations—may contribute to decentralizing water delivery functions. Thus it supports projects that introduce different forms of decentralized management, focusing on the division of responsibilities among the public and private entities involved.
   (d) Restoring and preserving aquatic ecosystems and guarding against overexploitation of groundwater resources, giving priority to the provision of adequate water and sanitation services for the poor.
   (e) Avoiding the waterlogging and salinity problems associated with irrigation investments by (i) monitoring water tables and implementing drainage networks where necessary, and (ii) adopting best management practices to control water pollution.
   (f) Establishing strong legal and regulatory frameworks to ensure that social concerns are met, environmental resources are protected, and monopoly pricing is prevented. The Bank requires legislation or other appropriate arrangements to establish effective coordination and allocation procedures for interstate water resources.

These issues are discussed in the project documents.

3. Individual water lending operations are explicitly linked to the country's priorities for reform and investment and to the Bank's program of support.
4. If inadequate progress by borrowers in these priority areas leads to serious resource misuse and hampers the viability of water-related investments, Bank lending is limited to operations that provide potable water for poor households or conserve water and protect its quality without additionally drawing on a country's water resources.

43

## 1. Study Design—The Approach Paper of October 21, 1998

The Bank's Water Policy has been operational since 1993. Since then the Bank has expanded its sector work and invested $16 billion in over 180 new operations costing $40 billion in 80 countries. Given this large and diverse portfolio, and CODE's request for an evaluation of the Policy, OED proposes to test compliance of recent operations with the Policy, assess its relevance to country needs, and estimate the efficacy, efficiency, and sustainability of its implementation.

## Background

The challenge for future water management is enormous. In 1995, 29 countries with populations totaling 436 million experienced water stress or scarcity. By 2025, about 48 countries will do so, and the number of people adversely affected will exceed 1.4 billion, the majority in the least-developed countries.[1] Many countries with limited water availability also have a large proportion of their total area in international river basins. Where water resources are scarce, dependence on shared water increases the risk of friction and social tensions—as is already the case along the rivers Euphrates, Jordan, and Nile.

The Bank's portfolio of water projects accounts for 14 percent of Bank lending. Between 1985 and 1998, the Bank invested more than $33 billion in water-related projects. Until the mid-1980s, however, the Bank treated the various water subsectors (water supply, irrigation, hydropower, drainage, flood control, etc.) separately. It recognized intersectoral impact but did not seek to systematically optimize water allocations. The damage to aquatic ecosystems inherent in some projects was treated, if at all, by limited add-on corrective actions, and rarely by substantive adjustments to project design. Irrigation and water supply/sanitation projects tried, with varying success, to implement pricing schedules and cost recovery agreements to help with recurrent costs and achieve more efficient water management within projects.

In 1993, the Bank issued a comprehensive statement—*Water Resources Management, A World Bank Policy Paper*. This paper took three years to complete, a measure of the range and intensity of the debate that surrounded it. There was little disagreement on the fundamental issue—to reverse the trend whereby demand was outrunning supply of fresh water, while its quality was declining due to user abuse. While the debate was over the practicality of proposed solutions, it also raised awareness at all levels in the Bank of the relevant issues and the need for a new approach.

### The Bank's Water Policy

The Bank's Water Policy has two functions. First, it seeks to encourage reforms in water management institutions, policies, and planning in borrowing countries. Second, it is intended to guide the Bank in helping borrowers create incentives to promote these reforms and the tools to implement them.

The Policy has three central themes: (i) a comprehensive analytical framework for identifying priorities (holistic planning); (ii) the institutional and regulatory systems, supported by legislation, that promote reform (with emphasis on decentralization and participation); and (iii) the financial and opportunity costs of water in all its competing uses (an economic good). Annex 1 organizes the recommendations in matrix form, and provides a structure for subsequent analysis and reporting. Two other important principles are that special attention should be given to participation by women because they are the primary managers of domestic water (the gender dimension), and that the requirements of the poor for water should take precedence (the poverty dimension).

### Conceptual Framework of the Study

The conceptual framework for the main analytical exercise of the study, depicted in figure B.1, is adapted from the logical framework underlying results-based management. The principal *impact* of the Bank's Policy is identified as the improvement of water sector performance: the provision of water services, such as irrigation and water supply/sanitation, in an economically viable and environmentally sustainable manner. The Policy meets the Bank's overarching objective of reducing poverty by giving priority to the water requirements of poor communities. The Policy recognizes that, to improve the performance of the water sector, it is first necessary to help borrowing countries reform their water management institutions,

policies, and planning systems. Thus, reform is identified as the principal *outcome* of Bank and other interventions.

Improvements in Bank capacity and specific Bank interventions are portrayed as *inputs* and *outputs* in figure B.1. The Policy recommends a number of ways for the Bank to intervene to help promote water management reforms. These include assisting governments through sector work and technical assistance in formulating priority policy, planning, and institutional reforms—and investments—that are consistent with the Bank's Water Policy. These priorities should guide the Bank's sector lending programs. Individual lending operations should be linked to and promote the priorities for reform and investment. The Policy also places a high priority on Bank support for upgrading the skills of country policy analysts, planners, managers, and technicians.

Bank actions are only a modest driving force behind water management reforms.[2] A host of country and region-specific variables influence reforms in borrowing countries. Countries differ in their water requirements and endowments, economic and political conditions,

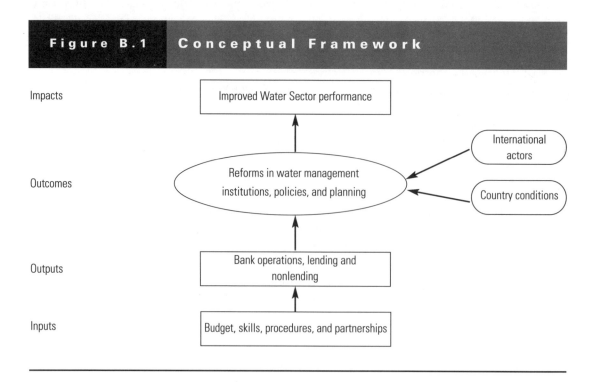

### Figure B.1    Conceptual Framework

Impacts — Improved Water Sector performance

Outcomes — Reforms in water management institutions, policies, and planning — International actors — Country conditions

Outputs — Bank operations, lending and nonlending

Inputs — Budget, skills, procedures, and partnerships

institutional capacities, and environmental problems. Other development institutions, including multilateral and bilateral development agencies, nongovernmental organizations, and the private sector, also influence the pace and direction of reform. And promoting collaboration with these international actors is an important element of the Water Policy. Thus, the design of relevant reforms, and the time frame for their implementation, crucially depend on the internal dynamics and water situation of the country, and on the quality of partnerships involved in water sector operations. Figure B.1 aligns country conditions and other international actors with Bank interventions as contributors to reform.

## Study Objectives

The purpose of the study is to evaluate the Bank's performance in implementing the Water Policy and derive lessons for improving Bank lending and nonlending activities and Bank staff capabilities. Five main issues will be examined:

- The extent to which Water Policy themes and priorities have been internalized into Bank procedures, staffing patterns, and staff development programs
- The quality of lending and nonlending instruments operational departments have used to implement Water Policy priorities
- The influence Bank interventions have had on national and international water resource policies and institutions, and how that influence was affected by conditions specific to particular countries and shared river basins
- The development effectiveness of Water Policy instruments in light of those results that can be observed
- And, most important, country-specific conditions most likely to induce water policy reforms—for example, severe water scarcity, fiscal deficits, liberalizing regimes—and the "levers" accessible to the Bank to encourage and shape government interventions.

The study will focus on water management reforms—the *outcomes*—as the measure of success in implementing the Bank's Water Policy. Since it is too early to estimate the *impact* of

Bank interventions on the ground, the study will reflect OED's conventional standards for assessing value added: the *relevance* to country conditions of recent Bank activities, including economic and sector work, portfolio and pipeline investment operations, and developments in organization and training; the *efficacy*, *efficiency*, and *sustainability* of activities showing results; and the contribution of the activities to *institutional development*.

## Methodology

The study has four components: a desk review, focus-country studies, thematic studies, and outreach. It will be conducted in three phases. The phase 1 review will concentrate on the Bank's actions, phase 2 will expand the analysis to include the country and other partner contributions, and phase 3 will consolidate and report the findings.

### Desk Review

The desk review will cover all Bank-financed water projects approved since 1993 as well as projects nearing approval, a total of about 190 operations. The evaluation format will use quantitative scoring to assess in particular the compliance of these projects with respect to the Water Policy. Compliance, in this context, refers to the extent to which the project's objectives and design are intended to promote, or already have prompted, reforms in water management institutions, policies, and planning consistent with the water policy matrix (table B.1). The relevance of Bank nonlending activities, such as sector work and policy dialogue with governments, will be examined because in many countries they have led, and even dominated, Bank involvement in water sector reform. The desk review will include in-depth evaluation (including some field visits where practicable) of up to 10 innovative projects promoting reforms to identify lessons for broader application.

### Focus-Country Studies

The study will examine the Bank's role in promoting water sector reforms in five countries. Brazil has been selected as a pilot because of the rapid evolution of its water management system

| Table B.1 | Water Policy Matrix of Recommended Reforms |
|---|---|

**Comprehensive Analytic Framework**

| National/State Level | Regional/Basin Level | Infrastructure Projects |
|---|---|---|
| National/state water strategy should reflect social, economic, and environmental objectives and be based on a sound assessment of water resources. The strategy deal should spell out priorities for providing water services; establish policies on water rights, water pricing and cost recovery, demand management, public investment, private sector participation; and meeting environmental management needs. Strategy formulation should be transparent and participatory. | Investments, policies, and regulations in one part of a river basin potentially affect other activities in the basin. The framework should be formulated in the context of a broad national/state strategy, be sensitive to socioeconomic concerns related to water, and incorporate environmental management needs. This is an indicative and dynamic planning process. Formulation of frameworks should be transparent and participatory, and based on accurate information. | Projects should be planned and assessed in the context of a broad river basin and national water strategy. Projects should internalize environmental management needs (e.g., water quality, in-stream flows). Socioeconomic assessments should accompany all projects. Project planning should be transparent and participatory, and based on accurate information. Projects should be reviewed by appropriate management agencies. |

**Institutional and Regulatory Systems**

| Legal, Policy and Planning | Regulatory and Management | Water Service Provision |
|---|---|---|
| Institutional structures—and laws—at the national and regional levels to coordinate the formulation and implementation of policies for improved water management, water service delivery, public investment programs and environmental management. Policy and planning institutions at the river basin level may also be appropriate. Stakeholders actively influence policy decisions, and policy-makers are ultimately responsible to the public. | Agencies for the regulation of water services and the management of water resources. Water services to be regulated with respect to pricing and quality of service. Water management responsibilities include *inter alia* setting standards, issuing permits, basin operations, and the collection and analysis of data. Regulatory and management decisions should take place at the lowest appropriate level with stakeholder participation. | Water service organizations should be financially and operationally autonomous—within an appropriate regulatory framework. Water services should be decentralized to the lowest appropriate level. Water service customers and users should participate in the formulation of management decisions. |

**Economic and Social Issues**

| Financing and Subsidies | Water Service Charges | Poverty Alleviation |
|---|---|---|
| Public sector financing should be focused on public goods. Water service organizations should be partially self-financing and use private capital markets; subsidies should be transparent and justified; subsidy programs should not create perverse incentives. | Water service organizations should be financially autonomous and operate under a hard budget constraint with explicit cost recovery targets. Service charge mechanisms should promote incentives for performance by providers and efficiency by users. Cross-subsidies between users and regions should be minimized, but equity pursued. | Special efforts should be directed to meeting the water supply and sanitation needs of the poor and redressing the neglect of the rural poor. Policies that undermine subsistence agricultural or fisheries should be carefully evaluated and, where necessary, there should be adjustments and compensation. |

in the last 10 years, and the Bank's large portfolio of projects and economic and sector work in that country. Selection of the other focus countries will be guided by studies already being undertaken by OED (such as the CAEs for China and India), the screening criteria developed from the desk review, and discussions with internal and external partners in the study. Country selection will be regionally balanced, cover a significant percentage of Bank-financed water projects, and reflect diversity in country-specific conditions. For each focus country the study will assess—by desk review and selected city/project visits—water management institutions, policies, and planning; the role played by the Bank and other actors; partnership with other development agencies; and country-specific conditions.

### Thematic Studies

During phase 2, at least three thematic studies will investigate important issues that cannot be adequately treated in the desk review and focus-country studies. Final selection of these themes will follow the workshop concluding phase 1. Three subjects have been tentatively programmed:

- *Bank Capacity.* The study would assess the evolution of Bank capacity in all water sectors—staff qualifications, training programs, documentation, coordination with other agencies, and so on.
- *International Watercourses.* The Water Policy advocates better management of shared international water resources. The Bank is currently supporting international cooperation in a number of international basins, including the Aral Sea, the Mekong Basin, Lake Victoria, the Nile River, and the Senegal River. This thematic study would evaluate the success of those interventions and include up to four case studies.
- *Implementation of Pricing and Cost Recovery Reforms.* Sustained progress toward the objectives of the Water Policy depends in many countries on successful implementation of higher tariffs for water. Commitment to such policy reforms depends on political will at the local level to execute the new pricing regimes. The objective will be to assess whether the Water Policy pricing prescriptions are effective in the focus countries and identify patterns of successful intervention. The 10 in-depth case studies proposed for the desk review may supply other examples.

### Internal and External Outreach

In an effort to tap the knowledge and opinions of Bank staff and other stakeholders, the following activities are planned: an *entry workshop* to discuss study methodology with Bank staff

and selected external participants and to help produce the design paper; five *focus-country workshops* to be held in-country with government officials, Bank task managers, relevant international organizations, and other stakeholders to discuss the evolution of water management reforms in the country and the Bank's role; *formal and informal interviews* to learn from the experience of Bank staff; a *phase 1 workshop* to discuss the results of the desk review and Brazil focus study and revisit the approach for phase 2; and *stakeholder workshops* near the end of the study to review the draft report. Some of the workshops will be professionally facilitated by a consultant with experience in water management issues and water policy evaluation.

### OED and Partner Roles

OED will link the study with ongoing QAG studies and OED's CAEs, the rural development study; the aid coordination study; and other thematic, country, and project evaluations. At the same time, OED will work closely with Bank country departments, national governments, other development banks and bilateral donors, NGOs, the Global Water Partnership (managed by ESDGW), and other partners, as appropriate. Because of ESDGW's strong interest in this topic, and because of its intention to build on the results of the study to formulate a revised Bank strategy for water resources management, OED will carry out the desk review, country case studies, and workshops in consultation with ESDGW. Guidance for the overall study would be provided by a three- or four-person review panel of senior international experts from developed and developing countries.

## 2. Implementation

The study has three components: a desk review, focus-country studies, and outreach. It was conducted in four phases. Phase 1 involved discussion with the Bank's Global Water Unit to develop the terms of reference for the study and discuss the methodology, which was subsequently discussed with Bank staff and selected external stakeholders. The study officially started after approval of the Approach Paper by the

Board's Committee on Development Effectiveness (CODE) on October 21, 1998. Phase 2 undertook detailed examination of Bank data and documents, reviewed the Bank's organizational response to the OP, and initiated a pilot country study in Brazil, and a Roundtable Conference to discuss findings in Brasilia, sponsored by OED. Subsequently, internal and external stakeholders met in June 1999 to review interim results and make suggestions for improvement. Phase 3 continued the documentary research and country studies. OED participated in two country studies and roundtables sponsored by ESSD: India (May 2000) and Yemen (October 2000). GWU undertook two further in-country country studies and roundtables in the Philippines and Nigeria during 2000. A special OED study was also made of China. At all four roundtables, a standard (anonymous) written questionnaire was applied, and these formed the basis for drawing cross-comparisons among study country views on Bank effectiveness. Phase 4, finalization of the draft report based on feedback received, started in November 2000 after review of the first draft OED evaluation report, which had been circulated within the Bank and to peer reviewers on September 2000. The revised draft was completed on December 20, 2000, and was sent for formal Bank review in order to present the final report to CODE in late February 2000.

## Desk Review

The desk review covered different sets of data:

- A comparison of OED's evaluation ratings and lessons learned from over 300 water and water-related operations completed in the period 1988–99. These data were then partitioned into pre- and post-*Strategy* groups centered on 1993, and comparisons were made to establish the differences in county operating conditions.
- A review of economic and sector work by *Strategy* elements for the same period and making the same comparison to establish how content—classified under *Strategy* elements—varied from one period to another.
- A content review of Bank 410 operations during 1988–99 (163 in 1988–93, and 247 in

1994–99) to determine how development and project objectives have changed.

- A review of 146 CASs covering 98 countries to determine responsiveness to the *Strategy*.
- An in-depth review of post-1994 operations against a standard evaluation process (Annex D) to determine responsiveness to the *Strategy*.
- A special study of 292 QAG evaluations covering the period 1997–99 to determine quality at entry and at supervision based on QAG typology.
- A special study of 103 randomly drawn operations to determine coverage and trends of social development issues pre- and post-*Strategy* (Annex E).

In addition to desk studies, many Bank task managers were interviewed to check and supplement the findings from the desk review.

## Focus Country Studies

The study examined the Bank's role in promoting water sector reforms in five countries. Brazil was selected as a pilot because of the rapid evolution of its water management system in the last 10 years, and the Bank's large portfolio of projects and economic and sector work in that country. Subsequent country studies were regionally balanced in order to cover a significant percentage of Bank-financed water projects and reflect diversity in country-specific conditions. For each focus country the study assessed—by desk review and selected city/project visits—water management institutions, policies, and planning, the role played by the Bank and other actors, partnership with other development agencies, and country-specific conditions.

## Thematic Studies

The thematic studies were not undertaken, as sufficient funds were not available.

## Internal and External Outreach

- An entry workshop with Bank staff was held in December 1998.
- Five focus-country workshops were held—two attended by OED, three by ESDGW.

- A series of informal workshops was held with Bank staff to discuss the methodology in the period November–April 1999.
- A phase I workshop organized by ESDGW was held in the Bank in June 1999.

- Stakeholder workshops to discuss the draft OED report were organized by the Water Resources Management Group in October 2000.

# ANNEX C:  SECTOR PERFORMANCE—RECOVERING FROM A TROUBLED PAST

At the time the Bank's water *Strategy* was under preparation, water-related projects were among the poorer performers in the Bank's portfolio. Since 1993 that performance has improved, although it remains below the Bank average. While the water *Strategy* may have contributed to the improving trend, the more immediate influence was the drive to improve overall Bank performance following the 1993 Wapenhans Report, which was highly critical of the quality of the Bank's lending, and the responses to OED sector reviews of water supply and sanitation in 1992 and of irrigation and drainage in 1995.

The recovery, however, has not been evenly distributed or the same for all subsectors. Water supply and sanitation has recovered more than irrigation and drainage since 1993. The principal reason for this is that the water supply and sanitation (WSS) subsector has benefited from multiple Project Improvement Plans (PIPs); irrigation and drainage has had no PIPs. The WSS portfolio, guided by the PIPs, was extensively restructured after 1993 to eliminate the most risky projects and to concentrate on institutional development and financial and organizational sustainability in the remainder. The irrigation and drainage subsector, in contrast, has been, and remains, weak on policy and institutional issues, focusing instead on costly participation approaches that enhance ownership among stakeholders but leave untouched some more important factors for sustainability. This Annex first reviews the issues contributing to the poor performance of the past, then analyzes current performance trends.

## Water and Sanitation Lacked a Unified Sector Approach

The 1992 OED evaluation of the WSS portfolio found that the lack of a sector approach under-

mined the Bank's mission to reduce poverty and missed the synergy from complementary investments in sanitation. Although there were sound sector policies, none addressed the need for development strategies that were environmentally sustainable or adequately addressed competing uses of water. Even so, almost half of the 120 country-specific projects evaluated were begun without an established policy for the sector, or without studies in the sector context. In many cases, the lack of a sector approach meant that there was insufficient provision for the poor, and that the Bank responded too much to the pressure from influential segments of the population for improved water and sanitation services. Thus many projects addressed immediate local problems, such as how best to get water supplies quickly into major cities, regardless of other demands for water. Sanitation and environmental protection were only ancillary considerations. Even when considered, sanitation was normally the first area to be scaled-down or eliminated when escalating costs forced borrowers to revise project plans.

The development effectiveness of Bank operations and their sustainability was frequently jeopardized by taking the easy option to increase a country's infrastructure rather than exercising the Bank's leverage to obtain sector reforms. Only 2 WSS projects demonstrated success in poverty relief; another 20 claimed success but provided no means of measuring it. The low priority given to sanitation services and environmental protection was often due to the failure of governments in setting up efficient sector organizations and management and well-balanced water resources management strategies. The Bank also failed to promote water tariffs and charges that reconciled economic efficiency, social equity, and financial criteria. Yet, enforcing such pricing policies is a necessary condition for efficiency savings and ensuring contributions to investment that would increase the share of the population with safe water and sanitation.

There was compelling evidence that the prerequisites for good utility performance are autonomy and an independent regulatory system. Water supply and sanitation organizations had relied too much on government involvement and public finances because the Bank did not use its influence to encourage governments to grant management and financial autonomy to utilities.[1] Experience showed that the time span on one project is too short for developing an enabling framework and building well-staffed and efficient utilities. Thus, OED recommended that the Bank should embark on medium-term programs focused on sectoral adjustment and technical assistance, followed by investment lending only when minimum and monitorable conditions are met for a healthy expansion.

## Irrigation's Success Was Built on Weak Policy and Institutional Foundations

The 1995 OED Irrigation and Drainage Sector Review cautioned that the success of irrigation may be its Achilles' heel. The review said that since irrigation was a major component of the green revolution that decreased food prices and allowed greater access by the poor, the success of irrigation might lead to complacency and reduced investment because of lower financial returns. Although irrigation projects were found to be effective in reaching the rural poor, their perceived success was strongly affected by macroeconomic conditions, further emphasizing the need for comprehensive appraisal.

As investment in new irrigation projects declined in the 1980s, many projects changed from a primarily engineering focus to become "rural development" projects with an irrigation component, and there was a marked shift from financing of specific irrigation schemes to sector loans. The evaluation found, however, that while sector loans appeared to promote reform, in many cases they contained minimal policy and institutional content. These projects were also more comprehensive and reminiscent of the integrated rural development loans of the 1970s—but may suffer from the problems of impracticality because of their complexity and dispersed geographical nature.

The evaluation argued that the Bank should continue to finance large irrigation schemes because of the economies of scale and high rates of economic return. Even so, there was a definite trend away from new construction toward rehabilitation, but not enough was being done to promote system upgrading, a process that uses engineering and social sciences to improve irrigation service to people, lower unit costs, and conserve water where it is scarce. In particular, OED argued that the Bank's traditional response to inadequate water service delivery—raising water charges—did not work because it ignored the incentive structure that enabled stakeholders to work together to improve performance. Nascent attempts at participatory irrigation management were starting to yield results, yet there was still insufficient recognition of the new institutions and governance—particularly financial autonomy—needed to make them successful.

The environmental and human impact of irrigation development was a cause for concern. Where health issues were incorporated into irrigation projects the results were outstanding, but too many opportunities for a synergistic approach, as for example with catchment management, were overlooked. Drainage was still the biggest single source of environmental problems stemming from irrigation and, in the worst cases, salinization of soils led to loss of productive land and livelihoods. The record on involuntary resettlement was mixed (Annex F). Sometimes its application was unsatisfactory, partly because of inadequate design due to peripheral Bank involvement and inherited problems, and partly because of borrowers' reluctance to fully embrace the Bank's resettlement policies because of additional costs and delays. As a result, there was an increasing aversion within the Bank and among borrowers to use Bank finance for projects with resettlement, particularly dams, even when there was sound economic justification for doing so.

Finally, the evaluation showed that there were a number of Bank institutional constraints to the "new agenda" for irrigation reforms. There was a pervasive concern that many of the issues raised by OED were either marginal or would prove to be costly to the Bank, such as resettlement. Irrigation professionals were also wary of increased user participation because they perceived it would lengthen the implementation period and may prejudice project results. A survey of staff revealed that they thought engineering design aspects were three to four times more important than design of agricultural support, production, and marketing facilities. Not surprisingly, there was concern at the declining pool of irrigation engineers and their replacement by nontechnical specialists and economists: "there is a risk of decline of quality of work in the future if this trend continues." Yet management rebutted the recommendation for increased supervision to ensure construction quality and land acquisition primarily because of the budget implications—small in terms of overall project cost, large in terms of Bank staff resources needed.

Many of the deficiencies noted in the two OED reviews were addressed by management and corrected through implementing the water strategy in the Bank's subsequent lending and nonlending operations. As Chapters 1 and 2 of the main report explain, a concerted effort was made after 1993 to shift the direction of Bank water activities.

## Portfolio Performance

The overall performance of 336 water projects completed in the period 1988–99 was below the Bank average, based on the assessment of project results along three related dimensions—outcome, institutional development impact, and sustainability of project benefits (figure C.1).[2] OED's exit ratings reflect performance over the life of the project and provide critical insight into the current policymaking environment of Bank clients and many valuable lessons. Almost half the water portfolio was active in the most recent six years of the period.[3]

**Outcome.** OED's outcome rating is based on whether the project achieved most of its major relevant goals efficiently and with few shortcomings, considering the importance of its major stated objectives and the associated costs and benefits. It takes account of how relevant the project's objectives were to the country's

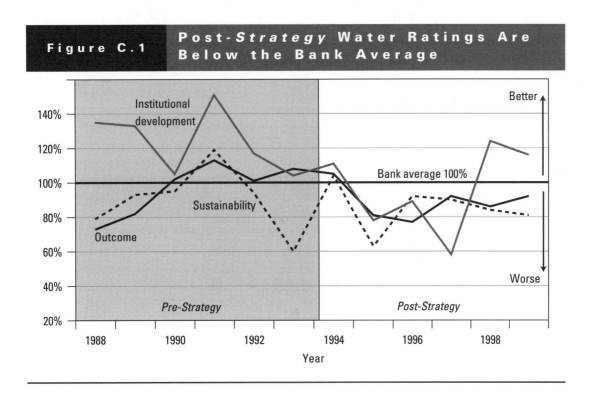

**Figure C.1** Post-*Strategy* Water Ratings Are Below the Bank Average

development strategy. The portfolio showed marked improvement, increasing from just over 40 percent satisfactory in 1988 to three-quarters satisfactory by 1991. Thereafter, satisfactory outcome ratings declined steadily until 1996, when they bottomed out at 53 percent. In the last three years of the period the score improved, but it remained 5–10 percent below the Bankwide average of 72 percent.[4] While this trend seems broadly correlated with the introduction of the Bank's water *Strategy,* this is purely coincidental, since a typical water project is implemented over seven years. Thus, the downward trend starting in 1991 reflects quality at entry in the early to mid-1980s.[5] When the outcome is related to the date of project approval, the results show that the upturn after 1996 follows improved quality at entry since 1992. Much of this was because the Bank increased its attention to portfolio quality following the 1993 Wapenhans Report.

Efficiency is an important component of the outcome rating. Two-thirds of all water projects had estimates of economic or financial efficiency. In line with water strategy recommendations, urban water supply projects increased their use of efficiency tests by almost 40 percent. Conversely, there was a decline of 9 percent for irrigation and drainage, and 38 percent for hydropower. There is a marked difference between the optimism shown at appraisal and outcomes for projects completed after 1993—most of it related to institutional performance. Table C.1 shows that the Bank has improved its

estimated rate of return in its water portfolio since 1993, and reduced the risks. The most risky sector was water supply adjustment lending, which delivered a rate of return 80 percent below expectations—not surprising, given that most of the benefits are predicated on relatively quick and substantial institutional reform. Economic returns from agricultural projects are not without risk either, and mature at about 20 percent less than planned. The least risky projects are urban water supply and hydropower, primarily because outcomes are determined by very clearly defined development objectives and well-defined costs.

**Institutional development.** This was higher for water projects than the Bankwide average before 1994. Emphasis on institutional development—and client ownership—is essential to move beyond project financing and to achieve long-lasting improvements in developing countries' utilization of human and financial resources. Despite a long decline between 1991 and 1995, institutional development ratings recovered because of greater private sector involvement, beneficiary participation, and the adoption of a tougher line with public sector implementing agencies (box C.1). One of the most notable features of the water portfolio is the high correlation of unsuccessful project outcomes (even though most projects substantially achieved their physical objectives) with modest or negligible institutional development, and vice versa (figure C.2).

| Table C.1 | Acceptable Levels of Efficiency (except for adjustment lending) | | | | |
|---|---|---|---|---|---|
| | Average subsectoral economic/financial rate of return (percent) | | | | |
| | Water sector adjustment[b] | Inland fisheries | Irrigation & drainage | Hydropower[c] | Urban water supply |
| Pre-*Strategy* | — | 21 | 13 | 12.9 | 10 |
| Post-*Strategy* | 3 | 23 | 20 | 12.9 | 11 |
| Pre-*Strategy* efficiency gap[a] | — | -10 | -9 | 0 | -1 |
| Post-*Strategy* efficiency gap[a] | -13 | -6 | -5 | -1 | -1 |

a. The "efficiency" gap is the difference between appraisal and exit economic or financial rate of return.

b. The rate of return is for those projects that had infrastructure investment components; adjustment per se cannot be explicitly measured by standard efficiency tests.

c. Returns and ratings for hydropower projects are heavily conditioned by the efficacy of power generation, regulation, and management and only weakly linked to water sector performance.

Box C.1 **High Borrower Ownership Ensures Success in Albania**

The political and economic collapse of Albania provided a window for reform of the irrigation sector through the Albania Irrigation Rehabilitation Project (1994–2000). The Bank moved quickly from appraisal to approval (10 months) and provided substantial supervision to respond quickly to an evolutionary and community-driven reform program. A new Irrigation Code and Regulation for Water Users' Associations was approved by Parliament in 1996. A comprehensive Law on Irrigation and Drainage covering restructuring of all existing public sector water enterprises into drainage boards was adopted by Parliament in 1999.

Irrigation sector reform succeeded because it had strong central government support and newly established local management. Conservative public sector agencies unwilling to reform were bypassed by government and replaced by the private sector. Water user associations (WUAs) were set up and given complete responsibility for operating all irrigation facilities (including reservoirs and primary irrigation canals) over an area of 70,000 ha, and 12 WAUs have federated. Rehabilitation significantly exceeded appraisal projections and at considerable cost savings (32 percent for irrigation and 57 percent for drainage). The ex-post economic rate of return is estimated to be 38 percent compared with 17 percent estimated at appraisal. Overall, 85 percent of WUAs have successfully managed WUA administration, water allocation and distribution, O&M, and fee collection and are beginning to become a focus for self-help on issues of social development and governance. Actual cost recovery by WUAs ranges from 35 percent to 100 percent, and averages 60 percent.

There are still unresolved problems. As the ECA Region notes: "despite their achievements, WUAs and federated WUAs have yet to prove their sustainability, simply establishing [them] is not a goal in itself . . . but the start of a long journey toward establishing sustainability." A large number of absentee landlords threatens the sustainability of many WUAs. Agriculture remains primarily at a subsistence stage and economically suboptimal farm sizes are a disincentive to farming. About 40 WUAs have ceased operation due to lack of interest in agriculture and mass urbanization of farmland around Tirana and Durres. Unresolved land drainage problems are causing waterlogging of the coastal plain and depressing agricultural production.

**Figure C.2** **Institutional Development Is Key to Satisfactory Outcomes (n = 306 projects)**

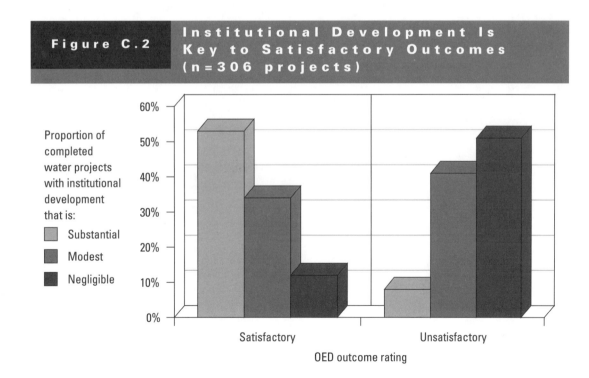

# ANNEX D: ASSESSING WATER PROJECT DESIGN UTILIZING THE WATER POLICY MATRIX DEVELOPMENT FOR THE BANK'S 1993 WATER *STRATEGY* PAPER

## Evaluation Methodology

1. Does the project intervene in a specific category? If yes, score the nature of the intervention according to the general criteria listed below.

2. If the project does not intervene in a specific category, is the category relevant to the project design? If yes, does the SAR/PAD discuss the issue?

Scores:

4. High: The project design addressed these issues with no major shortcomings.

3. Substantial: The project design addressed these issues with some major shortcomings.

2. Modest: The project design addressed these issues with numerous shortcomings.

1. Negligible: The project design addressed these issues in a completely inadequate manner.

N/R: Category not relevant (N/R) in this project context.

N/D: Category appears relevant, but no specific project component addresses it, and the SAR/PAD does not discuss the category (N/D) in sufficient detail. [Note: this mark has a negative connotation because, if the issue is relevant, the SAR/PAD **should** discuss it.]

D: Category is relevant, no specific project intervention, but the SAR analyzes the issue.

| Table D.1 | Assessment Criteria for Interventions |
|---|---|

### Comprehensive Management

| **National/state level** | **Regional/basin level** | **Projects** |
|---|---|---|
| National/state water resources Strategy/plan | Regional/basin water resources Strategy/plan | Water resource planning for physical infrastructure |

### Institutional Development

| **Legal and policy** | **Regulatory & management** | **Water service organizations** |
|---|---|---|
| *Water resources:* | *Water resource management:* | Urban water utilities |
| National/state water laws, policies, decrees | Water resource management agencies | Irrigation water user organizations |
| Water councils & commissions | Environmental management agencies | Rural water user groups |
| | | Hydropower companies |
| *Water services:* | *Water service regulation:* | |
| Laws for water service & regulatory organizations. Policy statements and government decrees | Public utility commissions | |

### Economic and Social Issues

| **Financing and subsidies** | **Water service charges** | **Disadvantaged groups** |
|---|---|---|
| Infrastructure financing terms and conditions | Financial management and tariff Structure for water service organizations | Low-cost WS&S for rural and urban poor Resettlement Gender Indigenous groups |

## 1. Comprehensive Management

### A. *National/State Level (alphanumerical score)*

I. Based on sound assessment of water resources and alternative development scenarios?

- Environmental/ecological issues an integral part of the framework?
- Stakeholders fairly represented in framework formulation?

II. The framework addresses policy issues, such as water rights, water pricing, cost recovery, private sector participation, capacity building, etc.?

III. Is there a clear relationship to national/state goals and policies?

IV. **B. *Regional/Basin Level (alphanumerical score)***

V. Based on sound assessment of water resources and alternative development scenarios?

- Environmental/ecological issues an integral part of the framework?
- Stakeholders fairly represented in framework formulation?
- Is there a clear relationship to the national/state framework?

### C. *Projects (alphanumerical score)*

- Based on a sound assessment of water resources?
- Environmental/ecological issues an integral part of project planning?
- Project embedded in broader regional/basin and national/state frameworks?
- Is project planning and review conducted in a transparent and participatory manner?

## 2. Institutional Development

### A. *Legal and Policy*

*Water Resource Policy and Legal Interventions* **(alphanumerical score)**

- Are there coordination mechanisms across agencies and jurisdictions?
- Do major stakeholders (water users, civil society, NGOs, etc.) participate in policy making?
- Do the policy institutions have sufficient power to be effective? i.e., budget authority, legal mandates, political backing, etc.?

VI. Are the policy institutions supported by competent water management agencies?

VII. *Water Service Policy and Legal Interventions* **(alphanumerical score)**

- Effective regulatory framework: pricing, service, environmental standards, etc.?
- Water service organizations operate on a commercial basis?
- Explicit policy statements regarding: service pricing, subsidy levels, etc.?
- Water service organizations appropriately decentralized?

### B. *Management and Regulation*

*Water Resource & Environmental Management Agencies* **(alphanumerical score)**

- Agency's monitoring and planning capability strengthened?
- Collaboration with other agencies involved in water management, i.e., environmental, fisheries, agriculture?
- Does the agency have an outreach/public education program?
- Plans and decisions reviewed and approved by an appropriate policy institution?

VIII. If the agency provides infrastructure (i.e., bulk water supply or flood control), is this unit a distinct financial and operational entity, separated from planning responsibilities?

*Water Service Regulation Bodies* **(alphanumerical score)**

- Does the body set cost recovery, tariff, and accounting policies?
- Does the body monitor the financial performance of water service organizations?
- Does the body review and approve tariff proposals for water service organizations?

### C. *Water Service Organizations (alphanumerical score)*

IX. Is the organization financially and operationally autonomous, and operating on a commercial basis?

- Is the organization under an appropriate regulatory framework for pricing and service quality?

- Is the water service organization appropriately decentralized?
- Do water service customers and users have a voice in management decisions?

## 3. Economic and Social Issues

### A. Financing and Subsidies (alphanumerical score)

- Financing terms *explicit*?
- Are subsidies explicit and justified?
- Does the water service organization/agency contribute some degree of self-financing?
- Are nonpublic sources of financing used (private banks, bonds, equity markets, etc.?)

### B. Water Service Charges (alphanumerical score)

- Are there explicit cost-recovery targets?
- Is there a sound financial analysis which examines the need for tariff increases and the impact on the financial health of the organization/agency?

- Is the tariff structure analyzed with respect to promoting water use efficiency and equity?
- Are the collected revenues put back into service provision?

### C. Disadvantaged Groups (alphanumerical score)

- Is there a social assessment of the people affected by the project?
- If there is a project component targeted at the poor (i.e., low-cost WS&S), does it take the special needs of affordability, appropriate technology, community participation, etc. into account?
- If resettlement is involved, is there an adequate resettlement plan?
- When relevant, are the specific needs and participation of women considered?
- When relevant, are the specific needs and participation of indigenous groups considered?

| Figure D.1 | Water Policy Review—Sample Project Design Analysis |
|---|---|

### 1. Project Data:

| | |
|---|---|
| Country: | China |
| Project Name—ID: | Shanxi Poverty Alleviation Project |
| Effectiveness Date: | September 5, 1996 |
| Closing Date: | December 31, 2002 |
| % Disbursed | 45.7 |
| Task Manager: | |
| Partners Involved: | |
| Reviewed By: | |
| Checked By: | |
| Date Posted: | 03/01/99 |

### 2. Project Objectives, Financing, Costs, and Components

| Project Costs (US $ million) | Appraisal |
|---|---|
| **Total** | 182.8 |
| **List Financing Sources** | |
| Shanxi Province | 45.7 |
| Prefectures/Counties | 7.3 |
| Farmers | 29.8 |
| IDA | 100.0 |

| Figure D.1 | Water Policy Review—Sample Project Design Analysis (continued) |
|---|---|

**Executing Agencies:**

**Objectives:** Help alleviate poverty in the 20 poorest counties of Yuncheng and Luliang Perfectures in Shanxi Province through activities aimed at raising incomes of about 3 million poor through rehabilitation of an existing irrigation system, improvement of rural roads and construction of village water supply schemes, land development, expansion of livestock raising and horticulture, and expansion of primary agriculture processing capacity.

**Components:**

(i).  Construction of a new Pumping Complex in Langdian on Yellow River for Yuncheng Irrigation System.

(ii).  Improvement and expansion of Yuncheng Irrigation System

(iii).  River beach development with irrigation and rural infrastructure on 13,000 ha in Yuncheng

(iv).  Construction of 78 village water supply schemes in Yuncheng (620,000 people) and Luliang (64,000 people).

(v).  Improvement of existing rural roads 209 km in Yuncheng and 118 km in Luliang.

(vi).  Soil and water conservation works (56 check dams, 4,200 ha of afforestation on sloping lands, 13,400 ha of terracing)

(vii).  Agricultural processing facilities, livestock raising and expansion of area under fruit and nut trees.

(viii).  Support for program targeted at poor and disadvantaged women.

(ix).  Project management, training and overseas study tours.

**3. Overall Design Rating: 3**

|   | Analytic Framework | | | Institutional & Regulatory | | | Economic and Social | | |
|---|---|---|---|---|---|---|---|---|---|
| National/ State Level | Basin/ Region Level | Infra- structure | Legal, Policy & Planning | Management & Regulatory | Water Services | Financing & Subsidies | Service Charges | Poverty/ Gender |
| 2.5 | 3.5 | 3.5 | (WR) ND  (WS) 3 | (WR) N/D  (WS) 3.5 | 3 | 3 | 3.5 | 3 |

**4. Water Policy Review Issues:**

(i).  Also the water sector policies and the implementation strategy have been presented and discussed for the region in the context of the project, their relevance to the national water policy is not discussed. At least one should know how the regional policies are dictated by the national policy and how the experience of the regional policies will influence the national policies and water management strategies.

(ii).  The water resources assessment for the region should have been more elaborate. The project discusses the water requirements of the area, but it does not discuss the resource availability nor does it give the regional or the basin water balance. The conjunctive use of the surface and groundwater is proposed without throwing some light on the water balance.

**5. Implementation Issues:**

(i).  Implementation is ahead of schedule, but the initial momentum of the project progress appears to have slowed down. This may reflect on some weakness in the project design and/or the implementation arrangements.

(ii).  Progress on many components and amongst the counties is uneven.

(iii).  The construction of Langdeng Pumping Station, the main source of water supply for the Yancheng Irrigation Area has hit some snag. There appears to be lack of commitment by the Government and uncertainty surrounding the financial viability of the scheme. The prefecture is not sure that it will be able to pay the province back for the investment on the pumping station. (A serious issue indeed!)

(iv).  Counterpart funding is insufficient in some cases.

| Figure D.1 | Water Policy Review—Sample Project Design Analysis (continued) |
|---|---|

**Evaluation Notes**

### *Analytic Framework*

| National/State Level: | There is no discussion of the national strategy. The Province has designed the project in accordance with the most plausible development plans. These take into consideration the participation, environmental and other policy issues. The relevance to or impact on the national strategies is not discussed. |
|---|---|
| Basin/Regional Level: | The project is designed for regional development. The strategy for the development and management of the resources as presented for the region is endorsed by the provincial government. (But, does the provincial government have a formal water sector management strategy?) |
| Infrastructure | An excellent presentation. The project fits in the China's poverty reduction strategy plans which aim at addressing poor areas through investments in land development, rural works and rural enterprise. |
| | However, the water resources assessment (p 3.3–3.6) lacks analysis of resource availability, its firmness and the regional water balance. |
| | EIA is prepared for each prefecture (p 3.40) and approved by NIPA (Annex 13). The stakeholder participation is ensured (p 3.53); the area targeting appears to be fine, but the community targeting may be problematic. (p 3.54). An elaborate and good discussion of the socio-economic aspects of the beneficiaries and the PAPs is given (p 2.9–2.95 and Annex 12). Resettlement Action Plan based on the Chinese Law of Land Management has been approved by IDA (p 3.49) |

### *Institutional & Regulatory*

| Legal, Policy & Planning: | The national water policy is not discussed. The provincial and the regional policies are presented. |
|---|---|
| Management & Regulatory: | The capabilities of the governmental agencies have been assessed and the strengthening of the institutional capacity is provided for, where needed. (p 4.2). The institutional framework provides for collaboration with the other agencies through the Project Leading Group, which also facilitates overseeing by the provincial government and reviewing the project plans etc. (p 4.1) The planning functions are with the provincial government while the operation is with the prefectures and its subordinate agencies. |
| Water Services: | The village committees appear to have some degree of financial and operational autonomy. However, the influence of the government is predominant. The water charges are based on volumetric assessment, but the funds go to the province through the perfecture. The prefectures, and the counties are responsible for O&M through funds provided by the provincial government. (p 4.8) |

### *Economic and Social*

| Financing & Subsidies: | Financing terms are explicit in table 3.2. The subsidies are implicit in the cost recovery arrangements, though the government's declared policy is to recover all costs from the beneficiaries. (p 4.7). There is qualitative discussion of the risks involved (p 5.26); financial implications and the impact on economic viability should have been presented. |
|---|---|
| Water Service Charges: | The cost recovery targets are explicit. The irrigation use is assessed on volumetric basis to recover for O&M and loan repayment.to the province. The cost recovery on terraces and check dams is 50%, beach land development 60%; rural roads full; and water supply schemes full O&M and 60% investment cost. (p 4.7) |
| Poverty/Gender Focus: | Technology for addressing poverty issue is fine. The project supports WID through support to China's Women Federation |

| Figure D.2 | Water Policy Review—Sample Project Design Analysis |
|---|---|

**1. Project Data:**

| | |
|---|---|
| Country: | Philippines |
| Project Name—ID: | Water Districts Development Project |
| Effectiveness Date: | Not Given in the last PSR of Dec 8, 1998 |
| Closing Date: | June 30, 2003 |
| % Disbursed: | Nil |
| Task Manager: | |
| Partners Involved: | |
| Reviewed By: | |
| Checked By: | |
| Date Posted: | |

**2. Project Objectives, Financing, Costs, and Components**

| Project Costs (US $ million) | *Appraisal* |
|---|---|
| **Total** | 80.7 |
| **List Financing Sources** | |
| IBRD | 56.8 |
| MWSS/City Government | 11.5 |
| User Installation Charges | 12.4 |

**Executing Agencies:**　　　　Land Bank of the Philippines, LWUA, City Governments and MWSS.

**Objectives:**

(i). Help participating LGUs and water districts plan and implement sewerage and sanitation investments based on the residents' wishes and willingness to pay.

(ii). Assist the Government of Philippines in developing a transparent regulatory mechanism in order to facilitate private sector participation in water utilities.

**Components:**

(i). TA designed to pilot and field-test a privatized public performance audit system.

(ii). Construction of sewerage, sanitation, and drainage infrastructure in the cities of Davao, Cotabato, Calamba and Cagayan de Oro.

**3. Overall Design Rating: 2.5**

| Analytic Framework | | | Institutional & Regulatory | | | Economic and Social | | |
|---|---|---|---|---|---|---|---|---|
| National/ State Level | Basin/ Region Level | Infra- structure | Legal, Policy & Planning | Management & Regulatory | Water Services | Financing & Subsidies | Service Charges | Poverty/ Gender |
| 3 | 3 | 3.5 | (WR) 3 | (WR) 2 | 3.5 | 2.5 | 3.5 | 2 |
| | | | (WS) 3 | (WS) 2.5 | | | | |

**4. Water Policy Review Issues:**

(i). Generally the water supply and sewerage (WSS) projects are designed in isolation from the national water resources development plans— though they conform to the specific strategies of the WSS sub-sector. The national water plans include those for the various sub-sectors; therefore, the development plans of the sub-sector components must link them to the national plans.

(ii). Discussion of gender issues, particularly the role of women, are usually not adequately discussed in the project documents for WSS projects.

| Figure D.2 | Water Policy Review—Sample Project Design Analysis (continued) |
|------------|-----------------------------------------------------------------|

**5. Implementation Issues:**

(i). This project is facing major implementation projects, which shows weakness of project design, particularly the financing and implementation arrangements.

(ii). The last supervision mission has rated the "DO" component unsatisfactory. Project restructuring and even cancellation are currently being discussed.

**Evaluation Notes**

### *Analytic Framework*

| | |
|---|---|
| National/State Level: | The Government strategies and the work plans are well defined for the water supply and sewerage sub sector. These are based on full stakeholder participation and aim at creating an enabling environment for a large and rapid infusion of private sector investments and to invest in sanitation infrastructure in a demand-driven, financially sustainable and technologically cost-effective manner. Unfortunately, in discussing the Government strategies, no reference is made to the Government's strategies and the on-going plan formulation. |
| Basin/Regional Level: | Same as above. |
| Infrastructure | A good participatory approach has been adopted in project formulation starting from the planning to the design stages. This would ensure that the project interventions are demand-driven. (p 4.6P and Annex 13) The project follows the Government's development objectives for the WSS sub-sector. The environmental considerations are taken into consideration in the project design. No resettlement is needed. The land for the facilities will be purchased at the market price. The water resources assessment is weak in the project documents. The discussion of the water quality aspects is inadequate. |

### *Institutional & Regulatory*

| | |
|---|---|
| Legal, Policy & Planning: | The National Economic development Agency (NEDA) of the Philippines is the nation's highest policy advisory committee, chaired by the President. The NEDA Board laid out policies for water supply and sanitation in 1994, which led to the formulation of strategies for the sub-sector development. These and the National Water Crisis Act of June 1995 provide the necessary regulatory framework for development. |
| Management & Regulatory: | The Land Bank of the Philippines would on-lend to the City Level Local Government Units (LGUs) to implement the project. The water districts would then operate the utilities. The implementation methodology is complex and risky. |
| Water Services: | The Local Water Districts is a "water supply franchise" and would be the water service organization. These are autonomous bodies and would have full O&M responsibility. |

### *Economic and Social*

| | |
|---|---|
| Financing & Subsidies: | The financing terms are explicit, but difficult. The risk analysis is routine sensitivity evaluation of the probable set backs to the project assumptions. |
| Water Service Charges: | The cost recovery targets are well set based on the beneficiaries' ability to pay for the services. |
| Poverty/Gender Focus: | It is not a poverty targeted operation. The discussion of the indigenous groups and the participation by women is weak. |

| | | | | | | | |
|---|---|---|---|---|---|---|---|
| **Table D.2** | | | | **Water Policy Analysis: Compliance with Water Policy According to the 9-Cell Water Policy Matrix** | | | |

| Project ID | Region | Year | Sector | Subsector | Instrument | Country | Project name |
|---|---|---|---|---|---|---|---|
| 43178 | ECA | 1999 | AI | ID | SIL | Albania | Second Irrigation and Drainage Rehabilitation |
| 3562 | EAP | 1994 | AI | WRM | SIL | China | Xiaolangdi Multipurpose |
| 1409 | AFR | 1998 | WY | WRM | SIL | Lesotho | Highland Water |
| 10478 | SAR | 1996 | UM | UWSS | SIL | Pakistan | Balochistan Natural Resources |
| 10501 | SAR | 1997 | AI | ID | SIL | Pakistan | National Drainage Program |
| 7105 | LAC | 1994 | AI | ID | TAL | Ecuador | Irrigation TA |
| 60132 | MNA | 1999 | UU | RWSS | SIL | Tunisia | Greater Tunis Sewerage & Reuse |
| 6522 | LAC | 1994 | WU | UWSS | SIL | Brazil | Espirito Santo |
| 38895 | LAC | 1998 | VM | WRM | SIL | Brazil | Federal Water Management |
| 8319 | ECA | 1994 | WU | UWSS | SIL | Bulgaria | Water Companies Restructuring and Modernization |
| 7713 | LAC | 1996 | VM | WRM | SIL | Mexico | Water Resources Management |
| 3637 | EAP | 1997 | WW | RWSS | SIL | China | National Rural Water III |
| 36405 | EAP | 1997 | AI | WRM | SIL | China | Wanjiazhai Water Transfer |
| 36414 | EAP | 1998 | VP | ENV | SIL | China | Guanxi Urban Environment |
| 49700 | EAP | 1998 | AI | ID | SIL | China | Irrigated Agriculture Intensification II |
| 35783 | ECA | 1996 | VP | WSM | SIL | Lithuania | Siauliai Environment |
| 40566 | MNA | 1998 | WR | RWSS | SIL | Morocco | Water Resource Management |
| 46052 | LAC | 1997 | AI | WRM | SIM | Brazil | Ceara Water Resource Management Pilot |
| 35805 | ECA | 1998 | WW | UWSS | SIL | Armenia | Municipal Development Project |
| 3644 | EAP | 1994 | VR | WRM | SIL | China | Xiaolangdi Resettlement |
| 4010 | EAP | 1994 | VM | HYDRO | SIL | Indonesia | Dam Safety |
| 39015 | AFR | 1998 | WW | UWSS | SIL | Mozambique | National Water Development I |
| 4799 | EAP | 1995 | PH | HYDRO | SIL | Thailand | Lam Takhong Pump Storage |
| 10500 | SAR | 1998 | AI | ID | SIL | Pakistan | Punjab Private Sector Ground Water |
| 7707 | LAC | 1994 | WW | UWSS | SIM | Mexico | Second Water Supply Sanitation |
| 7710 | LAC | 1994 | VP | UWSS | SIL | Mexico | Northern Border Environment |
| 50745 | SAR | 1999 | WY | RWSS | SIL | Bangladesh | Arsenic Control |
| 8037 | LAC | 1997 | AI | ID | SIL | Peru | Irrigation Sub Sector |
| 42442 | LAC | 1997 | AA | WSM | SIL | Peru | Sierra Natural Resources |
| 10463 | SAR | 1995 | VP | ENV | SIL | India | Industrial Pollution Prevention |
| 4611 | EAP | 1996 | WS | UWSS | SIL | Philippines | Manila 2nd Sewerage |

| Overall score | Comprehensive management | | | Institutional development | | | | | Economic and social issues | | |
|---|---|---|---|---|---|---|---|---|---|---|---|
| | | | | Legal and policy | | Management and regulation | | | | | |
| | National/state level | Regional/basin level | Projects | Water resource | Water service | Water resource & environmental management agencies | Water service regulation bodies | Water service organizations | Financing and subsidies | Water service charges | Disadvantaged group |
| 4 | 4 | 4 | 4 | 4 | 3.5 | 3.5 | 3 | 3.5 | 3.5 | 3.5 | 4 |
| 4 | 4 | 4 | 4 | 3.5 | 3.5 | 3.5 | 3.5 | 4 | 4 | 4 | N/R |
| 4 | 4 | 4 | 4 | 4 | 3.5 | 4 | 3.5 | 4 | 4 | 4 | 3 |
| 4 | 4 | 4 | 3 | 4 | D | 4 | D | N/R | 4 | D | 2 |
| 4 | 4 | 4 | 4 | 3 | 3 | 4 | 3 | 3 | 2 | 2 | 3 |
| 4 | D | 4 | N/R | 4 | N/R | 4 | N/R | 4 | N/R | N/R | N/R |
| 4 | D | D | 4 | N/R | D | N/D | 4 | D | 4 | 4 | 4 |
| 4 | N/R | N/D | 4 | 4 | N/D | 4 | 4 | 4 | 4 | 4 | 4 |
| 3.5 | 3 | 3 | 3 | 4 | 4 | 4 | 4 | 3 | 2 | 2 | 3 |
| 3.5 | 3 | 3 | 3.5 | 3.5 | 3.5 | 3.5 | 3.5 | 3.5 | 3.5 | 3.5 | 3 |
| 3.5 | 3 | 3 | N/R | 2 | N/R | 4 | N/R | N/R | D | N/R | N/R |
| 3.5 | 3.5 | 3.5 | 4 | 3.5 | 4 | 3.5 | 3.5 | 3.5 | 3.5 | 3.5 | 3 |
| 3.5 | 3.5 | 3.5 | 4 | 3.5 | 3.5 | 3.5 | 3.5 | 4 | 4 | 4 | 2 |
| 3.5 | 3.5 | 3.5 | 3.5 | 3.5 | 3.5 | N/R | 3.5 | 3.5 | 4 | 4 | 2 |
| 3.5 | 3.5 | 3.5 | 4 | 3.5 | 3.5 | 3.5 | 3.5 | 3.5 | 3.5 | 3.5 | 1.5 |
| 3.5 | 3.5 | 3.5 | 4 | 3.5 | 3.5 | 3.5 | 3.5 | 3.5 | 3.5 | 3.5 | 3 |
| 3.5 | 4 | 2 | 4 | D | N/R | 4 | N/R | N/R | N/R | 2 | N/R |
| 3.5 | 4 | 3 | 4 | 4 | N/R | 4 | N/R | 3 | 1 | 2.5 | 3 |
| 3.5 | 4 | 4 | 3.5 | NA | 3.5 | 3.5 | 3.5 | 4 | 3.5 | 3.5 | 3.5 |
| 3.5 | 4 | 4 | 4 | N/R | N/R | 3.5 | 3.5 | N/R | 4 | 3.5 | 3.5 |
| 3.5 | 4 | 4 | 4 | 3 | 3 | 3.5 | 3.5 | 3 | 3.5 | N/R | N/R |
| 3.5 | 4 | 4 | 4 | 3.5 | 3 | 3.5 | 3 | 3.5 | 3 | 3 | 3 |
| 3.5 | 4 | 4 | 4 | N/R | N/R | 3.5 | 3.5 | N/R | 3.5 | 3.5 | 2.5 |
| 3.5 | D | 2.5 | 3 | D | D | 4 | 4 | 4 | 4 | 3 | 2.5 |
| 3.5 | D | 3 | 4 | 4 | D | 4 | ND | 4 | 3 | 3 | 2 |
| 3.5 | D | 3 | 4 | D | D | 4 | ND | 4 | 3 | 3 | 3 |
| 3.5 | D | D | 4 | D | D | D | 3 | 4 | 3 | 3 | 4 |
| 3.5 | D | D | 3 | D | D | D | D | 4 | 4 | 3 | 2 |
| 3.5 | D | D | 4 | D | D | 1 | 3 | 3 | 4 | 4 | 4 |
| 3.5 | D | N/D | 3 | D | N/R | 3 | N/R | N/R | 4 | 4 | 4 |
| 3.5 | N/D | N/D | 3 | N/R | N/D | N/R | N/D | 3 | 3.5 | 3.5 | N/R |

*(continues on following page)*

| Table D.2 | Water Policy Analysis: Compliance with Water Policy According to the 9-Cell Water Policy Matrix (continued) | | | | | | |
|---|---|---|---|---|---|---|---|
| Project ID | Region | Year | Sector | Subsector | Instrument | Country | Project name |
| 51124 | LAC | 1998 | MY | UWSS | TAL | Panama | Utilities Restructuring |
| 3594 | EAP | 1996 | AI | ID | SIL | China | Gansu Hexi Corridor |
| 10480 | SAR | 1997 | WS | UWSS | SIL | India | Bombay Sewage Disposal |
| 41887 | SAR | 1999 | VV | UWSS | SIL | Bangladesh | Municipal Services |
| 3593 | EAP | 1994 | AM | ID | SIL | China | Songliao Plain Agriculture Dev |
| 10484 | SAR | 1996 | WW | RWSS | SIL | India | Uttar Pradesh Rural WSS |
| 10485 | SAR | 1996 | VM | WRM | TAL | India | Hydrology Project |
| 7701 | LAC | 1994 | AI | ID | SIL | Mexico | On Farm and Minor irrigation |
| 39022 | EAP | 1999 | | UWSS | APL | Philippines | LGU Urban Water and Sanitation |
| 1075 | AFR | 1997 | WU | UWSS | SIL | Guinea | Third Water Supply |
| 10516 | SAR | 1997 | WR | RWSS | SIL | Nepal | Rural Water Supply and Sanitation |
| 38570 | AFR | 1997 | AI | ID | SIL | Tanzania | River Basin Mngmt and Smallholder Irrig Improv |
| 3649 | EAP | 1996 | AI | ID | SIL | China | Sanxi Poverty Alleviation |
| 8173 | LAC | 1994 | AI | ID | SIL | Uruguay | NRM and Irrigation Development |
| 8288 | ECA | 1995 | WU | UWSS | SIL | Azerbaijan | Greater Baku Water Supply Rehabilitation |
| 9545 | SAR | 1995 | VM | WRM | SIL | Bangladesh | River Bank Protection |
| 45629 | EAP | 1998 | WY | UWSS | SIL | Cambodia | Urban Water Supply |
| 3596 | EAP | 1995 | AI | WRM | SIL | China | Yangtze Basin Water |
| 3599 | EAP | 1996 | VV | ENV | SIL | China | Yunnan Environment |
| 3648 | EAP | 1996 | US | ENV | SIL | China | Second Shanghai Sewerage |
| 8406 | ECA | 1995 | VP | WSM | SIL | Estonia | Haapsalu and Matsalu Bays Environment Project |
| 764 | AFR | 1996 | WU | UWSS | SIL | Ethiopia | Water Supply Development and Rehab |
| 39929 | ECA | 1998 | SA | RWSS | FIL | Georgia | Social Investment Fund |
| 8510 | ECA | 1996 | AI | ID | SIL | Kazakhstan | Irrigation and Drainage |
| 8595 | ECA | 1996 | WW | UWSS | SIL | Poland | Bielsko-Biala Water and Wastewater |
| 0 | ECA | 1999 | | UWSS | SIL | Poland | Wroclaw Water and Wastewater |
| 8867 | ECA | 1997 | WW | UWSS | SIL | Turkmenistan | Water Supply and Sanitation |
| 4830 | EAP | 1997 | WY | UWSS | SIL | Viet Nam | Water Supply |
| 3954 | EAP | 1994 | AI | ID | SIL | Indonesia | Java Irrigation Imp and WRM |
| 4834 | EAP | 1995 | AI | ID | SIL | Viet Nam | Irrigation Rehabilitation |
| 40720 | ECA | 1999 | WU | UWSS | SIL | Kazakhstan | Atyrau Pilot Water Supply and Sanitation |

| Overall score | Comprehensive management | | | Institutional development | | | | | Economic and social issues | | |
| | | | | Legal and policy | | Management and regulation | | | | | |
| | National/state level | Regional/basin level | Projects | Water resource | Water service | Water resource & environmental management agencies | Water service regulation bodies | Water service organizations | Financing and subsidies | Water service charges | Disadvantaged group |
|---|---|---|---|---|---|---|---|---|---|---|---|
| 3.5 | N/R | 2 | N/R | N/D | 3 | N/D | 4 | 4 | 4 | 3 | 3 |
| 3.5 | N/R | 3.5 | 3.5 | N/R | N/R | N/R | 3 | 2.5 | 3.5 | 3.5 | 3 |
| 3.5 | N/R | D | 4 | N/D | D | D | D | 3 | 4 | 3 | 4 |
| 3.5 | N/R | N/R | 3 | N/R | D | N/R | 4 | 4 | 3 | 2 | 3 |
| 3.5 | N/R | N/R | 4 | N/R | 3.5 | N/R | 3.5 | 3.5 | 3 | 3.5 | 3 |
| 3.5 | N/R | N/R | 3 | N/R | 3 | N/R | 3 | 4 | 3 | 4 | 4 |
| 3.5 | N/R | N/R | N/R | D | 3 | 4 | ? | N/R | 2 | 2 | N/R |
| 3.5 | N/R | N/R | 4 | D | D | D | 4 | 3 | 4 | 3 | 2 |
| 3.5 | N/R | N/R | 3 | N/R | D | N/R | D | 3 | 4 | 3 | N/D |
| 3.4 | 3 | 3 | 3 | 3 | 3 | 3 | 3 | 4 | 4 | 3.5 | 3 |
| 3.3 | N/R | N/R | 4 | N/R | 3 | N/R | 3 | 4 | 3 | D | 4 |
| 3.1 | 4 | 4 | 2.5 | 3 | 3 | 3 | 3 | 2.5 | 2.5 | 2.5 | 2.5 |
| 3 | 2.5 | 3.5 | 3.5 | N/D | 3 | N/D | 3.5 | 3 | 3 | 3.5 | 3 |
| 3 | 2.5 | N/D | 3 | D | 3 | 3 | D | 4 | 2 | 3 | 2.5 |
| 3 | 3 | 3 | 3 | 2 | 2 | 3 | 3 | 2 | 3 | 3 | 3.5 |
| 3 | 3 | 3 | 3 | 3 | N/D | 3 | D | 3 | 2 | N/D | 3 |
| 3 | 3 | 3 | 3.5 | N/D | 2.5 | D | 3 | 2.5 | 3 | 3 | 2 |
| 3 | 3 | 3 | 3.5 | 3.5 | 3.5 | 3.5 | 3.5 | 3 | 3.5 | 3 | 2.5 |
| 3 | 3 | 3 | 3.5 | N/D | 3.5 | N/D | 3.5 | 3 | 3 | 3 | 2 |
| 3 | 3 | 3 | 3 | N/R | 3.5 | N/R | 3.5 | N/R | 3.5 | 3 | 3 |
| 3 | 3 | 3 | 3.5 | 3 | 2.5 | 3 | 3 | 3 | 2.5 | 3 | 2.5 |
| 3 | 3 | 3 | 3 | 3 | 3 | 3 | 3 | 2.5 | 3 | 3 | 3 |
| 3 | 3 | 3 | 3.5 | NA | NA | 3.5 | NA | NA | 3 | 3 | 3.5 |
| 3 | 3 | 3 | 3 | 3 | 3 | 3 | 3 | 3 | 3 | 3 | 2 |
| 3 | 3 | 3 | 3.5 | 3 | 3 | 3.5 | 3.5 | 3.5 | 3.5 | 3.5 | 2.5 |
| 3 | 3 | 3 | 3 | 3 | 3 | 3.5 | 3.5 | 3.5 | 3.5 | 3.5 | 2.5 |
| 3 | 3 | 3 | 3 | 3 | 3 | 2.5 | 2.5 | 3 | 2 | 3 | 2.5 |
| 3 | 3 | 3 | 3.5 | N/D | 3 | N/D | 3.5 | 3.5 | 3 | 3 | 2 |
| 3 | 3 | 3.5 | 3.5 | 2.5 | 3 | 2.5 | 3 | 3 | 3 | 3.5 | 1 |
| 3 | 3 | 3.5 | 3.5 | 3 | 3 | 3.5 | 3.5 | 3.5 | 3 | 3 | 1.5 |
| 3 | 3 | NA | 3 | NA | NA | 3 | 3 | 3.5 | 3 | 3.5 | 2.5 |

*(continues on following page)*

69

| Table D.2 | Water Policy Analysis: Compliance with Water Policy According to the 9-Cell Water Policy Matrix (continued) | | | | | | |
|---|---|---|---|---|---|---|---|
| Project ID | Region | Year | Sector | Subsector | Instrument | Country | Project name |
| 46042 | ECA | 1998 | AI | ID | SIM | Kyrgyz Rep | Irrigation Rehabilitation |
| 38399 | ECA | 1998 | AI | ID | SIL | Macedonia | Irrigation Rehabilitation |
| 3602 | EAP | 1996 | US | ENV | SIL | China | Hubei Urban Environment |
| 43444 | ECA | 1998 | WS | UWSS | SIL | Croatia | Municipal Environmental Infrastructure Project |
| 50911 | ECA | 1999 | VM | ENV | SIL | Georgia | Integrated Coastal Management |
| 10530 | SAR | 1998 | AI | ID | SIM | Nepal | Irrigation Sector Development |
| 10418 | SAR | 1993 | WR | RWSS | SIL | India | Karnataka Rural WS and Env |
| 5435 | MNA | 1994 | WW | UWSS | SIM | Yemen | Taiz Water Supply Pilot |
| 5907 | MNA | 1999 | WU | UWSS | SIL | Morocco | Water Supply V |
| 10408 | SAR | 1993 | TR | ID | SIL | India | Bihar Plateau Development |
| 5731 | MNA | 1997 | WS | UWSS | SIL | Lebanon | Coastal Pollution Control and Water Supply |
| 9961 | SAR | 1993 | AI | ID | SIL | India | Uttar Pradesh Sodic Lands Reclamation |
| 6541 | LAC | 1993 | WY | UWSS | SIL | Brazil | Sao Paulo Water Quality |
| 6206 | LAC | 1996 | WR | RWSS | SIM | Bolivia | Rural Water and Sanitation |
| 43420 | LAC | 1998 | WU | UWSS | SIL | Brazil | Second Water Modernization |
| 3507 | EAP | 1996 | PH | HYDRO | SIL | China | Ertan Hydro II |
| 39983 | LAC | 1998 | WR | RWSS | SIL | Paraguay | Fourth Rural Water Supply and Sanitation |
| 49166 | MNA | 1998 | AY | ID | SIL | Jordan | TA for Agricultural |
| 35076 | AFR | 1998 | PH | HYDRO | SIL | Zambia | Power Rehabilitation Project |
| 6052 | LAC | 1997 | WY | FM | SIL | Argentina | Flood Protection |
| 50646 | SAR | 1999 | AY | ID | SIL | India | Uttar Pradesh Sodic Lands Reclamation II |
| 39281 | SAR | 1996 | PH | HYDRO | SIL | Pakistan | Ghazi Barotha Hydropower |
| 10453 | SAR | 1994 | VI | WSM | SIL | Pakistan | NWFP Community Infrastructure |
| 10482 | SAR | 1996 | AI | ID | SIL | Pakistan | Balochistan Com Irrig Agr |
| 1012 | AFR | 1999 | | UWSS | SIL | Guinea-Bissau | Water and Energy Project |
| 1750 | AFR | 1997 | UU | WRM | SIL | Mali | Urban Development and Decentralization |
| 1921 | AFR | 1998 | WW | ENV | SIL | Mauritius | Environmental Sewerage and Sanitation |
| 5173 | MNA | 1995 | AI | ID | SIL | Morocco | Rural Water Supply and Sanitation |
| 3241 | AFR | 1995 | WU | UWSS | SIL | Zambia | Urban Restructuring and Water Supply |
| 33965 | ECA | 1998 | VP | ENV | SIL | Bulgaria | Environmental Remediation Pilot |
| 8051 | LAC | 1995 | WU | UWSS | SIL | Peru | Lima Water Rehabilitation |

| Overall score | Comprehensive management | | | Institutional development | | | | | Economic and social issues | | |
|---|---|---|---|---|---|---|---|---|---|---|---|
| | | | | Legal and policy | | Management and regulation | | | | | |
| | National/state level | Regional/basin level | Projects | Water resource | Water service | Water resource & environmental management agencies | Water service regulation bodies | Water service organizations | Financing and subsidies | Water service charges | Disadvantaged group |
| 3 | 3 | NA | 3.5 | 3 | 3 | 3.5 | 3 | 3 | 2 | 2.5 | 3 |
| 3 | 3 | NA | 3 | 3.5 | 3 | 3 | 3 | 3 | 2 | 2 | 1.5 |
| 3 | 3.5 | 3.5 | 3 | N/D | 2.5 | N/D | 3 | 3 | 3 | 3 | 1 |
| 3 | 3.5 | 3.5 | 2.5 | 2.5 | 2.5 | 3 | 3 | 3.5 | 3.5 | 3.5 | 3 |
| 3 | 3.5 | 3.5 | 3.5 | 3.5 | NA | 3 | 3 | NA | 2 | 2 | 3 |
| 3 | 4 | 4 | 4 | D | 3 | 4 | 3 | 4 | 2 | 2 | 4 |
| 3 | D | 3 | 3 | D | 3 | N/D | 2.5 | 3 | 3 | 3 | 4 |
| 3 | D | 3 | 4 | 4 | D | 4 | 4 | D | 2 | 2 | 4 |
| 3 | D | D | 3 | N/R | D | N/R | 2 | 3 | 4 | 4 | 3 |
| 3 | D | N/D | 3 | N/R | D | N/R | 3 | 3 | 3 | N/D | 4 |
| 3 | D | N/D | 3 | N/R | 4 | N/R | 3 | 3 | D | D | N/D |
| 3 | D | N/R | 3 | 3 | N/D | 3 | N/D | 3 | 3 | 3 | 4 |
| 3 | N/D | 3 | 3 | 3 | N/R | 2 | N/R | D | 2 | 2 | 3 |
| 3 | N/D | N/D | 2 | N/D | 2 | N/D | 2 | 4 | 4 | 4 | 4 |
| 3 | N/D | N/D | 3 | N/D | 4 | 2.5 | | 4 | 3 | 2.5 | 4 |
| 3 | N/D | N/D | 3 | N/D | N/D | N/D | 3.5 | 3 | 3 | 3 | 1.5 |
| 3 | N/D | N/D | 2 | N/D | N/D | N/D | 3 | 4 | 4 | 3 | 4 |
| 3 | N/R | 3 | N/R | 3 | N/R | 3 | N/R | N/D | N/D | 2.5 | N/D |
| 3 | N/R | 3 | 3 | N/R | 2.5 | N/R | 3 | N/D | 3 | 3 | 3 |
| 3 | N/R | D | 4 | 4 | | | 3 | N/R | 1 | 1 | 3 |
| 3 | N/R | D | 4 | 3 | N/D | 4 | N/D | 3 | 3 | 3 | 4 |
| 3 | N/R | D | 4 | D | D | D | 3 | 3 | 3 | 3 | 4 |
| 3 | N/R | N/D | 2 | N/D | 3 | N/D | 3 | 4 | 3 | 3 | 4 |
| 3 | N/R | N/D | 2.5 | N/D | 3 | D | 2 | 4 | 4 | 2 | 4 |
| 3 | N/R | N/R | 3 | N/R | 2.5 | N/R | N/D | 3 | 3 | 3 | 3 |
| 3 | N/R | N/R | 2.5 | N/R | 3 | N/R | 3 | 3 | 3.5 | 3 | D |
| 3 | N/R | N/R | 3 | N/R | 3 | N/R | 3 | 3 | 4 | 4 | N/D |
| 3 | N/R | N/R | 3 | N/R | D | N/R | 3 | 3 | 3 | 2 | 3 |
| 3 | N/R | N/R | 3 | N/R | 3 | N/R | 3 | 3 | 2.5 | 3 | 3 |
| 3 | NA | NA | 2.5 | NA | NA | 3 | NA | NA | 3.5 | 3.5 | NA |
| 3 | N/R | 2 | 3 | 2 | D | 1 | 3 | 3 | 4 | 4 | 4 |

*(continues on following page)*

| Table D.2 | Water Policy Analysis: Compliance with Water Policy According to the 9-Cell Water Policy Matrix (continued) |
|---|---|

| Project ID | Region | Year | Sector | Subsector | Instrument | Country | Project name |
|---|---|---|---|---|---|---|---|
| 6540 | LAC | 1993 | WY | UWSS | SIL | Brazil | Minas Gerais Water Quality |
| 6541 | LAC | 1993 | WY | WRM | SIL | Brazil | National Water Quality |
| 7926 | LAC | 1995 | WS | UWSS | SIL | Paraguay | Asuncion Sewerage |
| 9093 | ECA | 1995 | WS | UWSS | SIL | Turkey | Antalya Water Supply and Sanitation |
| 8985 | ECA | 1998 | WY | UWSS | SIL | Turkey | CESME- ALACATI Water Supply and Sewerage |
| 1667 | AFR | 1995 | WU | UWSS | SIL | Malawi | National Water Development |
|  | AFR | 1997 | VM | ENV | SIL | Uganda | Lake Victoria Environment |
| 34212 | SAR | 1998 | AG | ID | SIL | Sri Lanka | Mahaweli Restructuring |
| 6010 | LAC | 1997 | AA | WRM | SIL | Argentina | Provincial Agricultural Development |
| 973 | AFR | 1996 | US | UWSS | SIL | Ghana | Urban Environmental Sanitation |
| 2669 | AFR | 1995 | UM | WSM | SIL | Swaziland | Urban Development |
| 924 | AFR | 1994 | WR | RWSS | SIM | Ghana | Community Water Sanitation |
| 8260 | ECA | 1994 | WS | UWSS | SIL | Albania | Durres Water Supply Rehabilitation |
| 121 | AFR | 1994 | WR | RWSS | SIM | Benin | Rural Water Supply and Sanitation |
| 45303 | ECA | 1997 | WU | UWSS | SIL | Kazakhstan | Pilot Water Supply Project |
| 9964 | SAR | 1994 | AI | ID | SIL | India | Haryana Water Resources Consolidation |
| 39455 | LAC | 1996 | AI | FM | SIM | St. Lucia | Watershed and Environment Management |
| 3586 | EAP | 1994 | VM | ENV | SIL | China | Shanghai Environment |
| 3598 | EAP | 1995 | VP | ENV | SIL | China | Liaoning Environment |
| 8417 | ECA | 1995 | UM | UWSS | SIL | Georgia | Municipal Infrastructure Rehabilitation |
| 50910 | ECA | 1998 | UU | UWSS | SIM | Georgia | Municipal Development and Decentralization |
| 10476 | SAR | 1995 | AI | ID | SIL | India | Tamil Nadu WRCP |
| 10529 | SAR | 1996 | AI | ID | SIL | India | Orissa Water Resources Consolidation |
| 34584 | ECA | 1996 | UM | UWSS | SIL | Latvia | Municipal Services Development |
| 8553 | ECA | 1995 | VP | ENV | SIL | Lithuania | Klaipeda Environment |
| 4613 | EAP | 1997 | AI | ID | SIL | Philippines | Water Resources Development |
| 9121 | ECA | 1998 | WW | RWSS | SIL | Uzbekistan | Rural Water Supply and Sanitation |
| 8778 | ECA | 1997 | WY | UWSS | SIL | Romania | Bucharest Water Supply Project |
| 8277 | ECA | 1995 | AI | ID | SIL | Armenia | Irrigation Rehabilitation |
| 37006 | LAC | 1995 | WW | UWSS | TAL | Trinidad and Tobago | Water Sector Institutional Strengthening |

| Overall score | Comprehensive management | | | Institutional development | | | | | Economic and social issues | | |
| :---: | :---: | :---: | :---: | :---: | :---: | :---: | :---: | :---: | :---: | :---: | :---: |
| | | | | Legal and policy | | Management and regulation | | | | | |
| | National/state level | Regional/basin level | Projects | Water resource | Water service | Water resource & environmental management agencies | Water service regulation bodies | Water service organizations | Financing and subsidies | Water service charges | Disadvantaged group |
| 3 | N/R | 3 | 3 | 4 | N/R | 3 | N/R | N/R | 2 | 3 | 3 |
| 3 | N/R | 3 | N/R | 3 | N/R | N/R | N/R | N/R | N/R | N/R | N/R |
| 3 | N/R | D | 3 | N/D | 2 | 2 | N/D | 2 | 1 | 2 | 1 |
| 2.9 | 2 | 2 | 3 | 3 | 3 | 3 | 3 | 3 | 3 | 3 | 2 |
| 2.9 | 3 | 3 | 3 | 2.5 | 3 | 3 | 3 | 3.5 | 3.5 | 3 | 2.5 |
| 2.8 | 3 | N/D | 3 | 3 | 3 | 3 | 3 | 2.5 | 3 | 2.5 | 2.5 |
| 2.8 | N/R | 3 | 3 | N/R | 2.5 | N/R | 2.5 | N/R | N/R | N/R | D |
| 2.8 | N/D | 2.5 | 3 | D | N/D | 3 | N/D | 4 | 3 | N/D | 2 |
| 2.8 | N/D | N/D | 2 | N/D | 2.5 | 2 | 3 | 4 | 3 | 4 | 3 |
| 2.7 | N/R | N/D | 2.5 | N/R | 3 | N/R | 3 | N/R | 3 | 2.5 | 3 |
| 2.7 | N/R | N/D | 2.5 | N/R | 3 | N/R | 3 | 3 | 2.5 | 2.5 | D |
| 2.7 | N/R | N/R | 3 | N/R | 3 | N/R | N/D | 2.5 | 3 | 3 | 3 |
| 2.6 | 2 | 2 | 3 | 2 | 2 | 3 | 3 | 2.5 | 2 | 2.5 | 3 |
| 2.6 | N/R | N/R | 3 | N/R | 3 | N/R | D | 2.5 | 3 | 3 | 2.5 |
| 2.5 | 2 | 2 | 3 | 2 | 2 | 2 | 2 | 2 | 2 | 2 | 2 |
| 2.5 | 2 | D | 3 | 2 | N/D | 3 | N/D | 2 | 1 | 1 | N/D |
| 2.5 | 2 | N/R | 3 | 2 | N/R | 3 | | N/R | N/D | N/R | N/R |
| 2.5 | 2.5 | 2.5 | 3 | N/D | 3 | N/D | 3 | 3 | 3 | 2.5 | 1 |
| 2.5 | 3 | 3 | 3.5 | N/D | 3 | N/D | 3.5 | 2.5 | 2.5 | 3 | 2 |
| 2.5 | 3 | 3 | 3 | 2 | 2 | 3 | 3 | 3 | 2.5 | 3 | 2 |
| 2.5 | 3 | 3 | 2.5 | 2.5 | 2.5 | 3 | 3 | 3 | 2.5 | 2 | 2 |
| 2.5 | 3 | 3 | 2 | D | 3 | 2 | 3 | 3 | 1 | 2 | 2 |
| 2.5 | 3 | 3 | 2 | D | N/D | 2 | 2 | 3 | 1 | 2 | 3 |
| 2.5 | 3 | 3 | 2.5 | 2.5 | 3 | 3 | 3 | 3 | 3 | 3 | 2.5 |
| 2.5 | 3 | 3 | 2.5 | 2.5 | NA | 3 | 2.5 | 2 | 3 | 2.5 | 2.5 |
| 2.5 | 3 | 3 | 3 | 2 | 3.5 | 3 | 3 | 3 | 1 | 2 | 2 |
| 2.5 | 3 | 3 | 3 | 2.5 | 2.5 | 2.5 | 2.5 | 2.5 | 2.5 | 2.5 | 2 |
| 2.5 | 3 | N/R | 3 | 2 | 2 | 3 | 3 | 3 | 3 | 3 | 2 |
| 2.5 | 3 | NA | 3 | 2 | 2 | 3.5 | 3.5 | 3.5 | 3.5 | 2 | 1 |
| 2.5 | 4 | N/D | N/R | N/D | 3 | 3 | 3 | 2.5 | 2 | 2.5 | N/D |

*(continues on following page)*

| Table D.2 | Water Policy Analysis: Compliance with Water Policy According to the 9-Cell Water Policy Matrix (continued) | | | | | | |
|---|---|---|---|---|---|---|---|
| Project ID | Region | Year | Sector | Subsector | Instrument | Country | Project name |
| 6436 | LAC | 1995 | UM | WRM | SIL | Brazil | Ceara (WRM compon.) |
| 5680 | MNA | 1995 | VM | UWSS | SIL | Yemen | Southern Governorates Rural Development Project |
| 5342 | MNA | 1997 | WS | UWSS | SIL | Jordan | Amman Water Sanitation Management |
| 5344 | MNA | 1994 | AI | ID | SIL | Morocco | Sewerage and Water Reuse |
| 7020 | LAC | 1995 | AI | ID | SIM | Dominican Republic | Irrigation Land and Watershed |
| 43728 | SAR | 1997 | VI | ENV | SIL | India | Environment Capacity Building TA |
| 8224 | LAC | 1996 | WW | UWSS | SIL | Venezuela | Monogas Water |
| 3493 | EAP | 1995 | TP | NAV | SIL | China | Inland Waterways |
| 48521 | MNA | 1999 | WW | UWSS | SIL | Egypt | Irrigation Improvement Project |
| 35158 | SAR | 1997 | AI | ID | SIL | India | Third Andhra Pradesh Irrigation |
| 49385 | SAR | 1998 | SY | ID | SIL | India | Andhra Pradesh Economic Restructuring |
| 34617 | AFR | 1996 | PH | HYDRO | SIL | Mali | Selingue Power Rehabilitation |
| 4576 | EAP | 1998 | WY | UWSS | SIL | Philippines | Water District Development |
| 3595 | EAP | 1994 | AP | WSM | SIL | China | Second Red Soils II Development |
| 35802 | ECA | 1999 | UU | UWSS | SIL | Lithuania | Municipal Development |
| 1994 | AFR | 1995 | AI | ID | SIL | Niger | Pilot Private Irrigation Promotion |
| 5902 | MNA | 1998 | AA | ID | SIL | Tunisia | Water Supply and Sewerage |
| 2957 | AFR | 1994 | WU | UWSS | SIL | Uganda | Small Town Water |
| 35728 | LAC | 1998 | VM | WRM | SIL | Brazil | Bahia Water Resource Management |
| 54667 | LAC | 1998 | TU | FM | ERL | Peru | El Nino Emergency |
| 1564 | AFR | 1998 | WR | RWSS | SIL | Madagascar | Rural Water Sector Pilot |
| 1738 | AFR | 1997 | AI | ID | SIL | Mali | Pilot Private Irrigation Promotion |
| 961 | AFR | 1994 | AM | ID | SIL | Ghana | Agricultural Sector Investment |
| 7607 | LAC | 1995 | AI | ID | SIL | Mexico | Rainfed Areas Development |
| 7257 | LAC | 1994 | WU | UWSS | SIM | Guyana | Guyana Water Sector TA and Rehab |
| 44942 | ECA | 1997 | WR | UWSS | SIL | Uzbekistan | Pilot Water Supply Engineering |
| 4207 | EAP | 1994 | SA | RWSS | SIL | Laos | Luang Namtha Provincial Development |
| 4974 | MNA | 1994 | WU | UWSS | SIM | Algeria | Water Supply and Sewerage |
| 10522 | SAR | 1995 | AI | ID | SIM | India | Asam Rural Infrastructure |
| 48522 | MNA | 1997 | AA | FM | ERL | Lebanon | Irrigation Rehabilitation and Modernization |

| Overall score | Comprehensive management | | | Institutional development | | | | | Economic and social issues | | |
| --- | --- | --- | --- | --- | --- | --- | --- | --- | --- | --- | --- |
| | | | | Legal and policy | | Management and regulation | | | | | |
| | National/state level | Regional/basin level | Projects | Water resource | Water service | Water resource & environmental management agencies | Water service regulation bodies | Water service organizations | Financing and subsidies | Water service charges | Disadvantaged group |
| 2.5 | D | 3 | 2 | 2 | 2 | 3 | 3 | 2 | 2 | 2 | 3 |
| 2.5 | D | 3 | 3 | N/D | N/R | 1 | N/R | N/R | 3 | N/R | 4 |
| 2.5 | D | D | 3 | N/D | D | N/R | 3 | 4 | 2 | 3 | 1 |
| 2.5 | D | D | 4 | N/R | D | N/R | D | 2 | 4 | 3 | 1 |
| 2.5 | D | N/D | 4 | N/D | N/D | N/D | 2.5 | 3 | 2 | 2.5 | 4 |
| 2.5 | N/D | 3 | N/R | 3 | N/R | 3 | N/R | N/R | 2 | 1 | N/R |
| 2.5 | N/D | 3 | 1 | 2 | 3 | N/D | 4 | 4 | 4 | 3 | 3 |
| 2.5 | N/D | N/D | 2.5 | N/R | N/R | N/R | 3 | N/R | 3 | 3 | N/R |
| 2.5 | N/D | N/D | 3 | N/D | D | 2 | N/D | 3 | 1 | 1 | 2 |
| 2.5 | N/D | N/D | 2 | N/D | N/D | 1 | N/D | 2 | 1 | 1 | 4 |
| 2.5 | N/D | N/D | 3 | N/D | N/R | 1 | N/R | 3 | 1 | 3 | 4 |
| 2.5 | N/D | N/D | N/R | N/R | 3 | N/R | 3 | 2.5 | 2.5 | 3 | N/R |
| 2.5 | N/D | N/D | 3 | N/D | 3 | D | 4 | 2 | 2 | 2 | N/D |
| 2.5 | N/R | N/R | 3 | N/R | 3 | N/R | 3 | 2.5 | 3 | 3.5 | 2 |
| 2.5 | N/R | N/R | 3 | N/R | N/R | 3 | N/R | N/R | N/R | N/R | 2 |
| 2.5 | N/R | N/R | 2.5 | N/R | D | N/R | 2.5 | 2 | 2 | 2 | 2.5 |
| 2.5 | N/R | N/R | 2 | N/R | D | N/D | N/D | 2 | 4 | 3 | 3 |
| 2.5 | N/R | N/R | N/D | N/R | 2.5 | N/R | 2.5 | 2.5 | 2.5 | 2.5 | 2.5 |
| 2.5 | N/D | 3 | 2 | 2 | 2 | 3 | 3 | 2 | 1 | 1 | 3 |
| 2.5 | N/R | N/D | 3 | N/D | N/R | 3 | N/R | N/D | 1 | 1 | 4 |
| 2.4 | D | N/D | 2 | N/R | 2.5 | N/R | 2.5 | 2.5 | 2.5 | 2 | 2 |
| 2.3 | N/R | N/D | D | N/R | 3 | N/R | 2.5 | 3 | 2 | 2.5 | 2 |
| 2.3 | N/R | N/R | 2.5 | N/R | 2.5 | N/R | N/D | 2.5 | 3 | 3 | 2.5 |
| 2.3 | N/D | N/D | 2 | N/D | N/D | N/D | N/D | 3 | 2 | N/D | 3 |
| 2 | 1 | 1 | 2 | 1 | N/D | 1 | N/D | 3 | 2 | 3 | 2 |
| 2 | 2 | 2 | 3 | 2 | 2 | 2 | 2 | 2 | 3 | 3 | 2 |
| 2 | 3 | 3 | 3 | N/D | 2 | N/D | 2 | 2 | 2 | 2 | 3 |
| 2 | D | 3 | 3 | N/D | 2 | 3 | 2 | 3 | 2 | 2 | 1 |
| 2 | D | D | 4 | N/D | N/D | N/D | N/D | 2 | 1 | 1 | 4 |
| 2 | D | D | 2 | N/D | D | 2 | N/D | 2 | 2 | 2 | 1 |

*(continues on following page)*

| Table D.2 | | Water Policy Analysis: Compliance with Water Policy According to the 9-Cell Water Policy Matrix (continued) | | | | | |
|---|---|---|---|---|---|---|---|

| Project ID | Region | Year | Sector | Subsector | Instrument | Country | Project name |
|---|---|---|---|---|---|---|---|
| 10467 | SAR | 1995 | US | UWSS | SIL | Sri Lanka | Colombo Env Improvement |
| 1967 | AFR | 1996 | VM | WRM | SIL | Niger | Natural Resources Management |
| 6894 | LAC | 1996 | WW | UWSS | SIM | Colombia | Bogata/Santafe WSS Rehab |
| 1331 | AFR | 1996 | AL | ID | SIL | Kenya | Arid Land Resource Management |
| 1522 | AFR | 1995 | AI | ID | SIL | Madagascar | Second Irrigation Rehabilitation |
| 9482 | SAR | 1997 | WU | UWSS | SIL | Bangladesh | Fourth Dhaka Water Supply |
| 55974 | LAC | 1998 | TU | FM | ERL | Bolivia | El Nino Emergency |
| 3985 | EAP | 1994 | VM | WSM | SIL | Indonesia | National Watershed Conservation |
| 5521 | MNA | 1998 | AI | WRM | SIL | Yemen | Second Public Works |
| 3937 | EAP | 1994 | AI | ID | SIL | Indonesia | Integrated Swamps Development |
| 5321 | MNA | 1995 | AI | WRM | SIL | Yemen | Emergency Flood Rehabilitation |
| 50418 | MNA | 1998 | AY | ID | SIL | Tunisia | Agricultural Sector Investment Loan |
| 5721 | MNA | 1994 | AI | ID | SIM | Egypt | East Delta Agr Serv |
| 5503 | MNA | 1996 | | UWSS | SIL | Tunisia | Second Agricultural Sector Investment Loan |
| 43367 | MNA | 1997 | WU | UWSS | SIL | Yemen | Sana'a Water Supply Sanitation |
| 6541 | LAC | 1993 | WY | UWSS | SIL | Brazil | Parana Water Quality & Pollution Control |
| 10461 | SAR | 1995 | WU | UWSS | SIL | India | Madras Water Supply II |

| Overall score | Comprehensive management | | | Institutional development | | | | | Economic and social issues | | |
| | | | | Legal and policy | | Management and regulation | | | | | |
| | National/state level | Regional/basin level | Projects | Water resource | Water service | Water resource & environmental management agencies | Water service regulation bodies | Water service organizations | Financing and subsidies | Water service charges | Disadvantaged group |
|---|---|---|---|---|---|---|---|---|---|---|---|
| 2 | D | D | 2.5 | N/D | N/D | N/D | 2 | 2.5 | 3 | 2.5 | 1 |
| 2 | D | N/D | 2 | N/R | 3 | N/R | 3 | N/R | 2.5 | 2.5 | 3 |
| 2 | N/R | D | 2 | D | D | D | D | 4 | 4 | 4 | 2 |
| 2 | N/R | N/D | 2.5 | N/R | N/D | N/R | N/D | N/R | N/D | N/R | 3 |
| 2 | N/R | N/D | 2 | N/R | N/D | N/R | 2 | 2 | 1.5 | 2 | 1 |
| 2 | N/R | N/R | 3 | N/R | D | N/R | 2 | 2 | 2 | 2 | 2 |
| 2 | N/R | N/R | D | N/D | N/D | N/R | N/R | N/D | D | N/R | 3 |
| 2 | N/R | N/R | 3 | 1 | 2 | 1 | 2 | N/R | 2 | N/R | 2 |
| 2 | N/R | N/R | 2 | N/R | N/D | N/R | N/D | 2 | 2 | 1 | 4 |
| 1.5 | 2 | 2 | 3 | 2 | 3 | 2 | 3 | 1.5 | 3 | 2 | 1 |
| 1.5 | 3 | D | 2 | N/R | N/R | N/D | N/R | N/R | 1 | 1 | 1 |
| 1.5 | D | N/D | 2 | N/D | N/D | N/D | N/D | 2 | 1 | 2 | 1 |
| 1.5 | N/D | N/D | 1 | N/D | N/R | N/D | N/D | 2 | 1 | 1 | 3 |
| 1.5 | N/D | N/D | 2 | N/D | N/D | 2 | N/D | 3 | 1 | 1 | 1 |
| 1.5 | N/D | N/D | 1 | 3 | N/D | N/D | D | 3 | 1 | 1 | 1 |
| 1.5 | N/R | 2 | 1 | 3 | 3 | 3 | 3 | D | 3 | 2 | 1 |
| 1 | D | D | 1 | N/D | N/D | N/D | N/D | D | 3 | 3 | 2 |

## ANNEX E:   SOCIAL DEVELOPMENT DIMENSIONS OF BANK-FINANCED
WATER SECTOR PROJECTS

## Objectives

The Social Assessment Team (SAT) within the Social Development Policy Cluster collaborated with Operations Evaluation Department (OED) to analyze the extent to which Bank-financed water sector projects focus on poverty and social development issues. Given the explicit attention paid to social development issues in the 1993 World Bank Water Resources Management (WRM) Policy, the review focuses on a comparison of samples from pre- and post-1993 water sector projects. The comparison of the pre- and post-policy projects aims to establish the extent to which progress has been made with respect to these issues and the areas that require further improvements. In so doing, urban and rural water supply and sanitation, irrigation, and other water resources management project documents were reviewed. In addition, water sector projects that were subjected to a quality review by the Quality Assurance Group (QAG) were also identified and analyzed for their social development aspects.

## Approach

The analyses relied solely on Project Appraisal Documents (PADs) and Staff Appraisal Reports (SARs) for analysis of the project. To this end, a comprehensive social development database (SDD) was created. The database consists of sections on the poverty focus of the project, key social issues identified in the project document, stakeholders involved in the design and implementation stages of the project, participation of the poor in project design and implementation, social studies completed for the project design, applicability of resettlement issues to the project, and the availability of monitoring systems, with an emphasis on social impact monitoring.

## Methodology

To estimate the changes brought about by the Bank's 1993 water *Strategy*, a stratified random sample was drawn from the whole cohort of Bank water projects. Stratification involved selecting samples until each subsector had the same relative proportion of projects in the Bank portfolio. No attempt was made to stratify to ensure matching regional representation. Two sets of sample were drawn, one representing projects approved in the pre-policy period, 1988–93, and one for the post-policy period, 1994–99. Each project selected was then extensively analyzed by a team of researchers according to the variable listed in table 2 and database. It is important to note that quality assessment of poverty/social analyses included in SARs/PADs was not a part of the stock-taking exercise. No qualitative indicators are thus in the database. Also, a large number of poverty-focused projects do not provide sufficiently informing analyses of poverty, its impact, or of social issues. Nor is there an adequate treatment of institutional arrangements to bring about targeted changes. A great deal of what would otherwise be considered as "basic minimum information" is not consistently provided. For instance, the numbers of direct/indirect beneficiaries and directly/indirectly affected populations are missing from many documents.

## Poverty and Social Development Focus

Several indicators were used to characterize the poverty focus of water sector projects. The first was based on the formal determination made by the project team, often noted on the first page of a project document. Generally, the formal poverty applicability of a project is defined by whether the project targets specific groups within its components. If no specific targeting is done, then the project is categorized as "Poverty: Not Applicable." According to this indicator, 42 percent of the water sector projects completed after 1993 targeted poverty. This indicator was not used in a majority of the pre-1993 projects; the Bank did not have a policy to address poverty applicability in project summaries.

To cope with the problem of defining poverty focus in a consistent manner in water sector projects, the SA team developed a less stringent definition of poverty focus. According to this definition, if a project involved an analysis of poverty issues in project regions, made provisions for rehabilitating poverty in project regions, or analyzed the poverty impacts in project areas, it was considered poverty focused. The quality of the poverty focus and targeting of poor people were not judged; rather, the project was deemed poverty focused if it had one or more of the elements of focusing on poverty levels of people in project areas. Throughout the report, comparisons between poverty-focused and non-poverty projects are based on these less stringent criteria.

## Main Findings

Water projects have a significant, but not universal, focus on poverty. In comparing the pre- and post-policy periods, an increased focus on social development and poverty concerns in project appraisals is evident. Participation of the poor, gender issues, and evaluation of social capital constitute a greater focus of social development concerns mentioned in project documents, and this was increasingly evident in the projects completed after 1993. As such, the main findings of the study can be summarized as follows:

**There is a growing emphasis in integrating poverty and social development issues in Bank-financed water sector projects, particularly after the adoption of the Bank's 1993 *Water Resources Management* policy paper.**

- The focus on poverty increased from 57 percent prior to 1993 to 63 percent after 1993. The poverty focus was enhanced through an increase in conducting poverty analysis (36 percent pre- to 53 percent post-1993), better

consideration of poverty impacts (52 percent pre- to 63 percent post-1993), and establishing institutional mechanisms to target the poor (23 percent pre- to 53 percent post-1993) and to monitor poverty impacts (16 percent pre- to 46 percent post-1993).

- Involving gender dimensions has become an integral part of the water sector, particularly in the water and sanitation subsector. Gender and other social groups are less of a concern in other subsectors. As accepted in the Dublin Statement and reiterated in The Hague Water Forum 2000, women play a central role in all aspects of water. Among the projects reviewed, gender is addressed in 30 percent of the pre-1993 projects, but only 54 percent of the post-1993 projects. The number of projects that involved an NGO specializing in gender at the appraisal doubled from 8 percent to 19 percent from one period to the other.
- As the Bank has focused more on community-driven approaches, projects that involve community participation have nearly doubled over the past 12 years. Forty-four percent of the projects completed prior to, and 67 percent of the projects completed after, 1993 consider community participation issues and can be considered CDD projects.
- The focus on distribution issues and equity, while remaining at a modest level, quadrupled from one period to the other.

**There are systematic project characteristics that account for differences in poverty/ social development focus.**

- IDA projects are more likely to target poverty, have a higher share of Bank financing, and a higher level of partnerships compared to IBRD projects. IDA projects also have greater poverty focus than IBRD-financed projects, both prior to and after 1993.
- Projects with smaller financing (in dollar terms) have a sharper poverty focus; both pre- and post-policy projects show that where the Bank invests large sums, it tends to ignore poverty/social development issues.
- It appears that the Bank has achieved greater cost-effectiveness in its water sector invest-

ments. Per beneficiary costs of projects decreased for both poverty-focused and non-poverty projects after 1993. However, per beneficiary costs of poverty-focused projects are still higher than are others.

- Partnerships with other donors have come to enhance the Bank's poverty/social development focus. Especially during the post-policy period, 74 percent of the projects prepared with other donors are poverty-focused. There is also a clear increase in the participation of NGOs and civil society organizations in project implementation in poverty-focused projects; non-poverty projects have low levels of civil society participation in implementation. An analysis of private sector institutions was included in only 30 percent of pre- and 37 percent of post-1993 projects.

- The sample size is insufficient to make regional comparisons. There are indications that the Southeast Asia Region projects have a more consistent emphasis on poverty and social development dimensions. However, a separate analysis of Middle East/North Africa (MNA) Region projects, undertaken at the request of the Global Water Unit (GWU) as part of a larger quality review process, looked into social development aspects of MNA water sector projects. This analysis shows that a somewhat larger than average number of these projects also had a focus on poverty and social development issues. Details of this analysis can also be found in the report.

- Of the projects completed after 1993, resettlement was considered in 68 percent of the projects, and 41 percent of all projects had a resettlement action plan (RAP) available in their PAD/SAR. This contrasts sharply with the pre-1993 data that reflected consideration of resettlement in only 34 percent of the projects and RAPs in only 19 percent.

- Cultural property issues are considered in fewer than 10 percent of all projects; most of these involve resettlement.

- Indigenous peoples are considered in close to 20 percent of the projects after 1993; most of these involve resettlement. While this percentage is low, it nearly doubled in comparison with the pre-1993 period.

**Even though 38 percent of the projects used the "four-pillar approach" in their social assessments, this number is nearly doubled in the community-driven water sector projects.**

- *Social analysis:* There was a remarkable increase in use of participatory methods to address social development concerns. For instance, use of broad-based stakeholder consultations more than doubled from one period to the other, together with qualitative beneficiary assessments and direct consultations with the poor.

- *Participation:* There was an increase in community participation and consultations with the poor in both project appraisal and project implementation during the post-1993 period (for example, community participation in appraisal increased from 30 percent to 61 percent).[1] Household and nonhousehold user as well as community participation in project financing also increased in the post-1993 period (26 percent of projects pre-1993, and 38 percent post-1993); average contributions were $4.44 million in pre-1993 and $5.3 million after 1993.

- *Institutional analysis:* Both prior to and after 1993, most projects involved analyses of technical institutions, municipal water systems, and local government institutions. However, social and informal private institution analyses are much less common.

- *Social Impact Monitoring (SIM)* is in place in 49 percent of the post-1993 projects and the vast majority of these had a focus on social development issues. This reflects a significant improvement in addressing these issues when compared with the pre-1993 data, in which only 30 percent of projects show SIM in place and of these, only a few have a focus on social development issues.

## Lessons Learned and Areas for Further Improvement: A Summary

**Policy matters.** There have been major improvements in the pro-poor emphasis of Bank-financed water projects since the 1993 WRM policy paper across a wide variety of dimensions, such as poverty analysis, direct participation of the poor in projects, attention to gender, assisting client institutions to target poverty groups, and the like. While the data indicate an overwhelming change in the social dimensions of water resource management projects since 1993, they also indicate areas where enhanced attention to a more consistent mainstreaming of poverty and social sustainability would improve the Bank's contribution to the holistic WRM policy that is the consensus of the international community.

**Partnership with other development agencies enhances the Bank's focus on poverty and social development; further emphases on partnership matters**: Partnership in designing and cofinancing projects with other donors helps the Bank to sharpen its social development/poverty focus in water resource projects. This finding suggests that the Bank would benefit from improved partnership with other donors and civil society organizations in future WRM projects.

**Pro-poor/pro-social focus and its quality can be enhanced.**
- There is substantial room for improvement of priority-setting in targeting the poor and vulnerable populations within water sector projects. Many projects provide a relatively superficial analyses of poverty, its social dimensions, and specific measures for its alleviation through water sector interventions.
- Since IBRD-financed projects do not have as much of a focus on poverty and social issues as IDA projects, there is scope for improvement of water resource project objectives in countries with higher income levels.
- The per beneficiary cost of poverty-focused projects continues to be higher than non-poverty projects, suggesting the Bank can sharpen its skills to deliver assistance to the poor more efficiently.
- Urban water supply and sanitation projects can sharpen their poverty focus to catch up with the greater progress made in this area by water projects in agriculture and water resource management generally.
- Larger projects (measured in dollar terms) can improve their poverty and social devel-

opment focus. The quality of poverty and social analyses is of particular concern for the projects that lend large sums for water sector investments.
- There is substantial room for improvement in the quality of poverty analyses incorporated in water sector projects; a more detailed evaluation that would assess both documentation and results on the ground would be needed to better specify areas for quality improvement.
- Analysis of gender issues, often formulated within the framework of poverty and/or exclusionary policies for service delivery, has been integrated into the design of many projects; but attention to gender is seldom translated into action or monitored.
- The focus of social analysis of water projects is relatively narrow. Most projects incorporate a focus on one or another social issue, and a holistic social assessment is missing from the majority of projects. Some key issues, such as water rights, are largely neglected, but require future focus, especially as they relate to poverty.
- The low level of poverty/ social monitoring and evaluation (M&E), especially impact monitoring, incorporated in water sector projects is a serious concern and mirrors the findings for Bank projects in other sectors. Measuring impact, monitoring implementation, and promoting a culture of continuous learning can only be done through improved M&E, both in client institutions and in the Bank itself. The recommendations of the Bankwide task force on M&E should be implemented without delay in water resource management units.

**Projects increasingly show that participation is more than a tool for cost recovery, it is also a mechanism for promoting stakeholder involvement and community-driven (CDD) initiatives. There is particular need to formulate CDD approaches to WRM.**
The greater the share that communities and households contribute to project financing, the greater responsibility they take with respect to operations and maintenance There have been increases in the frequency of consultations

directly with the poor and/or with civil society organizations for project design, and in NGO involvement in implementation. However, the data also suggest that decentralized and/or sub-regional projects are not consistently more poverty focused. Since communities are not monolithic entities and they respond to micro-level socioeconomic characteristics, a closer examination of poverty focus in decentralized projects might be needed. Full community ownership is yet to be evidenced in the Bank-financed projects[2] and is an area for future focus, with particular attention to the institutional aspects.

**The water sector compares favorably in its social development focus with other sectors. Given this strong start, social analyses of water sector projects can be broadened.**
Pro-poor projects are also pro-social; they concern themselves more with social dimensions of development. Inclusion of a focus on one element of social sustainability generates focus on other aspects and opens doors for other social considerations. Water sector projects are highly variable in their treatment of social issues: not all incorporate holistic consideration of social, environmental, and economic objectives, not all use social analysis or aim to maximize sustained stakeholder participation. Experience indicates that the inadequate social and political analysis of watersheds and river basins may result in the dominance of power groups in key decisions. Landless farmers, pastoralists, smallholders, and minority communities have little voice in planning and tend to get further marginalized in implementation.

In Bank project appraisal, poverty, participation, and gender are more frequently addressed than other social issues. Of the safeguard policies, resettlement receives a more routine consideration than indigenous populations and cultural heritage. Issues relating to equity, ethnic and tribal concerns, and those concerning water rights and their poverty/social impacts do not receive the attention they deserve. The limited treatment of social development issues within the water sector is apparent in Bank-produced publications, as well as in water sec-

tor learning efforts of the World Bank Institute (WBI). The learning programs in the Social Development family also place little emphasis on the water sector, and the SD literature insufficiently exemplifies how a broad range of social issues play key roles in the design and implementation of water sector projects. Therefore, the water-sector-related learning exercises and client capacity building efforts of WBI might consider giving more attention to poverty and social development. The Social Development family may likewise sharpen its skills to further improve the quality of social assessments of water sector projects.

**There is a need to incorporate a more systematic, quantified, and well-documented approach to social assessment in water sector projects.**
Learning about peoples' actual behavior and opinions in a continuous fashion is essential to ensuring that project objectives are relevant to people's needs, and that project implementation takes account of local realities. The water sector projects that are included in this analysis have not only a narrow treatment of the behavioral and social structural elements, but provide little evidence that an in-depth knowledge has been acquired. Indeed, only a small percentage of the analyzed projects have all elements of the World Bank's four-pillar approach to social assessment in place, including; (i) social analysis; (ii) participation; (iii) institutional analysis; and (iv) impact monitoring. Rather, projects documents suggest that social assessment is deferred to the implementation stage without specific budget allocation. The findings of the Quality Assurance Group also show that a holistic integration of social development concerns lags behind the performance of other quality concerns (economic, financial, and technical), despite the indication that the water sector performs better than others in its treatment of poverty and social issues.

The analyses show that CDD projects are more systematic in being built on organized social assessment than projects with a more centralized design. Indeed, CDD projects have a visibly broader treatment of social development issues and tend to monitor progress with respect to these more often than other projects.

Needless to say, as the focus on WRM, integrated river basin, and watershed management increases, the need for a better understanding of human activities that affect these will also. Co-existing social structures and the historical patterns of their interrelationships are particularly needed as watershed boundaries and political/administrative boundaries diverge, the number and diversity of stakeholders become more complex, and as the design of incentives with respect to soil erosion, waterlogging, salinization, flood runoff, and so forth, become critical.

While technical information needs become more relevant in establishing aquatic resources, providing this information to the people whose activities affect these resources becomes more challenging. Yet human societies are dynamic and their information and communications structures require careful assessment, which is consistently lacking in the water sector projects.

**There is room for a better understanding of behaviors, attitudes, informal rules, and local modifications of formal laws.**

A large number of social analyses are based primarily on secondary data and qualitative observations. A deeper understanding of behavioral and attitudinal patterns as displayed by different socioeconomic and water user groups could substantially improve the design and implementation of WRM projects. How do large-scale investments impact landlords, smallholders, and the landless? How do the marginal groups cope with forces that may force their displacement? Who are the full range of stakeholders, formal and informal suppliers and users of water? What could be the modality of community participation in large-scale river basin management? Who are the key stakeholders in groundwater management? The relevant inquiries can benefit from greater analytical focus on the institutions as defined as the "rules of the game." These institutions also influence information/communication structures, as do values, attitudes, and culture. To the extent that information is a basic requirement for informed stakeholders, this has to be provided in a timely and effective way.

These are among the many concerns that are inadequately addressed by many water sector projects.

**There is room to further enhance stakeholder involvement, especially of communities and the informal sector.**

Water sector projects continue to place their institutional focus on the formal state and/or municipal agencies. Other suppliers of water, the providers of goods and services for water quality enhancement, including the informal sector, have received less comprehensive attention. An accurate understanding of all uses of water and establishing an appropriate stakeholder participation process also require knowledge of local social systems. While community involvement is a more common feature of rural water supply and low-cost urban sanitation projects, the modalities of community involvement in river basin and/or groundwater management are less well described except in cases where water for a single urban community is to be imported from one or two rural communities. Even in these cases, there is more concern with the supply of water than with the quality of water resources management. Indeed, there is remarkably little emphasis on the social dimensions of water quality management in WRM projects. This is an area where an accurate understanding of relevant patterns of behavior, values, and social institutions would substantially contribute to the formulation of quality and quantity enhancement strategies that would involve local communities.

**There is room to involve the local, small-scale, and informal private sector.**

Despite consistent and continued emphasis on private sector development, the current deficiencies in the operation of this sector and the requirements for improvement are less well documented. Equally important, insufficient attention is given to the small-scale and informal private sector and the incentives that would be needed to build the capacity of local private initiatives. Indeed, it appears that "the private sector" is largely associated with large-scale private firms and, often, international concerns, and the question of how to build on the efforts of existing informal and small-scale private initiatives is not pursued; nor is a description of their activities provided. This goes hand-in-hand with the lack of a behavioral focus on coping strategies or an attempt to understand how users meet their needs when governmental institutions fail to do so.

**There is need to further debate social safety arrangements and cost recovery issues with respect to poor groups and/or communities.** There is an increasing recognition within the international community that full cost recovery in water sector projects may not always be feasible. In infrastructure and irrigation projects, it is reasonable to assume that at least part of the target population will not be willing or will not have the capacity to pay for water. For instance, there are communities with depleted underground resources to whom providing low-cost water is not easy. Therefore, it may be necessary to subsidize the water access of some groups, or, in cases where the whole community is poor, the whole community.[3] In so doing within a specific project context, the Bank ought to strengthen its partnership with communities, other donors, and civil society organizations, as this partnership has proved to have a positive impact on the poverty and social focus of its projects.

An underlying concern in determining water pricing issues is to anticipate behaviors involving traditional practices. Traditional rights and governance practices must be fully understood prior to implementing water pricing to avoid social disruption. Inasmuch as inefficient water use in water-scarce societies negatively impacts the poor, any proposed policy interventions should be attentive to the disrupting effects of implementing water demand management in situations where these systems are operating effectively and efficiently.

**There is need to give more emphasis to gender concerns.**
As mentioned before, incorporation of a balanced gender approach into water sector project design has been increasing, yet is still low compared with the poverty focus of these proj-

ects. If water sector projects are to face gender issues in project communities and to utilize them effectively for successful implementation, then they need to pay increasing attention to the following issues:

- **It is important to carry out social analysis for better understanding of gender issues.** Since water has both domestic and productive uses, deciphering existing behaviors and mechanisms is integral to examining equity between men and women with respect to access to and use of water. Detailed social analysis, with a focus on interactions among community members and their behavioral patterns and disaggregated by age and gender, therefore, is the most important prerequisite for systematic consideration of gender issues.[4]
- **Women's participation can be increased in all phases of the project cycle through adoption of an appropriate participatory framework.** Integration of the gender dimension in a project calls for equitable participation of both men and women, especially in management and the decisionmaking process. Related to that, both women's and men's involvement in projects may go beyond consultations during the project planning phase to proactive participation in decisionmaking, management, control, and monitoring throughout the project cycle. The participation framework and mechanisms that are put in place need to take into account the possible constraints to women's participation. These include time allocation, feasibility of meeting locations, and avoiding burdens on women who already contribute with unpaid, manual work, yet do not have any say in decisionmaking in the existing system.
- An appropriate method of overcoming the additional burdens women may face in participating in water sector projects is to invest in programs to build on women's capacity in technical, managerial, social, and organizational skills. Such capacity-building activities could aim to enhance women's knowledge on an array of issues, ranging from leadership skills to financial management. Increased capacity, in turn, is likely to equip the women

with the necessary skills to have their voices heard in the system.

- **It is important to pay special attention to women's right to water and ensure that existing formal and informal institutional arrangements do not disadvantage women.** Mainly because of patriarchal relations, most women do not have the right to land, and water rights are tied to land rights. This leaves women in a particularly disadvantaged and vulnerable position. They are not allowed to participate in decisionmaking for water allocation, they cannot voice their needs and concerns, and they have to find coping mechanisms to access water. If the Bank wants to discourage policies and institutional formats that would disadvantage women in water sector projects, it need to be careful in assessing the existing formal and informal institutional arrangements. Water sector project design and implementation, therefore, need to encourage policies and institutional structures that would allow women a more equitable say in allocation and use of water. There are a number of ways of achieving such impact—

working with local NGOs in identifying women's problems and involving communities in decisionmaking processes upfront are two effective solutions.

**The water sector offers good opportunities to further strengthen the pro-poor/pro-social emphasis. To do so would require social impact monitoring of trends. This can be done by using the database established for purposes of the analysis presented here. However, an institutional host for the database needs to be identified.**

The improvement in the policy environment for water resource management agreed upon by the international community has led to a trend for World Bank projects to be more socially sustainable and more "pro-poor." This trend could become a permanent way of doing business for all WRM projects, with an emphasis on learning systematically from results and realities on the ground, establishing clear definitions of and commitment to quality, and dealing through social assessment and stakeholder participation with local specificity that, in the end, is the key to achieving an impact on peoples' lives.

| Table E.1 | Variables in Data File |
|---|---|
| **Variable (field) name** | **Description** |
| Report No | Report number written on the face of the document. |
| Project ID | Unique project identification number; can be used to merge the SDD with other Bank databases. |
| Double-check | Indicates whether project entries are double-checked by B. Ozbilgin for accuracy of recorded information. |
| QAG (Quality Assurance Group) | Overall QAG rating for project. Most of those projects do not have QAG ratings, and QAG does not give out information on individual projects. However, for compatibility with the analytical SPSS database, the variable has been retained in the database. |
| OED (Operations Evaluation Department) | Project OED rating. This variable is obtained from the OED database, if it exists. |
| Country | Project country. |
| Region | Bank Region for the project country. |
| Name | Full name of the project. |
| Sector | Main project sector. |
| Type | Project focus (infrastructure provision, or people focused). |
| Nationwide | If the project covers the whole country, this variable is checked. |

## Table E.1    Variables in Data File (continued)

| Variable (field) name | Description |
|---|---|
| Regional | If the project covers a particular region/province or a number of regions in the country, this variable is checked. |
| Number of provinces | For a regional project, indicates the number of provinces and/or cities involved. |
| Total number of beneficiaries | Total number of expected direct and/or indirect beneficiaries from the project. This number is obtained directly from the PAD/SAR; it is not independently confirmed and not available for all the projects. |
| Population | Country population. If the project document gives a figure, it has been noted here. Otherwise, figures are obtained from WB indicators for the country. |
| Project area population | Population of the project area. This value was taken from the project document; it was not available for all the projects. |
| Partnership with UN agencies | Indicates if there is a partnership within the project with various UN agencies. |
| Partnership with regional development banks | Partnership with regional development banks, which include mainly ADB, IDB, and EBRD. |
| Partnership with JOECF | Partnership with bilateral aid agencies. While the code suggests the JOECF, the scope of the variable includes other bilateral agencies. |
| Partnership with IFC | Indicates partnership with IFC in the project. |
| Partnership with USAID | Indicates partnership with USAID. |
| Partnership with others | Indicates partnership with other donors. |
| Poverty targeted | Poverty applicability as defined by the project. Each project document, on its description page, has information on whether any poverty category is applicable to the project or not. Usually, only projects incorporating strict, targeted interventions have considered themselves poverty targeting. This variable reflects that information. |
| Poverty focused | Poverty focus in the project. Even though a project may not technically be termed poverty targeting, a number of projects involved poverty issues and analysis of poverty for project regions, and made some provisions and analyzed impact of the project on poverty. These projects, within the scope of this variable, have been rated as "focusing on poverty." |
| Poverty specialist | Indicates if a poverty specialist is involved in project design. This variable is checked "yes" if there is an economist involved in project design, although it is not always possible to figure out the responsibilities of the individuals involved if the information is not available in the project document. |
| Poverty analysis | Indicates if an analysis of poverty is undertaken in the project document. It does not necessitate a separate, full analysis of poverty, and the variable does not make any assertions of quality. |
| Institutional mechanisms to target the poor | Indicates if there are institutional mechanisms established to target the poor (with the exception of compliance issues) in the project design. |
| Mechanisms to monitor poverty | Indicates if there are mechanisms established to monitor poverty impacts (with the exception of compliance issues) during the project implementation. |
| Budget allocated to monitor poverty | Indicates if there are explicit funds allocated to monitor poverty within the project documentation. |
| Poverty impact | Indicates if the project's impact on poverty levels is considered in design. |
| Poverty impact calculated | Indicates if the project's expected impact on poverty is quantified and articulated. |
| Indirect poverty impact | Indicates if the indirect impact of the project on poverty levels is considered. |
| International social scientist | Indicates if there is an international social scientist (Bank staff) involved in project preparation. It is not always possible to figure out the responsibilities of the individuals involved if that information is not available in the project document. *(continues on following page)* |

| Table E.1 | Variables in Data File (continued) |
|---|---|
| **Variable (field) name** | **Description** |
| Local social scientist | Indicates if local social scientists have been involved in design. This is also difficult to assess. |
| International social scientist peer review | Indicates if there have been international social scientists in the peer review of projects. This variable has the same limitations as those listed above. |
| CAS consistency | Indicates if the project is linked and consistent with the poverty reduction objective in the CAS. A project may be consistent with CAS, but unless it has a direct linkage to poverty reduction objective in the CAS, this question is coded "no." |
| Nationwide sectoral institutional analysis | Indicates whether nationwide sectoral institutions are analyzed during the appraisal stage. |
| Other formal institutions | Indicates whether other formal sector institutions analysis is included in appraisal. |
| Local sector institutions | Indicates whether local sector institutions analysis is included in design. |
| Municipalities analysis | Indicates an analysis of municipalities and/or local governments. |
| University analysis | Indicates an analysis universities and local intelligentsia. |
| Local formal institutions | Indicates analysis of other formal local institutions. |
| Private sector institutions | Indicates institutional analysis of private sector capacity. |
| State-owned enterprise | Indicates institutional analysis of state-owned enterprise. |
| Local informal institutions | Indicates whether local informal institutions and civil society analysis is included in the project.. |
| Social conditionality | Indicates whether or not a social conditionality exists in the legal agreement. |
| Resettlement-specific social conditionality | Indicates if there is a social conditionality in the legal agreement, it is compliance (resettlement, indigenous people, cultural property) specific. |
| Broader conditionality | Indicates if there is a broader social condition in the legal agreement, than mere compliance issues. |
| Environmental assessment | Indicates that the project has an environmental assessment. |
| Social assessment according to 4 pillars | Indicates that the project has an SA as defined by the 4-pillar approach. It may not explicitly state it, but if the project has all 4 pillars of the SA (social development issues analysis, institutional analysis, participation framework, and impact monitoring) then it is regarded as following the 4-pillar approach. |
| Affordability | Indicates whether affordability and/or willingness to pay has been calculated for appraisal. |
| Monitoring of social development issues | Indicates whether there is an explicit monitoring system for social development concerns. |
| Budget allocated for social impact monitoring | Indicates that explicit funds are allocated in budgeting documents for social impact monitoring. If the budget does not allocate a line item specially for social impact monitoring, the answer is coded as "no." |
| Funds for baseline survey | Indicates that explicit funds are allocated for a baseline survey/study. This is not necessarily socially oriented. |
| Funds available for baseline update | Indicates that explicit funds are allocated for an update of the baseline monitoring and evaluation. |
| Resettlement | Indicates that the project considers the relevancy of the resettlement issues and mentions them in the documentation. |
| Resettlement action plan available | Indicates that there is a resettlement action plan available in the project document. |
| Resettlement action taken | If resettlement issues are considered but a resettlement action plan (RAP) is not available, what is the action taken? |
| Resettlement cost | Is the resettlement cost clearly indicated? |
| Resettlement cost ($) | If the resettlement and/or land acquisition cost is indicated in the RAP, what is it in US$ (foreign currency converted at the rate indicated in the PAD). |
| Indigenous people | Indicates that the project considers the relevancy of indigenous people issues. |

| Table E.1 | Variables in Data File (continued) |
|---|---|
| **Variable (field) name** | **Description** |
| Indigenous people plan | Indicates that there is an indigenous people action plan available. |
| Cultural property | Indicates that the project considers the relevancy of cultural property issues. |
| Cultural property plan | Indicates that there is a cultural property action plan available. |
| Other interesting | Other interesting issues about the project. |
| Beneficiaries | Lists the names/types of beneficiaries identified within the project documentation. |
| Stakeholders in project design | Lists the stakeholders involved/consulted during the design of the project. |
| Stakeholders | Lists the stakeholders expected to be involved in the implementation of the project, as indicated by the PAD/SAR. |
| Stakeholder involvement in budget | Lists the stakeholders who are expected to be involved in the project if their involvement is explicitly budgeted in the project. |
| Community driven | The project is considered as a community driven project if it has a dimension that involves community groups, civil society, NGOs, or user associations. |
| Ethnicity | Indicates that the project takes into account ethnicity factors in its design. |
| Urban-rural equity | Indicates that the project takes into account urban/rural equity issues. If adjustments are made, these issues are assumed to be taken into account. |
| Sub-regional equity | Indicates that the project takes into account sub-regional equity issues (i.e., equity between different regions in the project area). |
| Land ownership equity | Indicates that the project takes into account differences between types of landowners (e.g., landless farmers vs. big landowners, medium-size holders; etc.). |
| Gender | Indicates that gender issues are considered in the project design. |
| Gender NGOs | Indicates that NGOs/civil society organizations specialize in gender issues are involved in preparation and/or implementation. |
| Participation | Indicates that the project involves participation from the low income and poor population. |
| Equity between rich and poor | Indicates that the project takes into account equity issues between the rich and the poor. |
| Direct consultations | Indicates that the project involves direct consultations with the poor. |
| Participation plan | Indicates that the project mentions participation for the implementation phase. It does not suggest existence of a structured detailed participation action plan, if the project cites participation for implementation, this variable is coded "yes." |
| Adverse impacts | Indicates that the project design has/reflects discussions with adversely affected populations. |
| EA consultations | Indicates that environmental assessment consultations have been done. |
| Benefits of participation considered | Indicates that benefits of decentralization/community participation are specifically considered. |
| NGO involvement | Indicates that civil society organizations/NGOs are involved in project implementation. |
| Consultations during implementation | Indicates that there will be consultations with the poor during project implementation. |
| Consultations with extracted | Indicates that people from whose area water will be extracted are consulted. |
| Compensation for water extraction | Indicates that these people will be compensated. |
| Land acquisition | Indicates that land acquisition is involved in the project. |
| Affected populations | Number of affected population (if available). |
| Relocated populations | Number of population to be relocated (if available). |
| Enterprise acquired effected | Indicates if there are enterprises affected by acquisition/relocation. |
| Empirical research | Indicates that there is systematic, quantifiable, project-specific empirical research for project design. |

*(continues on following page)*

| Table E.1 | Variables in Data File (continued) |
|---|---|
| **Variable (field) name** | **Description** |
| Rapid rural appraisal | Indicates that there is a rapid rural appraisal or other qualitative research. |
| Stakeholder consultation | Indicates that there is broad stakeholder consultation (meetings, seminars, conferences, etc.). |
| Secondary data | Indicates that secondary social development oriented data been used. |
| International experience | Indicates that there specific use of international experience, e.g., a similar project done in another country. |
| Resettlement surveys | Indicates that there is resettlement survey(s). |
| Indigenous population | Indicates that there are indigenous population studies. |
| Beneficiary assessment | Indicates that there is there a beneficiary assessment. |
| Board | Approximate date that the project went to the board (based on PAD/SAR). |
| Total cost | Total project cost in US$ million. |
| IDA | IDA financing for the project (US$ million). |
| IBRD | IBRD financing for the project (US$ million). |
| Other | Other (unspecified) World Bank financing (US$ million). |
| Regional fund | Regional development fund financing (US$ million). |
| Environmental fund | Environmental fund financing (US$ million). |
| Other | Other financing (US$ million). |
| Central government | Central government financing US($ million). |
| Households | Households and individuals financing (US$ million). |
| Non-household | Non-household users financing (US$ million). |
| Communities | Communities financing (US$ million). |
| Local government | Financing from local governments (US$ million). |
| WSS financing | Water and sewerage company financing (US$ million). |
| Component | Project components. |
| Cost | Component cost (US$ million). |
| Component poverty focused | Indicates that the component has a specific poverty focus. |
| Component other social | Indicates that the component accounts for other social issues (excluding safeguards). |

*Note:* Available answers to questions: yes/no/not applicable/unspecified. Variables involving population, cost, etc. are indicated in numbers and $ terms. All other variables are text-based, unless otherwise indicated. Detailed variable types and descriptions are also available in the MS Access file.

ANNEX F: RESETTLEMENT IN BANK WATER PROJECTS—RESULTS
FROM A RANDOM SAMPLE OF 108 WATER PROJECTS

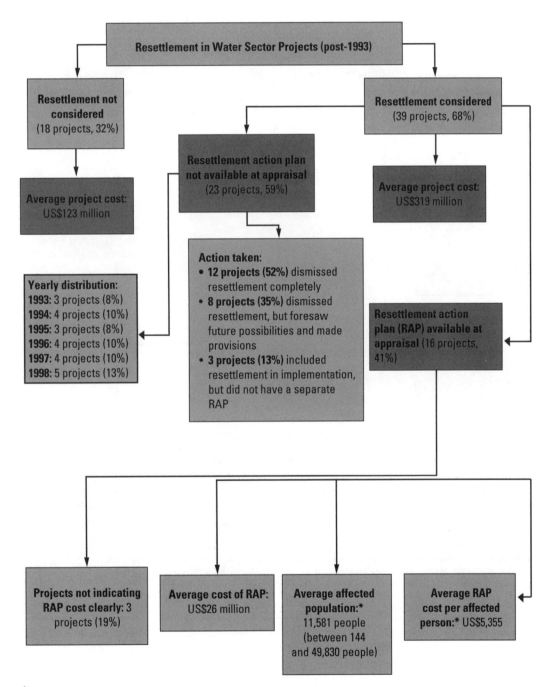

**Resettlement in Water Sector Projects (post-1993)**

**Resettlement not considered**
(18 projects, 32%)

**Average project cost:**
US$123 million

**Yearly distribution:**
**1993:** 3 projects (8%)
**1994:** 4 projects (10%)
**1995:** 3 projects (8%)
**1996:** 4 projects (10%)
**1997:** 4 projects (10%)
**1998:** 5 projects (13%)

**Resettlement action plan not available at appraisal**
(23 projects, 59%)

**Action taken:**
- **12 projects (52%)** dismissed resettlement completely
- **8 projects (35%)** dismissed resettlement, but foresaw future possibilities and made provisions
- **3 projects (13%)** included resettlement in implementation, but did not have a separate RAP

**Resettlement considered**
(39 projects, 68%)

**Average project cost:**
US$319 million

**Resettlement action plan (RAP) available at appraisal** (16 projects, 41%)

**Projects not indicating RAP cost clearly:** 3 projects (19%)

**Average cost of RAP:**
US$26 million

**Average affected population:***
11,581 people
(between 144 and 49,830 people)

**Average RAP cost per affected person:*** US$5,355

*This number is an approximation, because a number of RAPs present the number of people affected in terms of household; therefore, the analysis used an average household size of four to calculate the approximate number of affected people. Hence, the average cost per person value is also approximate and is highly sensitive to the level of resettlement financing in individual projects.

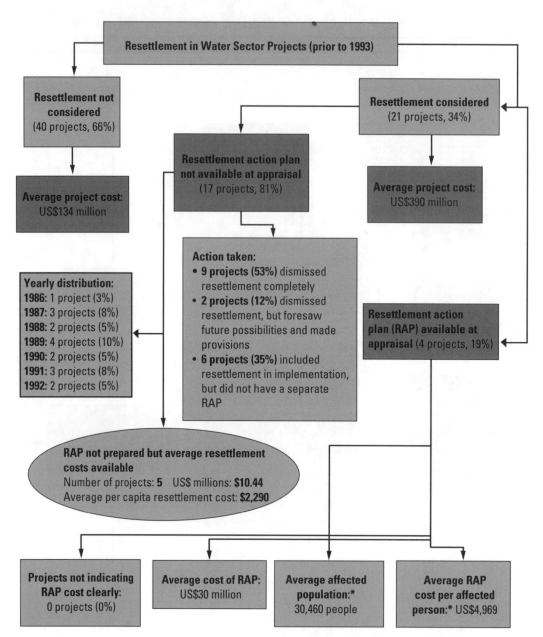

**Resettlement in Water Sector Projects (prior to 1993)**

**Resettlement not considered**
(40 projects, 66%)

**Average project cost:**
US$134 million

**Resettlement considered**
(21 projects, 34%)

**Average project cost:**
US$390 million

**Resettlement action plan not available at appraisal**
(17 projects, 81%)

**Yearly distribution:**
**1986:** 1 project (3%)
**1987:** 3 projects (8%)
**1988:** 2 projects (5%)
**1989:** 4 projects (10%)
**1990:** 2 projects (5%)
**1991:** 3 projects (8%)
**1992:** 2 projects (5%)

**Action taken:**
- **9 projects (53%)** dismissed resettlement completely
- **2 projects (12%)** dismissed resettlement, but foresaw future possibilities and made provisions
- **6 projects (35%)** included resettlement in implementation, but did not have a separate RAP

**Resettlement action plan (RAP) available at appraisal (4 projects, 19%)**

**RAP not prepared but average resettlement costs available**
Number of projects: **5**    US$ millions: **$10.44**
Average per capita resettlement cost: **$2,290**

**Projects not indicating RAP cost clearly:**
0 projects (0%)

**Average cost of RAP:**
US$30 million

**Average affected population:***
30,460 people

**Average RAP cost per affected person:*** US$4,969

*This number is an approximation, because a number of RAPs present the number of people affected in terms of household; therefore, the analysis used an average household size of four to calculate the approximate number of affected people. Hence, the average cost per person value is also approximate and is highly sensitive to the level of resettlement financing in individual projects.

WATER RESOURCES MANAGEMENT POLICY QUESTIONNAIRE
TO BANK STAFF

The questionnaire was sent to Bank staff in the period January–March 2000. It was preceded by two rounds of pre-testing among a random sample of 20 Bank water staff in the period November–December 1999. The questionnaire was designed using commercial software developed specifically for market and opinion surveys, and an external Website was used as a post box to collect responses to the questionnaire. This remote Website enabled the responses of Bank staff to remain anonymous.

Considerable difficulty was encountered in setting up a list of potential respondents. It was the intent to send the questionnaire to all Bank staff and recent retirees who were connected to water development. The names on the Bank's Global Water Unit circulation list formed the initial participant list. Subsequently, this was expanded to include all task managers responsible for water or water component projects—many of those on the larger list were general economists or specialists in other disciplines, such as sociology. In all, a list of about 420 names was compiled. It included about 150 staff who form the Bank's core water group.

After several reminders, a total of 107 staff responded. Judging by the answers to the initial questions, almost all of these were from the core Bank water group, although the exact proportion cannot be determined because of the guaranteed anonymity.

---

| Figure G.1 | Staff Questionnaire |
|---|---|

**Q1 and Q2 delt with administrative issues.**

| Q3 | **Which of the following best describes your position?** | | | | |
|---|---|---|---|---|---|
| | Task manager | 53% | Other | 4% | |
| | Other Bank Staff | 20% | Retired Bank Staff | 2% | |
| | Lead Specialist | 9% | Young Professional | 0% | |
| | Outside Consultant | 7% | | | |
| | Sector Manager | 5% | | | |

| Q4 | **Please give your position title:** | **Response not classified** |
|---|---|---|

| Q5 | **How much of your time in the Bank has been spent on water or water-related work?** | | |
|---|---|---|---|
| | | **Answer** | **Cumulative** |
| | 75–100% | 53% | 53% |
| | 50–75% | 15% | 68% |
| | 25–50% | 16% | 84% |
| | Less than 25% | 14% | 98% |
| | None | 2% | 100% |

*(continues on following page)*

| | | | |
|---|---|---|---|
| **Figure G.1** | **Staff Questionnaire (continued)** | | |

| Q6 | Recent Bank reports have expressed concern that the retirement of technical water staff since the early 1990s has undermined the Bank's ability to manage lending and ESW for water. Do you agree the Bank should be concerned? | Yes | 60% |
| | | No | 40% |

| Q7 | How long before you plan to retire? | | | |
|---|---|---|---|---|
| | Within a year | 1–2 years | 3–5 years | > 5 years |
| | 6% | 8% | 11% | 76% |

| Q8 | How many years (of cumulative experience) have you been working for the Bank ? | | |
|---|---|---|---|
| | | **Answers** | **Cumulative Bank experience** |
| | More than 20 years | 11% | 11% |
| | 15 to 20 | 5% | 16% |
| | 12 to 14 | 11% | 27% |
| | 9 to 11 | 11% | 37% |
| | 6 to 8 | 25% | 62% |
| | 3 to 5 | 14% | 77% |
| | Less than 3 years | 23% | 100% |

| Q9 | How many years of professional water or water-related experience do you have? | | |
|---|---|---|---|
| | | **Answers** | **Cumulative professional experience** |
| | More than 30 years | 17% | 17% |
| | 25 to 30 | 13% | 30% |
| | 20 to 24 | 16% | 46% |
| | 15 to 19 | 8% | 54% |
| | 10 to 14 | 11% | 65% |
| | 5 to 9 | 15% | 80% |
| | 1 to 4 | 18% | 98% |
| | less than 1 year | 2% | 100% |

| Q10 | Which of the following Bank Regions have you worked in? | | | |
|---|---|---|---|---|
| | East Asia and Pacific | 50% | Middle East and North Africa | 39% |
| | Africa | 45% | Latin America and Caribbean | 37% |
| | South Asia | 42% | E. Europe and Central Asia | 23% |
| | | | None | 2% |

| Q11 | Are You HQ or country based | | | |
|---|---|---|---|---|
| | HQ based (DC) | 65% | Country based | 26% |
| | Non-Bank staff—Not relevant | 8% | Don't know | 1% |

| Figure G.1 | Staff Questionnaire (continued) |

**Q12** How much time in total have you spent working in a developing country?
(either in the Bank or in another job?)

|  | Answers | Cumulative Profile |
|---|---|---|
| More than 20 years | 23% | 23% |
| More than 11 but less than 20 years | 33% | 56% |
| More than 5 but less than 10 years | 2% | 58% |
| Less than 5 years | 12% | 70% |
| More than 6 months but less than 1 year | 3% | 73% |
| Short trips, with no trip exceeding 6 months | 8% | 81% |
| No experience | 2% | 83% |

**Q13 & Q14** Select any of the following subjects in which you have professional expertise (Q13) and you have been significantly involved in (more than 5% of your time) over the past 5 years as water-related activities (Q14)

|  | Q13 Personal with expertise | Q14 Bank Work with experience |
|---|---|---|
| Water Resources and WR Management | 56% | 47% |
| Water Supply and Sanitation | 50% | 51% |
| Economics | 44% | 40% |
| Water Planning | 39% | 30% |
| Participatory Management | 38% | 41% |
| Rural Water Supply | 37% | 32% |
| Cost Recovery & Tariff | 29% | 32% |
| Irrigation Management | 28% | 25% |
| Evaluation | 27% | 24% |
| Finance | 27% | 22% |
| Sewerage and Waste Disposal | 26% | 26% |
| Water Quality | 22% | 16% |
| Utility Operation and Management | 22% | 22% |
| Privatization | 22% | 30% |
| Training | 21% | 20% |
| Irrigation Engineering | 18% | 13% |
| Environmental Management/Science | 16% | 15% |
| Other | 14% | 3% |
| Public & Environmental Health | 12% | 6% |
| Legal & Regulatory | 11% | 10% |

**Q15** To which Network(s) do you belong?

| | | | |
|---|---|---|---|
| ESSD | 44% | FPSI | 46% |
| HD | 3% | OCS | 2% |
| PSD | 1% | PREM | 6% |
| None | 6% | Don't know | 10% |

*(continues on following page)*

| Figure G.1 | Staff Questionnaire (continued) |
| --- | --- |

| Q16 | **Which of the following water-related mailing lists are you on?** | | | |
| --- | --- | --- | --- | --- |
| | Water Sector (WATER HELP DESK) | 77% | Rural WS&S (WSINF) | 48% |
| | Water Thematic Group (RSBG16) | 57% | Other (not listed above) | 13% |

| Q17 | **Have you read, or are you familiar with, the contents of the "Water Resources Management: A Policy Paper" published by the Bank in 1993?** | | |
| --- | --- | --- | --- |
| | Yes | No | Don't know |
| | 72% | 22% | 6% |

Q18 **Indicate how much you agree or disagree with the following statements about the Water Resources Management Policy Paper**

| | True | Somewhat true | Somewhat untrue | Untrue | Don't know |
| --- | --- | --- | --- | --- | --- |
| I found this helpful | 54% | 37% | 8% | 1% | 0% |
| WRMP is consistent with the Bank's objectives | 41% | 33% | 14% | 6% | 6% |
| The document is thorough | 27% | 46% | 20% | 4% | 3% |
| The paper is too long | 17% | 41% | 17% | 23% | 3% |
| The document is clear and unambiguous | 13% | 56% | 28% | 3% | 1% |

Q19 **Indicate how much you agree or disagree with the following statements about the Water Resources Management Policy Paper**

| | True | Somewhat true | Somewhat untrue | Untrue | Don't know |
| --- | --- | --- | --- | --- | --- |
| The document is practical for Bank staff to use | 29% | 24% | 32% | 11% | 4% |
| The paper only responded to the Dublin Statement of 1992 to show the bank had a water policy | 13% | 20% | 31% | 12% | 24% |
| The policy document has actionable recommendations | 38% | 32% | 21% | 6% | 3% |
| The policy described in this document is monitorable | 17% | 25% | 35% | 19% | 4% |
| The WRMP document is relevant to my Bank work | 49% | 25% | 18% | 1% | 6% |

Q20 **Indicate how much you agree or disagree with the following statements about the Water Resources Management Policy Paper**

| | Agree | Somewhat agree | Somewhat disagree | Disagree | Don't know |
| --- | --- | --- | --- | --- | --- |
| The paper is too complex | 7% | 30% | 23% | 25% | 16% |
| This document is mainly a set of platitudes | 7% | 41% | 24% | 12% | 16% |
| The text is too dense | 10% | 34% | 23% | 17% | 16% |
| The document gives realistic advice | 14% | 27% | 33% | 8% | 19% |
| The Paper is relevant to Borrowers' needs | 22% | 34% | 24% | 4% | 17% |

## Figure G.1    Staff Questionnaire (continued)

**Q21** **Indicate how much you agree or disagree**

| | Disagree | Somewhat disagree | Somewhat agree | Agree | Don't know |
|---|---|---|---|---|---|
| The different sectoral/sub-sectoral units in my region work harmoniuosly on water policy issues | 20% | 26% | 30% | 6% | 18% |
| Cross-sectoral cooperation in the Bank has improved since the 1993 water policy | 10% | 17% | 22% | 8% | 44% |
| There is insufficient FINANCE for comprehensive & holistic approaches to water in ESW/operations | 4% | 10% | 27% | 32% | 27% |
| There are insufficient PERSONNEL for comprehensive/holistic approaches to water in ESW/operations | 4% | 9% | 32% | 29% | 27% |
| Senior councils are effective in helping to implement the water policy | 12% | 17% | 22% | 5% | 44% |
| Bank staff do not have the skills to implement the water policy | 21% | 29% | 23% | 3% | 25% |

**Q22** **Indicate how true you think the following statements are**

| | True | Somewhat true | Somewhat untrue | Untrue | Don't know |
|---|---|---|---|---|---|
| The Bank has shown a high degree of leadership in promoting integrated water resources management | 19% | 33% | 28% | 9% | 11% |
| The Bank has practiced what it preaches with water policy | 13% | 26% | 27% | 15% | 20% |
| The water policy HAS been institutionalized my REGION | 8% | 28% | 22% | 10% | 33% |
| The water policy HAS NOT been institutionalized in my Sector | 8% | 31% | 20% | 14% | 28% |
| The water policy HAS NOT been institutionalized in my UNIT | 10% | 26% | 20% | 19% | 25% |

**Q23** **Indicate how much you agree or disagree**

| | Agree | Somewhat agree | Somewhat disagree | Disagree | Don't know |
|---|---|---|---|---|---|
| There is not enough continuity in Bank staff to implement the water policy | 16% | 37% | 17% | 11% | 19% |
| I/we (my team) are dependent on non-Bank funding (e.g., trust funds) to implement the policy | 37% | 23% | 6% | 8% | 27% |

*(continues on following page)*

| Figure G.1 | Staff Questionnaire (continued) |
|---|---|

**Q23** (continued)

| | Agree | Somewhat agree | Somewhat disagree | Disagree | Don't know |
|---|---|---|---|---|---|
| Bank staff do have sufficient experience to implement the water policy | 17% | 40% | 20% | 8% | 15% |
| Adding integrated water resources management to specific water operations is very difficult | 26% | 32% | 15% | 15% | 13% |
| Most of our clients support the integrated water resources management policy | 15% | 34% | 26% | 7% | 17% |

**Q24** Indicate how true you think the following statements are true

| | True | Somewhat true | Somewhat untrue | Untrue | Don't know |
|---|---|---|---|---|---|
| Staffing needs to implement the policy HAVE been quantified at unit level | 5% | 12% | 14% | 19% | 51% |
| Staffing needs to implement the policy have NOT been quantified at regional level | 17% | 18% | 5% | 7% | 54% |
| Staffing needs to implement the policy have NOT been quantified at sectoral level | 13% | 15% | 9% | 5% | 58% |
| Staffing needs to implement the policy at network level HAVE been quantified | 4% | 7% | 12% | 11% | 66% |

**Q25** Indicate how much you agree or disagree

| | Agree | Somewhat agree | Somewhat disagree | Disagree | Don't know |
|---|---|---|---|---|---|
| I have taken advantage of the EDI/WBI Water Resources Management programs | 14% | 14% | 41% | 18% | 12% |
| EDI/WBI is effective at disseminating the water policy with borrwers and development partners | 10% | 27% | 25% | 3% | 34% |
| The Bank has been effective at building international cooperation for water resources management | 19% | 32% | 23% | 3% | 23% |
| The Bank has been more careful in incorporating health safeguards in water projects since the policy | 13% | 25% | 28% | 4% | 31% |

**Q26** Indicate how effective you think the Bank has been at the following activities

| | Effective | Somewhat effective | Not very effective | Not effective | Don't know |
|---|---|---|---|---|---|
| Partnering with bilaterals to coordinate and implement water policy reforms | 14% | 51% | 19% | 8% | 9% |
| Dealing with water in a more integrated cross-sectoral manner | 8% | 44% | 37% | 8% | 4% |
| Paying attention to environmental impact of water operations | 10% | 73% | 12% | 2% | 3% |

| Figure G.1 | Staff Questionnaire (continued) |
|---|---|

**Q26** (continued)

| | Effective | Somewhat effective | Not very effective | Not effective | Don't know |
|---|---|---|---|---|---|
| Developing relationships with NGOs to further the water policy agenda | 3% | 52% | 35% | 6% | 5% |
| Treating water as an economic good (opportunity costing of water) in its project appraisal of loans/credits | 10% | 54% | 24% | 7% | 5% |
| Integrating watershed management and river basin planning/management activities | 9% | 32% | 39% | 5% | 16% |

**Q27** **Indicate how effective you think the Bank has been at the following activities**

| | Effective | Somewhat effective | Not very effective | Not effective | Don't know |
|---|---|---|---|---|---|
| Coordinating with UN partners on implementing water reform | 13% | 45% | 22% | 10% | 10% |
| Focusing on the poverty implications of water management | 6% | 43% | 38% | 10% | 4% |
| Institutionalizing the Bank's water policy | 4% | 44% | 33% | 6% | 14% |
| Enhancing the participation of women in water operations | 2% | 41% | 38% | 5% | 15% |
| Getting private participation in the water supply sector | 15% | 58% | 19% | 4% | 4% |
| Recruiting enough new water specialists to replace retiring Bank staff | 3% | 24% | 30% | 25% | 17% |
| Integrating water quality and environmental issues with institutional designs for water allocation | 5% | 35% | 32% | 9% | 19% |

## Table G.1 — Staff Expertise and Bank Work Experience (first line/column shows the number of respondents in each category, body of table shows number of staff in both categories)

Cross-tabulation of the responses of 105 survey participants

Q14: Areas in which Bank Staff have significant BANK water experience

| Q13 Bank staffs' professional expertise | Number | Economics (42) | Finance (23) | Water planning (31) | Water resources and WR management (49) | Environmental management or science (16) | Water supply and sanitation (54) | Rural water supply (34) | Sewerage and waste disposal (27) | Public environmental health (6) | Water quality (17) | Legal regulatory (10) | Participatory management (43) | Irrigation engineering (14) | Irrigation management (26) | Utility operation and management (23) | Training (21) | Cost recovery/tariff (34) | Privatization (31) | Evaluation (25) | Other (3) | Percentage of expertise utilized in Bank work |
|---|---|---|---|---|---|---|---|---|---|---|---|---|---|---|---|---|---|---|---|---|---|---|
| Economics | 47 | 37 | 13 | 13 | 26 | 8 | 19 | 13 | 7 | 1 | 7 | 3 | 19 | 5 | 13 | 9 | 6 | 18 | 18 | 13 | 2 | 79 |
| Finance | 28 | 12 | 18 | 3 | 9 | 2 | 19 | 6 | 10 | 3 | 4 | 6 | 7 | 1 | 5 | 11 | 7 | 16 | 17 | 10 | - | 64 |
| Water planning | 41 | 16 | 7 | 29 | 27 | 10 | 21 | 10 | 12 | 3 | 13 | 3 | 19 | 5 | 13 | 13 | 13 | 11 | 10 | 13 | 1 | 71 |
| Water resources and WR management | 59 | 27 | 8 | 26 | 47 | 11 | 21 | 11 | 12 | 1 | 11 | 5 | 20 | 14 | 22 | 14 | 16 | 18 | 15 | 13 | 2 | 80 |
| Environmental management/science | 17 | 7 | 2 | 6 | 8 | 9 | 6 | 8 | 6 | 2 | 8 | 4 | 8 | 3 | 6 | 1 | 4 | 2 | 2 | 6 | - | 53 |
| Water supply and sanitation | 52 | 16 | 14 | 16 | 15 | 4 | 49 | 25 | 25 | 5 | 13 | 5 | 21 | 1 | 4 | 16 | 11 | 20 | 21 | 12 | - | 94 |
| Rural water supply | 39 | 11 | 6 | 11 | 16 | 4 | 29 | 27 | 15 | 1 | 6 | 3 | 18 | 6 | 9 | 5 | 7 | 11 | 6 | 10 | 2 | 69 |
| Sewerage and waste disposal | 27 | 9 | 11 | 9 | 8 | 3 | 25 | 11 | 21 | 4 | 9 | 3 | 12 | 1 | 2 | 10 | 6 | 13 | 10 | 12 | - | 78 |
| Public/environmental health | 13 | 4 | 5 | 6 | 4 | 3 | 10 | 6 | 5 | 4 | 6 | 3 | 8 | - | 2 | 2 | 1 | 3 | 3 | 3 | - | 31 |
| Water quality | 23 | 8 | 4 | 12 | 12 | 7 | 14 | 5 | 10 | 3 | 14 | 4 | 8 | 1 | 4 | 7 | 6 | 9 | 8 | 5 | 1 | 61 |
| Legal/regulatory | 12 | 7 | 7 | 4 | 6 | 4 | 5 | 4 | 4 | 2 | 4 | 7 | 6 | 1 | 3 | 2 | 5 | 5 | 6 | 5 | 1 | 58 |
| Participatory management | 41 | 14 | 8 | 16 | 19 | 6 | 24 | 17 | 11 | 4 | 6 | 5 | 34 | 6 | 13 | 9 | 12 | 11 | 6 | 9 | 2 | 83 |
| Irrigation engineering | 19 | 8 | 3 | 9 | 18 | 4 | 2 | 5 | - | - | 4 | 2 | 9 | 10 | 14 | 1 | 6 | 4 | 1 | 5 | 2 | 53 |
| Irrigation management | 30 | 14 | 4 | 11 | 26 | 7 | 4 | 8 | - | - | 4 | 3 | 16 | 12 | 23 | 4 | 9 | 5 | 2 | 7 | 1 | 77 |
| Utility operation and management | 23 | 7 | 10 | 8 | 9 | - | 18 | 5 | 10 | 2 | 5 | 4 | 7 | 2 | 4 | 16 | 8 | 14 | 13 | 8 | - | 70 |
| Training | 22 | 8 | 4 | 12 | 9 | 3 | 11 | 5 | 5 | - | 4 | 4 | 10 | 2 | 9 | 9 | 14 | 9 | 9 | 6 | 1 | 64 |
| Cost recovery/tariff | 31 | 14 | 12 | 7 | 12 | 2 | 19 | 11 | 11 | 2 | 6 | 6 | 9 | 3 | 7 | 10 | 9 | 21 | 18 | 8 | 1 | 68 |
| Privatization | 23 | 10 | 11 | 5 | 5 | 1 | 16 | 8 | 10 | 3 | 3 | 6 | 8 | - | 2 | 9 | 7 | 16 | 22 | 7 | - | 96 |
| Evaluation | 29 | 8 | 10 | 8 | 9 | 2 | 15 | 8 | 10 | 2 | 5 | 6 | 11 | 2 | 9 | 10 | 11 | 12 | 11 | 19 | 2 | 66 |
| Other | 14 | 5 | 1 | 3 | 6 | 5 | 4 | 1 | 1 | - | 1 | - | 8 | 2 | 6 | 1 | 3 | 1 | - | 4 | 3 | 21 |
| Percentage of Bank experience using expertise | | 88 | 78 | 94 | 96 | 56 | 91 | 79 | 78 | 67 | 82 | 70 | 79 | 71 | 88 | 70 | 67 | 62 | 71 | 76 | 100 | |

# ANNEX H: THE DIFFICULTIES OF INTEGRATED RIVER BASIN MANAGEMENT

Recognizing that it would be difficult to implement the water strategy in client countries, the Bank and the UNDP produced a guide on capacity-building for countries interested in forming strategies for managing water resources (Le Moigne and others 1994), and its prescriptions were reinforced by all the UN family (UN/WMO 1997). A key principle was to build national capacity to manage water resources through the process of strategy formation adapted to country conditions. It was envisaged that the country strategies would be a set of medium- to long-term action programs and measures to support achievement of broad development goals and to implement water-related policies. Most important, measures would include developing managerial capacity, building institutions, and enhancing human resources.

Critical elements for successful strategy formulation were specified as a clear national statement of development objectives and key water policies, supported by government commitment at the highest level to using a comprehensive approach in formulating a water strategy. Once committed, a high-level policy committee would guide a team of national experts charged with determining partners and processes for strategy formulation.

In practice, however, there have been few successes, and this approach has failed when ownership was low and many of the critical elements were imposed as lending conditions. That was a fate similar to that imposed on National Environmental Action Plans, with a similarly chilling effect on local ownership and capacity building. Most notably, the Bank's desire to time-table strategy formulation and resulting investment plans has resulted in importation of expatriate specialists to "assist" the national effort, but who in practice substitute for inadequate local capacity. The most notable examples of this have been in Bangladesh and Mozambique. In Bangladesh, large expatriate teams undertook the national water planning effort in the late 1980s and early 1990s, and in a clear demonstration that no local capacity was created, a new expatriate team is currently producing a third iteration of the national water plan. Mozambique suffered a similar experience.

The MNA Region is notably successful in assisting clients to develop an orderly regional and country strategy framework (box H.1), but this has not led to investment lending that is better than in other Regions because it is difficult to mainstream water strategies and improve performance of line agencies.

Successes in strategy adoption are linked with good local capacity and ownership, with the country in the driver's seat. An irony is that low-key Bank advisory support under these circumstances is generally more successful (for example, in Mexico, Colombia, and Venezuela) than highly visible Bank-sponsored national water strategies and plans (Bangladesh). The recent Argentina and Ghana water resources management strategies put together by national experts are best-practice examples. It is salutary to compare the pragmatic Argentine approach that recognizes local problems and only recommends a few tasks in the short term, to the Bank-driven agenda in India that made 52 recommendations for reform in 1991, achieving little, and the 1998 water resources strategy that makes even more recommendations.

Regrettably, the global experience with implementing strategies for integrated water resources management is that while the concept is sound, it is extraordinarily difficult to implement suc-

**Box H.1     MNA Water Strategy Development**

MNA, along with AFR, is one of the regions in the Bank where its water activities in agricultural, industrial and potable water development and management is integrated under one sector leader—and this has led to a more comprehensive approach. Agriculture is the biggest consumer of water in the region accounting for about 85 percent of demand. Consequently, the Bank initiated its water strategy work in 1993 with a regional examination of the MNA's regional experience of improving the efficiency of water use in agriculture. The following year MNA published its regional water strategy for managing water. In line with this strategy, the focus turned on detailed water sector reviews of individual countries with significant water problems: Egypt (1993), Tunisia (1994), Morocco (1995), Jordan (1997) and currently Yemen. These studies were followed up by a series of regional roundtables of stakeholders that discussed common water development issues and solutions—*the Bank was there to listen and learn how to tailor investments to felt needs.* The most recent roundtable on *Policy Reforms in Water Resources in MNA (1999)* looked at case studies developed by stakeholders in Jordan, Oman, Tunisia and Yemen.

cessfully, even in OECD countries (Barrow 1998; OECD 1998; Millington 2000). Even where there is local ownership, there is a danger that the most dominant water agency—typically the irrigation department, frequently cosmetically renamed as the water resources agency—will capture the strategy for its traditional vested interests. This happened in Turkey, for example, under two bank-financed projects. In Brazil, the PLANSA model of the 1970s and 1980s created powerful state water companies, based on the premise that institutional strengthening alone would be sufficient to improve and sustain the efficiency of state water companies. Instead, it produced a large and inefficient bureaucracy and a highly politicized management culture with few incentive structures to serve the poor or address environmental issues. Similar problems arose in Sub-Saharan Africa, particularly in Nigeria's Lake Chad Basin Commission and the Niger Basin Authority. Indeed, one reviewer found he could not "recognize a single . . . body that had . . . played an effective role in planning and coordinating the development of a single river basin" (Scudder, 1989, 1994).

The Bank's strategy advocates setting-up river basin organizations (RBOs) to implement water strategy. However, there is no single global model that has proved successful, since each must adapt itself to local realities and needs. A review of 11 RBOs (Millington 2000) indicated that only the most mature (The Rhine Commission, Murray Darling Basin Commission) have evolved to limit themselves to resource manager and standard-setter/regulator, while the Mekong Commission and Niger River Basin Authority limit themselves primarily to resource management. The rest adopt a dual role of resource manager and operator and service provider—the most notable being the TVA and the Jordan Valley Authority. Unfortunately, earlier Bank initiatives have advocated design of RBOs that measured everything against fixed targets and did not allow for a natural evolution (Frederiksen 1992b): "the nature of reform of water institutions demands a will to attack the situation in a coherent, comprehensive manner. Piece-meal or simple solutions do not exist." Unfortunately, this blanket mechanistic approach is frequently politically impracticable and tends to fail, while an organic, adaptive approach succeeds (Maxwell and Conway 2000).

A recent global review of holistic approaches to planning (OED 2000b) found that it is best to avoid delegating responsibility for integrated planning problems to "super-institutions" created specifically for the task. Experience suggests that these are either ineffectual in the short term or unproductive or unsustainable in the long term. The biggest problem for RBOs is that they tend to take the form of regional structures that attempt to claim (but often merely duplicate) the responsibilities of existing regional departments of national ministries. This happened to the River Basin Councils and Aquifer Committees in Mexico. Additionally, a pervasive problem facing these new organizations is securing adequate funds for water resources management activities. To mitigate these problems, new bodies should instead be given responsibility for coordinating the relevant elements of existing organizations and ensuring participation of stakeholders, including NGOs, civil society, and the private sector: integrated planning, but not integrated implementation. Decentralized governance—subsidiarity—is a key component of this approach. Notwithstanding this new paradigm, lack of baseline data and adequate monitoring leads to decisions based on false assumptions.

# ENDNOTES

## Chapter 1

1. This document was the basis for the Bank's Operational Policy (OP) 4.07 (Annex A). However, the OP is limited to core mandatory provisions. For evaluation, the full Policy Paper (*Strategy* hereafter) is the appropriate reference, since it incorporates the guidance needed to achieve development effectiveness.

2. Annex C contains an evaluation of 306 completed Bank water and water-related projects exiting between 1988 and 1999.

3. Indeed, 78 percent of countries participating in sector operations did not live up to financial covenants, and the Bank took remedial action in one case only. One reason, OED found, was that the Bank may have required reforms to be implemented too quickly or before the borrowers were fully committed.

4. OD 4.00, Annex B: Environmental Policy for Dam and Reservoir Projects (1989); OD 4.01: Environmental Assessment (1991); OD 4.02: Environmental Action Plans (1992); OD 4.15: Poverty Reduction (1991); OD 4.20: Indigenous People (1991); OD 4.30: Involuntary Resettlement (1990); OD 7.50: Projects on International Waterways (1990); OD 14.70: Nongovernmental Organizations in Bank-Supported Activities (1989); OMS 2.12: Project Generation and Design—Local Involvement (1978); OMS 2.22: Financial Performance Covenants for Revenue-Earning Enterprises (1984); OMS 3.72: Energy, Water Supply, Sanitation and Communications (1987).

5. Bank Management disagrees with the projected reduction of investment going to agriculture shown in table 1.1 and states that it should show an increase. Management argues that according to the results of long-term food supply and demand forecasts by the International Water Management Institute and the International Food Policy Research Institute, additional investment in irrigation and drainage will be key to ensuring adequate and affordable food supplies, particularly for the poor. In addition to financing a modest increase in irrigated area, new investment will be required for technology to improve water use efficiency and to redress historically inadequate investment in drainage and irrigation rehabilitation.

## Chapter 2

1. Bank Management is currently evaluating issues and recommendations made in Dam Commission's Report and has indicated that it will address these in the context of the forthcoming Water Sector Strategy Paper.

2. Thirteen countries ceased borrowing because of graduation from the Bank, civil wars, or economic mismanagement. Forty countries started borrowing, most as a result of economic liberalization (Europe and Central Asia and East Asia and Pacific Regions), others as a result of successful peace negotiations (Lebanon, West Bank and Gaza, Angola).

3. Water investment in other sectors averaged 44 percent of the loan when its share could be determined.

4. The hydropower portfolio after 1993 includes 11 dam projects and 49 environmental projects. The ratio before 1993 was 16 dam projects to 11 environmental projects.

5. The Bank's Quality Assurance Group (QAG) has independently evaluated the quality of 292 projects at entry over the period 1997–99 against consistent Bankwide standards. OED disaggregated these data to compare the quality at entry of water and non-water projects.

6. OED, together with a social assessment team from the Bank's ESSD network, evaluated the social concerns and poverty focus of 103 randomly selected project appraisal documents, half completed before the water strategy came into effect and half after (details are given in Annex E).

7. The WSS Sector Board observed in 2000 that: "the key step to turning around our portfolio is to first put all the problems on the table as the MNA Region has done over the last two years, which helps explain the fact that it now tops (along with ECA) the problem projects league table in W&S" (internal Bank communication). In the MNA case there is clear evidence that this leads to better policy even though it is a painful process in the short term. The same is true of the water supply and sanitation sector as a whole.

## Chapter 3

1. There are 146 CASs covering 98 countries. Some countries had only one CAS, some two,

and a few had three. OED analyzed all the CASs for a number of specific water issues.

2. An aggregate CAS water strategy index was developed taking account of the main water strategy issues—countries were scored on this basis. To answer the CAS issue fully would require that all countries be assessed for the nature of their water problems, and that all external assistance and the countries' own efforts be evaluated together. Only then could the country lacunae in the Bank's water operations be clearly identified.

3. A joint team from the Operations Evaluation Department and Environmentally and Socially Sustainable Development Network team evaluated the design of 170 projects (a 100 percent sample of the 1993–99 cohort) for responsiveness to the 1993 water *Strategy* document against 11 criteria grouped under three categories: comprehensive framework, institutions, and economic and social considerations. Methodology and details are described in Annex B. The group of evaluators graded each project into one of four classes: high, substantial, modest, and negligible. For this report, the high and substantial classes were merged for simplicity.

4. Members of the Bank's Water Resources Management Group express strong reservations about the validity of using management information data in this section of the report for deriving conclusions of a cross-sectoral and cross-regional nature.

5. The total cost of all projects involving watershed management since 1990 is $2.37 billion.

6 A recent QAG review revealed significant problems with the forestry subcomponents and supervision.

7. Dam safety is a consideration for 104 Bank projects. Many are not classified within the Bank's water sectors and include mine-tailings dams.

8. The section is based upon an ongoing survey by the QAG RSA3 of FY 99 that contained 200 randomly selected projects, of which 50 were subjected to detailed review by a group of environmental specialists. Water projects were only part of this sample. Evaluative questions were directed at determining whether there was adequate supervision of environmental conditionalities; sufficient action to ensure satisfactory implementation, M&E, and mitigation and management; continued stakeholder consultation; and appropriate action if compliance with safeguards was inadequate.

9. Of course, these tariffs would be higher if the full opportunity costs of the water were added.

## Chapter 4

1. Domestic, industrial, and irrigation use tends to pollute downstream supplies or groundwater, while irrigation accounts for more than 70 percent of global fresh water consumption. Dams modify seasonality and bring the need to reconcile the competing objectives of power generation, flood control, and irrigation supply.

2. Annex H: The Difficulties of Integrated River Basin Management.

3. Administrative measures include defining supplies volumetrically and qualitatively, watershed protection, registering water rights, and enforcement of permits. Economic instruments include extraction and pollution fees, and regulating water markets.

4. This section is based on the results of stakeholder workshops held to discuss country experience of water development and the role of the Bank. Country studies for Brazil, India, the Philippines, and Yemen were prepared by a team drawn from ESSD's Global Water Unit (ESGWU) and OED. These studies were circulated prior to the workshops in Brazil (March 1999), prepared jointly; in Yemen (September 1999) and the Philippines (April 2000), prepared by ESGWU; and in India (May 2000), prepared by OED.

5. Latvia, Morocco, Mozambique, Peru, and the Philippines.

6. QAG used a 15 percent random sample of ESW products for the period FY98–99 that included five water studies, for: India (1998), Yemen (1998), Indonesia and Brazil (1999), and Indonesia (sewerage, 1999).

7. QAG, 1998. The areas where particular attention needs to be paid in future ESW are in ensuring that the work meets its own stated objectives (less than two-thirds achieved this) and

that recommendations are realistic. Only half (53 percent) of the ESW satisfactorily included recommendations that were realistic in light of social, political, and administrative constraints and that were suitably prioritized. These all work to undermine the likely impact of ESW.

8. Management commented that while resettlement planning quality has improved significantly since the 1994 Bankwide resettlement review, there has not been a comprehensive review of resettlement implementation for projects prepared since the early 1990s. However, feedback from task teams suggests that systematic efforts would need to be undertaken to strengthen the institutional, technical, and organizational skills of borrowers to meet Bank requirements on social policies.

9. There were also major recommendations about how compensation packages should be restructured, particularly regarding the land-for-land deal. As these are adequately dealt with within the Environmentally and Socially Sustainable Development Network and are outside the scope of this review, they are not discussed.

10. 6 India UP Tubewells Cr 1332; Pakistan Private Tubewells Development project Cr 2004. Much could have been learned from Bangladesh, where at the same time the Bank had been successful in enabling private sector participation in groundwater development—and this learning experience was hindered by the split of the South Asia Region among two independent operating departments.

11. Bank management objects to this statement, which is based on the findings of OED's recent Lesotho Country Assistance Evaluation (Hassan 2002).

12. The ideas summarized in this paragraph are derived from Ellerrman 2000.

## Chapter 5

1. Senior Water Advisor, personal communication.

2. A strong letter from an NGO group was sent to the U.S. Executive Director's office.

3. Overall, 72 percent of the 107 staff surveyed had read the Bank's water strategy paper. However, only two-thirds of the FPSI staff had read it compared with 80 percent of ESSD staff.

## Annex A

1. *Bank* includes IBRD and IDA, and *loans* include credits.

## Annex B

1. This is based on the UN (1995) low population projection. The medium-growth projection would increase those at risk to 2.8 billion.

2. Globally, approximately US$60 billion per year is invested in water projects. Only 10 percent is funded by external sources, of which the Bank contributes half.

## Annex C

1. Indeed, 78 percent of countries participating in sector operations did not live up to financial covenants, and the Bank took remedial action in one case only. One reason, OED found, was that the Bank may have required reforms to be implemented too quickly or before the borrowers were fully committed.

2. The analysis is based on project numbers only as each project represents an opportunity to implement Bank strategy; an analysis weighted on Bank commitment gives a better outcome, typically 5–10 percent higher.

3. A total of 157 projects (47 percent of the portfolio) were active after 1993, and 92 (27 percent) after 1995; 38 projects were approved after 1990 and half their implementation was in the post-*Strategy* period.

4. The number of project exit results declines sharply after 1995.

5. Only 9 of the 336 were approved after 1993.

## Annex D

1. Africa in this context is Sub-Saharan Africa only, north Africa is covered under the Bank's MNA Region.

## Annex E

1. The analysis also looked into common variables such as GNP per capita, country population, and national and/or regional scope of the project in a multiple regression analysis to determine if those differences have an effect on community participation, consideration of gender issues, and consultations with the poor. The analysis concluded that the relationship between

these factors and the inclusion of a community-driven approach, gender issues, and participation is not significant.

2. As also supported by OED's evaluation of rural water projects, insufficient focus on institutional capacity retards sustainability of CDD initiatives.

3. A case in point is communities in the Aral Sea area. Within that area, water diversions have had disastrous effects on these communities' livelihood and contributed to declines in their incomes, living standards, and health.

4. The Methodology for Participatory Assessment is a useful toolkit that combines gender- and poverty-sensitive indicators for conducting a thorough social analysis. See Dayal, van Wijk, and Mukherjee 2000.

# BIBLIOGRAPHY

Abernethy, Charles L., Hilmy Sally, Kurt Lonsway, and Chegou Maman. 2000. *Farmer-Based Financing of Operations in the Niger Valley Irrigation Schemes.* Research Report 37, International Water Management Institute. Colombo.

Adams, Adrian. 2000. *The River Senegal: Flood Management and the Future of the Valley.* Issue Paper 93. London: International Institute for Environment and Development.

Ahmad, Masood, and Gary P. Kutcher. 1992. *Irrigation Planning with Environmental Considerations: A Case Study of Pakistan's Indus Basin.* World Bank Technical Paper 106. Washington, D.C.

Alcázar, Lorena, Lixin Colin Xu, and Ana Maria Zuluaga. 2000. *Institutions, Politics, and Contracts: The Attempt to Privatize the Water and Sanitation Utility of Lima, Peru.* World Bank Policy Research Working Paper 2478. Washington, D.C.

Bandaragoda, D.J. 1999. *Institutional Change and Shared Management of Water Resources in Large Canal Systems: Results of an Action Research Program in Pakistan.* Research Report 36, International Water Management Institute. Colombo.

Barghouti, Shawki. 2002. "Growing Challenges to Water Resources Management." *Sustainable Development International* (1) 43–52.

Barlow, Maude. 1999. *Blue Gold: The Global Water Crisis and the Commodification of the World's Water Supply.* San Francisco: International Forum on Globalization.

Barrow, Christopher J. 1998. "River Basin Development Planning and Management: A Critical Review." *World Development* 26(1): 171–86.

Berger, Thomas R. 1994. "The Independent Review of the Sardar Sarovar Projects, 1991–92." *Water Resources Development* 10(1): 55–66.

Berkoff, D. J. W. 1990. *Irrigation Management on the Indo-Gangetic Plain.* World Bank Technical Paper 129. Washington, D.C.

Bhatia, Ramesh, Rita Cestti, and James Winpenny. 1995. *Water Conservation and Reallocation: Best Practice Cases in Improving Economic Efficiency and Environmental Quality.* A World Bank-ODI Joint Study. Washington, D.C.: World Bank.

Bird, Ashley, and Riki Therivel. 1996. "Post-auditing of Environmental Impact Statements Using Data Held in Public Registers of Environmental Information." *Project Appraisal* 11(2): 105–16.

Black, Maggie. 1998. *Learning Water and Sanitation Cooperation 1978–1998.* UNDP-World Bank Water and Sanitation Program. Washington, D.C.: UNDP-World Bank.

Brew, Douglas, and Norman Lee. 1996. "Reviewing the Quality of Donor Agency Environmental Assessment Guidelines." *Project Appraisal* 11(2): 79–84.

Briscoe, John. 1999a. "The Changing Face of Water Infrastructure Financing in Developing Countries." *Water Resources Development* 15(3): 301–8.

———. 1999b. "The Financing of Hydropower, Irrigation and Water Supply Infrastructure in Developing Countries." *Water Resources Development* 15(4): 459–91.

———. 1996. "Water as an Economic Good: The Idea and What it Means in Practice." International Commission on Irrigation and Drainage, Cairo Conference, Special Session R.11: 177–201.

———. 1995. *The German Water and Sewerage Sector: How Well It Works and What This Means for Developing Countries.* Transportation, Water, and Urban Development Department. Washington, D.C.: Water and Sanitation Division, the World Bank.

Byrnes, Kerry J. 1992. "Water Users Associations in World Bank-Assisted Irrigation Projects in Pakistan." World Bank Technical Paper 173. Washington, D.C.

Chowdhury, Mushtaque, Md Jakariya, Md Ashiqul H. Tareq, and Jalaluddin Ahmed. 1998. "Village Health Workers Can Test Tubewell Water for Arsenic." *Dhaka Monday Focus,* March 30, 1998.

Clarke, Robin. 1991. *Water: The International Crisis.* London: Earthscan.

Correia, Francisco Nunes (ed). 1998. *Institutions for Water Resources Management in Europe.* Rotterdam: Balkerma.

Cosgrove, William. 1997. *Water Policy Reform Program.* Evaluation Report, Economic

Development Institute. Washington, D.C.: World Bank.

Cosgrove William J., and Frank R. Rijsberman. 2000. *World Water Vision: Making Water Everybody's Business.* London: World Water Council.

Dayal, Rekha, Christine van Wijk, and Nilanjana Mukherjee. 2000. "Methodology for Participatory Assessments: With Communities, Institutions and Policy Makers." Water and Sanitation Program. Washington, D.C.: World Bank.

de Silva, Samantha. 2000. *Community-based Contracting: A Review of Stakeholder Experience.* Washington, D.C.: World Bank.

DFID (United Kingdom Department for International Development). 1998. *Maintaining the Value of Irrigation and Drainage Projects.* TDR Project R 6650. London.

Donahue, John M., and Barbara Rose Johnston (eds.). 1998. *Water, Culture, and Power: Local Struggles in a Global Context.* Washington, D.C.: Island.

DSE (German Foundation for International Development). 1998. "Global Water Politics: Cooperation for Transboundary Water Management." In lst Petersberg Round Tables, International Dialogue Forum. Berlin: DSE.

Easter, K. William, Mark W. Rosegrant, and Ariel Dinar. 1999. "Formal and Informal Markets for Water: Institutions, Performance, and Constraints." *World Bank Research Observer* 14(1): 99–116.

EC (Commission of the European Community). 2000. "Communication from the Commission to the Council, the European Parliament and the Economic and Social Committee: Pricing Policies for Enhancing the Sustainability of Water Resources." Brussels.

EDI (Economic Development Institute). 1997. "Capacity Building for Implementing PIM." International Network on Participatory Irrigation Management (INPIM) Newsletter 6. Washington, D.C.: World Bank.

EIB (European Investment Bank). 1999. *An Evaluation Study of 17 Water Projects Located Around the Mediterranean Financed by the European Investment Bank.* Luxembourg.

El-Ashry, Mohamed T. 1991. "Policies for Water Resource Management in Semi-arid Regions." *Water Resources Development* 7(4): 230–34.

Ellerman, David. 2000. *Hirschmanian Themes of Social Learning and Change.* World Bank Policy Research Working Paper, Washington, D.C.

Eriksen, John, and Roger Poulin. 1993. *Contrasting Approaches for Water Policy Development in Tunisia and Sri Lanka: Lessons Learned from USAID Mission Experience.* USAID ISPAN, Bureau for Asia and the Near East, Washington, D.C.: AID.

Euroconsult, Delft Hydraulics Laboratory, and Royal Tropical Institute. 1987. *Study on Options and Investment Priorities in Irrigation Development. Synthesis Report.* Arnhem, Delft, and Amsterdam.

Evans, Alison. 2000. *Poverty Reduction in the 1990s: An Evaluation of Strategy and Performance.* Operations Evaluation Department Study Series. Washington, D.C.: World Bank.

Evenson, Robert E., Carl E. Pray, and Mark W. Rosegrant. 1999. *Agricultural Research and Productivity Growth in India.* Washington, D.C.: International Food Policy Research Institute.

FAO (Food and Agriculture Organization of the United Nations). 1997. "Irrigation Technology Transfer in Support of Food Security: Proceedings of a Subregional Workshop in Harare, Zimbabwe, April 14–17, 1997." *Water Reports 14.* Rome.

——. 1996. *Guidelines for Planning Irrigation and Drainage Investment Projects.* FAO Investment Centre Technical Paper 11. Rome.

——. 1995. *Water Resources Policy Review and Strategy Formulation.* Rome.

Faruqee, Rashid. 1995. *Structural and Policy Reforms for Agricultural Growth: The Case of Pakistan.* Washington, D.C.: World Bank.

Feitelson, Eran, and Marwan Haddad. 1996. *Identification of Joint Management Structures for Shared Aquifers: A Cooperative Palestinian—Israeli Effort.* World Bank Technical Paper 415. Washington, D.C.

Foster, Stephen, John Chilton, Marcus Moench, Franklin Cardy, and Manuel Schiffler. 2000. *Groundwater in Rural Development: Facing the Challenges of Supply and Resource Sustainability."* World Bank Technical Paper 463. Washington, D.C.

Fox, James. 2000. "Applying the Comprehensive Development Framework." OED Working Paper Series 15. Washington, D.C.: OED.

Frederiksen, Harald D. 1992a. *Drought Planning and Water Efficiency Implications in Water Resources Management*. World Bank Technical Paper 185. Washington, D.C.

———. 1992b. *Water Resources Institutions: Some Principles and Practices*. World Bank Technical Paper 191. Washington, D.C.

Frederiksen, Harald D., Jeremy Berkoff, and William Barber. 1993. *Water Resources Management in Asia: Volume I, Main Report*. World Bank Technical Paper 212. Washington, D.C.

———. 1994. *Principles and Practices for Dealing with Water Resources Issues*. World Bank Technical Paper 233. Washington, D.C.

Frederiksen, Kenneth D. 1993. *Balancing Water Demands with Supplies: The Role of Management in a World of Increasing Scarcity*. World Bank Technical Paper 189. Washington, D.C.

GEF (Global Environmental Facility). 1997. "GEF Operational Programs." Washington, D.C.

———. 1996a. "Project Implementation Review." Washington, D.C.

———. 1996b. *Annual Report 1996*. Washington, D.C.: World Bank.

Ghana, Ministry of Works & Housing. 1998. *Ghana's Water Resources: Management Challenges and Opportunities*. Accra.

Griffin, Charles, John Briscoe, Bhanwar Singh, Radhika Ramasubban, and Ramesh Bhatia. 1995. "Contingent Valuation Meets the Cold Truth of Actual Behavior: Predicting Connections to New Water Systems in Kerala, India." *World Bank Economic Review* 9 (3).

Grigg, Neil S. 1996. *Water Resources Management: Principles, Regulations, and Cases*. New York: McGraw-Hill.

Groenfeldt, David, Mark Svendsen, and Anju Sharma. 1996. *Proceedings of the Second International Seminar on Participatory Irrigation Management: Antalya, Turkey, April 10–17, 1996*. The Economic Development Institute of the World Bank and the General Directorate of State Hydraulic Works. Antalya: DSI.

GWP (Global Water Partnership). 2000a. "Integrated Water Resources Management." Technical Advisory Committee Background Paper 4. Stockholm.

———. 2000b. *Towards Water Security: A Framework for Action*. Stockholm: GWP.

———. 1997. *Global Water Partnership: Building a Network for Sustainable Water Management*." Stockholm: GWP.

Hanna, Nagy. 2000. "Implementation Challenges and Promising Approaches for the Comprehensive Development Framework." OED Working Paper Series 13. Washington, D.C.: OED.

Hassan, Fareed. 2002. *Lesotho: Development in a Challenging Environment*, A Joint World Bank–African Development Bank Evaluation. OED Study Series. Washington, D.C.: World Bank.

Hirschman, Albert O. 1994. "A Propensity to Self-Subversion." In *Rethinking the Development Experience: Essays Provoked by the Work of Albert O. Hirschman*, L. Rodwin and D. Schon, eds. Washington, D.C.: Brookings Institution.

———. 1961. *The Strategy of Economic Development*. New Haven: Yale University Press.

Head, Chris. 2000. *Financing of Private Hydropower Projects*. World Bank Discussion Paper 420. Washington, D.C.

ICID (International Commission on Irrigation and Drainage). 1998. *Planning the Management, Operation, and Maintenance of Irrigation and Drainage Systems: A Guide for the Preparation of Strategies and Manuals*. World Bank Technical Paper 389. Washington, D.C.

IDB (Inter-American Development Bank). 1998a. *Beyond Tradeoffs: Market Reforms and Equitable Growth in Latin America*. Washington, D.C.: Brookings Institution.

———. 1998b. "Strategy for Integrated Water Resources Management." IDB Strategy Paper. Washington, D.C.

Israel, Arturo. 1987. *Institutional Development: Incentives to Performance*. Washington, D.C.: World Bank.

IUCN–World Conservation Union. 2000. *Vision for Water and Nature Project*. Monitoring and Evaluation Report. Gland, Switzerland.

———. 1997. *Large Dams: Learning from the Past Looking at the Future. Workshop Proceedings*. Gland, Switzerland.

Johansson, Robert D. 2000. *Pricing Irrigation Water: A Literature Survey*. World Bank Policy Research Working Paper 2449. Washington, D.C.

Katz, Travis, and Jennifer Sara. 1997a. "Making Rural Water Supply Sustainable: Recommendations from a Global Study." UNDP-World Bank Water and Sanitation Program, Washington, D.C.

———. 1997b. "Making Rural Water Supply Sustainable: Report on the Impact of Project Rules." UNDP-World Bank Water and Sanitation Program, Washington, D.C.

Keller, Andrew, R. Sakthivadivel, and David Seckler. 2000. *Water Scarcity and the Role of Storage in Development*. Research Report 39, International Water Management Institute. Colombo.

Kinzer, Stephen. "A Slow, Dusty Death for the Parched Aral Sea." *International Herald Tribune,* October 30, 1997.

Kirmani, Syed, and Guy Le Moigne. 1997. *Fostering Riparian Cooperation in International River Basins: The World Bank at Its Best in Development Diplomacy*. World Bank Technical Paper 335. Washington, D.C.

Kloezen, Wim H., Carlos Garces-Restrepo, and Sam H. Johnson III. 1997. *Impact Assessment of Irrigation Management Transfer in the Alto Rio Lerma Irrigation District, Mexico*. International Irrigation Management Institute. Colombo.

Langford, K. John, Christine L. Forster, and Duncan M. Malcolm. 1944. *Toward a Financially Sustainable Irrigation System: Lessons from the State of Victoria, Australia, 1984–1994*. World Bank Technical Paper 413. Washington, D.C.

Laos, Ministry of Public Health. 1998. "The Laos Experience: Indigenous, Sustainable, Replicable." Background paper to the International Conference on Water and Sustainable Development. Vientiane.

Lee, Terence Richard. 1999. *Water Management in the 21st Century: The Allocation Imperative*. U.K.: Edward Elgar.

Le Moigne, Guy, Ashok Subramanian, Mei Xie, and Sandra Giltner. 1994. *A Guide to the Formulation of Water Resources Strategy*. World Bank Technical Paper 263. Washington, D.C.

Le Moigne, Guy, K. William Easter, Walter J. Ochs, and Sandra Giltner, eds. 1994. *Water Policy and Water Markets: Selected Papers and Proceedings from the World Bank's Ninth Annual Irrigation and Drainage Seminar, Annapolis, Maryland, December 8–10, 1992*. World Bank Technical Paper 249. Washington, D.C.

Le Moigne, Guy, Shawki Barghouti, and Lisa Garbus, eds. 1992. *Developing and Improving Irrigation and Drainage Systems: Selected Papers from World Bank Seminars*. World Bank Technical Paper 178. Washington, D.C.

Le Moigne, Guy, Shawki Barghouti, Gershon Feder, Lisa Garbus, and Mei Xie, eds. 1992. *Country Experiences with Water Resources Management: Economic, Institutional, Technological and Environmental Issues*. World Bank Technical Paper 175. Washington, D.C.

Liebenthal, Andres. 2002. *Promoting Environmental Sustainability in Development: An Evaluation of the World Bank's Performance*. OED Study Series. Washington, D.C.: World Bank.

Livingston, Marie Leigh. 1993. *Designing Water Institutions: Market Failures and Institutional Response*. World Bank Policy Research Working Paper 1227. Washington, D.C.

Lobo, Crjspino, and Gudrun Kochendorfer-Lucius. 1995. *The Rain Decided to Help Us: Participatory Waterthed Management in the State of Maharashtra, India*. EDI Learning Resources Series. Washington, D.C.: World Bank.

Marcus, Amy Dockser. "Water Fight: Egypt Faces Problem It Has Long Dreaded: Less Control of the Nile." *The Wall Street Journal,* August 22, 1997.

Maxwell, Simon, and Tim Conway. 2000. "New Approaches to Planning." OED Working Paper Series 14. Washington, D.C.: OED.

Meinzen-Dick, Ruth, Richard Reidinger, and Andrew Manzardo. 1995. *Participation in Irrigation*. Environmental Department Participation Series Paper 003. Washington, D.C.: World Bank.

Merrett, Stephen. 1997. *Introduction to the Economics of Water Resources: An International Perspective*. Lanham, MD: Rowman & Littlefield.

Millington, Peter. 2000. *River Basin Management: Its Role in Major Water Infrastructure Projects.* WCD Thematic Reviews. Cape Town: World Commission on Dams.

Molden, D. 1997. *Accounting for Water Use and Productivity.* SWIM Paper 1, International Irrigation Management Institute. Colombo.

Moore, D., and L. Sklar. 1998. "Reforming the World Bank's Lending for Water: the Process and Outcome of Developing a Water Resources Management Policy." In *The Struggle for Accountability—The World Bank, NGOs and Grassroots Movements*, J.A. Fox, and L.D. Brown). Cambridge, MA: MIT Press.

Ochs, Walter J., and Bishay G. Bishay. 1934. "Drainage Guidelines." World Bank Technical Paper 195. Washington, D.C.:

OECD (Organization for Economic Co-operation and Development). 1998. "Water Consumption and Sustainable Water Resources Management." OECD Proceedings. Paris: OECD.

OED (Operations Evaluation Department). 2000a. "Moving from Projects to Programmatic Aid." OED Working Paper Series. Washington, D.C.

——. 2000b. "New Approaches to Planning." OED Working Paper Series. Washington, D.C.

——. 2000c. "Rural Water Project: Lessons from OED Evaluations." OED Working Paper Series 3. Washington, D.C.

——. 1998a. *India Impact Evaluation Report—Comparative Review of Rural Water Systems Experience.* Report 18114. Washington, D.C.: World Bank.

——. 1997. *Lessons of Fiscal Adjustment: Selected Proceedings from a World Bank Seminar.* Washington, D.C.: World Bank.

——. 1994. *A Review of World Bank Experience in Irrigation.* Report 13676. Washington, D.C.: World Bank.

——. 1992. *Water Supply and Sanitation Projects: the Bank's Experience—1967–1989.* Report 10789. Washington, D.C.: World Bank.

——. 1981. *Water Management in Bank-Supported Irrigation Project Systems: An Analysis of Past Experience.* Report 3421. Washington, D.C.: World Bank.

Pitman, G.K. 2002. "India: World Bank Assistance for Water Resource Management." OED India CAE Working Paper Series. Washington, D.C.

Plusquellec, Herve. 1997. "The Future of Irrigation." Keynote speech for EDI Regional Seminar on Sustainable Irrigation. Washington D.C.: World Bank. Photocopy.

Plusquellec, Herve, and Thomas Wickham. 1985. *Irrigation Design and Management: Experience in Thailand and Its General Applicability.* World Bank Technical Paper 40. Washington, D.C.

Plusquellec, Herve, Charles Burt, and Thomas Wickham. 1994. *Modern Water Control in Irrigation: Concepts, Issues, and Applications.* World Bank Technical Paper 246. Washington, D.C.

Renault, D., and I.W. Makin. 1999. *Modernizing Irrigation Operations: Spatially Differentiated Resource Allocations.* Research Report 35, International Water Management Institute. Colombo.

Rodts, Roland P.A. 2000. "Netherlands Support to the Water Sector in Mozambique: Evaluation of Sector Performance and Institutional Development." The Netherlands Ministry of Foreign Affairs, Policy and Operations Evaluation Department, The Hague.

Rogers, Peter. 1992. *Comprehensive Water Resources Management—A Concept Paper.* Washington, D.C.: World Bank.

Rosegrant, Mark W. 1997. *Water Resources in the Twenty-First Century: Challenges and Implications for Action.* Discussion Paper 20. Washington, D.C.: International Food Policy Research Institute.

Rosegrant, Mark W., and Shobha Shetty. 1994. "Production and Income Benefits from Improved Irrigation Efficiency: What is the Potential?" *Irrigation and Drainage Systems* 8: 251–70.

Rosegrant, Mark W., and Mark Svendsen. 1993. "Asian Food Production in the 1990s: Irrigation Investment and Management Policy." *Food Policy* 18 (1): 13–32.

Rosegrant, Mark W., Genato Gazmuri Schleyer, and Satya N. Yadav. 1995. "Water Policy for Efficient Agricultural Diversification: Market-based Approaches." *Food Policy* 20(3): 203–23.

Sadoff, Claudia. 1996. *The Price of Dirty Water: Pollution Costs in the Sebou Basin.* Environmental Economics Series Paper 038. Washington, D.C.: World Bank.

Saleth, R. Maria, and Ariel Dinar. 1955. *Evaluating Water Institutions and Water Sector Performance.* World Bank Technical Paper 447. Washington, D.C.

Salman, Salman M.A. 1997. *The Legal Framework for Water Users' Associations: A Comparative Study.* World Bank Technical Paper 360. Washington, D.C.

Scudder, T. 1994. "Recent Experiences with River Basin Development in the Tropics and Subtropics." *Natural Resources Forum* 18(2): 101–114.

———. 1990. "Victims of Development Revisited—The Political Costs of River Basin Development." *Development Anthropology Network* 8(1): 1–5.

———. 1989. "River Basin Projects in Africa." *Environment* 31 (2): 4–32.

Seckler, David. 1996. *The New Era of Water Resources Management: From 'Dry' to 'Wet' Water Savings.* Research Report 1, International Irrigation Management Institute. Colombo.

Seckler, David, Upali Amarasinghe, David Molden, Rhadika de Silva, and Randolph Barker. 1998. *World Water Demand and Supply, 1990 to 2025: Scenarios and Issues.* International Water Management Institute. Colombo.

Semedema, Lambert. 2000. *Irrigation-Induced River Salinization: Five Major Irrigated Basins in the Arid Zone.* International Water Management Institute. Colombo.

Serageldin, Ismail. 1994. *Water Supply, Sanitation, and Environmental Sustainability: The Financing Challenge.* Directions in Development Series. Washington, D.C.: World Bank.

Sharma, N. P., T. Damhang, E. Gilgan-Hunt, D. Grey, V. Okaru, and D. Rothberg. 1996. *African Water Resources: Challenges and Opportunities for Sustainable Development.* World Bank Technical Paper 331. Washington, D.C.

Shiklimanov, Igor A. 2000a. *World Water Resources at the Beginning of the 21st Century.* Summary of the Monograph. IHP Unesco.

Soussan, John. 2000a. "Institutional Development: Netherlands Support to the Water Sector, 1988–1998, Case Studies." The Hague: Netherlands Ministry of Foreign Affairs.

———. 2000b. *Netherlands Support to the Drinking Water Sector in India: Impacts on Institutional Development and Change.* The Hague: The Netherlands Ministry of Foreign Affairs.

Spulber, Nicolas, and Asghar Sabbaghi. 1998. *Economics of Water Resources: From Regulation to Privatization.* 2d ed. Norwell, MA: Kluwer Academic.

Sri Lanka, Ministry of Housing and Urban Development. 1998. *Community Water Supply and Sanitation Project.* Battaramulla, Sri Lanka.

Svendsen, M., and others. 2000. "A Synthesis of Benefits and Second-Generation Problems." In *Proceedings of the Second International Seminar on Participatory Irrigation Management,* Anlalya, Turkey. Analya: DSI.

Thomas, Robert, Michael Colby, Richard English, William Jobin, Bechir Rassas, and Peter Reiss. 1993. *Water Resources Policy and Planning: Towards Environmental Sustainability.* USAID ISPAN, Bureau for Asia and the Near East. Washington, D.C.: AID.

Umali, Dina L. 1993. *Irrigation-Induced Salinity: A Growing Problem for Development and the Environment.* World Bank Technical Paper 215. Washington, D.C.

UNDP-World Bank. 2000. *Voice & Choice for Women: Water is Their Business.* Water and Sanitation Program, South Asia Region. Washington, D.C.: World Bank

———. 1999. *Water and Sanitation Services for the Poor: Innovating through Field Experience Program Strategy: 1999–2003.* Washington, D.C.: World Bank.

United Nations/World Meteorological Organization. 1997. *Comprehensive Assessment of the Freshwater Resources of the World.* New York: United Nations.

USAID (U.S. Agency for International Development). 1994a. *Future Directions for Implementing Water Policy: Report on a USAID-Sponsored Workshop, April 28–29, 1994.* ISPAN, Bureau for Asia and the Near East. Washington, D.C.: AID.

———. 1994b. *A Strategic Framework for Water in Asia.* ISPAN, Bureau for Asia and the Near East. Washington, D.C.: AID.

———. 1994c. *Water Strategies for the Next Century: Supply Augmentation vs. Demand Man-*

*agement*. ISPAN, Bureau for Asia and the Near East. Washington, D.C.: AID.

USEPA (U.S. Environmental Protection Agency). 1995. *Watershed Protection: A Statewide Approach*. Assessment and Watershed Protection Division. Washington, D.C.

van Hofwegen, Paul J.M., and Frank G.W. Jaspers. 1999. *Analytical Framework for Integrated Water Resources Management: Guidelines for Assessment of Institutional Frameworks*. Rotterdam: Balkema.

van Koppen, Barbara. 1998. "More Jobs Per Drop: Targeting Irrigation to Poor Women and Men." Amsterdam: Royal Tropical Institute, Ministry of Foreign Affairs.

Vermillion, Douglas L., Madar Samad, Suprodjo Pusposutardjo, Sigit S. Arif, and Saiful Rochdyanto. 2000. *An Assessment of the Small-Scale Irrigation Management Turnover Program in Indonesia*. Research Report 38, International Water Management Institute. Colombo.

Walker, Ian, Fidel Ordonez, Pedro Serrano, and Jonathan Halpern. 2000. "Pricing, Subsidies, and the Poor: Demand for Improved Water Services in Central America." World Bank Policy Research Working Paper 2468. Washington, D.C.

Wang, Rusong, Zhiyun Ouyang, Hongjun Ren, and Qingwen Min. 1999. *China Water Vision: The Eco-sphere of Water, Environment, Life, Economy & Society*. Beijing: Research Center for Eco-Environmental Sciences and Chinese Academy of Sciences.

Whittington, Dale, Jennifer Davis, and Elizabeth McClelland. 1999. "Implementing a Demand-driven Approach to Community Water Supply Planning: A Case Study of Lugazi, Uganda." *Water International* 23: 134–45.

Whittington, Dale. 1998. "Administering Contingent Valuation Surveys in Developing Countries." *World Development* 26(1): 21–30.

Williams, Meryl. 1996. "The Transition in the Contribution of Living Aquatic Resources to Food Security." Food, Agriculture, and the Environment, Discussion Paper 13. Washington, D.C., International Food Policy Research Institute.

Winpenny, Jim. 1997. *Water Policy Issues*. DFID Water Resources Occasional Paper 2. London.

Wolf, Aaron T. 1996. "Middle East Water Conflicts and Directions for Conflict Resolution." Food, Agriculture, and the Environment, Discussion Paper 12. Washington, D.C., International Food Policy Research Institute.

World Bank, ADB, FAO, UNDP, and NGO Water Resources Group, Institute of Water Resources Planning, Vietnam. 1996. *Vietnam: Water Resources Sector Review, Main Report*. Washington, D.C.: World Bank.

World Bank. 2000a. "Bolivia Urban Water Supply: Main Issues and Recommendations." Latin America and Caribbean Regional Office. Washington, D.C..

——. 2000b. "Brazil: Private Participation in the Water Sector: Case Studies, Lessons, and Future Options." Report. 19896-BR. Washington, D.C. Photocopy.

——. 2000c. "Argentina: Water Resources Management—Policy Elements for Sustainable Development in the XXI Century." Report 20729-AR. Washington, D.C. Photocopy.

——. 2000d. *Maintaining Utility Services for the Poor: Policies and Practices in Central and Eastern Europe and the Former Soviet Union*. Washington, D.C.

——. 2000e. "Micro Infrastructure: Regulators Must Take Small Operators Seriously." *Viewpoint*, Private Sector and Infrastructure Network. Washington, D.C.

——. 2000f. *Private Solutions for Infrastructure: Opportunities for the Philippines*. Public-Private Infrastructure Advisory Facility. Washington, D.C.

——. 2000g. "The World Bank and the Water Sector." Brazil Country Management Unit, Brasilia.

——. 2000l. "Water and Sanitation Report, 98–99." Water and Sanitation Program. Washington, D.C.

——. 2000m. "Water Concessions." *Viewpoint* 217. Washington, D.C.

——. 1999. *Groundwater: Legal and Policy Perspectives—Proceedings of a World Bank Seminar*. World Bank Technical Paper 456. Washington, D.C.

——. 1998a. "Brazil: Second Water Sector Modernization Project—PMSS II." Appraisal Report 16771. Washington, D.C.

———. 1998b. *India Water Resources Management Sector Review: Initiating and Sustaining Water Sector Reforms*. Report 18356-IN. Washington, D.C.

———. 1998c. *Recent Experience with Involuntary Resettlement: Overview*. Report 17538, Operations Evaluation Department. Washington, D.C.

———. 1998d. *International Watercourses: Enhancing Cooperation and Managing Conflict—Proceedings of a World Bank Seminar*. World Bank Technical Paper 414. Washington, D.C.

———. 1997a. "United Arab Emirates: National Water Strategy Study." Middle East Department, Washington, D.C. Photocopy.

———. 1997b. "Water for Life." World Bank Water Program Communications Campaign, FY98–99. Washington, D.C.

———. 1997c. *Environment Matters at the World Bank: World Bank Environmental Projects July 1996–June 1997*. World Bank Environment Department. Washington, D.C.

———. 1995d. *From Scarcity to Security: Averting A Water Crisis in the Middle East and North Africa*. Washington, D.C.

———. 1994a. *Pakistan Irrigation and Drainage: Issues and Options*. Washington, D.C.

———. 1994b. *World Development Report 1994: Infrastructure for Development*. New York: Oxford University Press for the World Bank.

———. 1994c. "Multipurpose River Basin Development in China." Economic Development.

———. 1994d. *Water Resources Management*. A World Bank Policy Paper. Washington, D.C.

———. 1993. *A Strategy for Managing Water in the Middle East and North Africa*. Washington, D.C.

———. 1991. *Environmental Assessment Sourcebook*. Washington, D.C.

Wouters, Patricia K. 1996. "An Assessment of Recent Developments in International Watercourse Law through the Prism of the Substantive Rules Governing Use Allocation." *Natural Resources Journal* 36.

WWC (World Water Commission). 2000. *World Water Vision: A Water Secure World*. Commission Report. London.

WWC (World Water Council). 1998. *Water in the 21st Century*. Paris.

WWF (World Wildlife Fund) 1994. *Economic Evaluation of Danube Floodplains*. A WWF Case Study. Rastatt.

Xie, Mei, Ulrich Kuffner, and Guy Le Moigne. 1960. *Using Water Efficiently: Technological Options*. World Bank Technical Paper 205. Washington, D.C.

# OPERATIONS EVALUATION DEPARTMENT PUBLICATIONS

The Operations Evaluation Department (OED), an independent evaluation unit reporting to the World Bank's Executive Directors, rates the development impact and performance of all the Bank's completed lending operations. Results and recommendations are reported to the Executive Directors and fed back into the design and implementation of new policies and projects. In addition to the individual operations and country assistance programs, OED evaluates the Bank's policies and processes.

*Summaries of studies and the full text of the Précis and Lessons & Practices* can be read on the Internet at http://www.worldbank.org/html/oed

## How To Order OED Publications

Operations evaluation studies, World Bank discussion papers, and all other documents are available from the World Bank InfoShop.

Documents listed with a stock number and price code may be obtained through the World Bank's mail order service or from its InfoShop in downtown Washington, D.C. For information on all other documents, contact the World Bank InfoShop.

For more information about this study or OED's other evaluation work, please contact Elizabeth Campbell-Pagé or the OED Help Desk.

Operations Evaluation Department
Partnerships & Knowledge Programs (OEDPK)
E-mail: ecampbellpage@worldbank.org
E-mail: eline@worldbank.org
Telephone: (202) 458-4497
Facsimile: (202) 522-3200

## Ordering World Bank Publications

Customers in the United States and in territories not served by any of the Bank's publication distributors may send publication orders to:

The World Bank
P.O. Box 960
Herndon, VA 20172-0960
Fax: (703) 661-1501
Telephone: (703) 661-1580
The address for the World Bank publication database on the Internet is: http://www.worldbank.org (select publications/project info).
E-mail: pic@worldbank.org
Fax number: (202) 522-1500
Telephone number: (202) 458-5454

The World Bank InfoShop serves walk-in customers only. The InfoShop is located at:

701 18th Street, NW
Washington, DC 20433, USA

All other customers must place their orders through their local distributors.

## Ordering by e-mail

If you have an established account with the World Bank, you may transmit your order by electronic mail on the Internet to: **books@worldbank.org**. Please include your account number, billing and shipping addresses, the title and order number, quantity, and unit price for each item.